Locked Dimensions out of Reach: The Lost Stories of H. P. Lovecraft

J.-M. Rajala

I try always to keep a supply of story-ideas on hand—recording all bizarre notions, moods, dreams, images, concepts, &c. (& keeping all press clippings involving such) for future use. I do not despair if they seem to have no logical development. Each one may be worked over gradually—surrounded with notes & synopses, & finally built into a coherent explanatory structure capable of fictional use. I never hurry . . . The best stories sometimes grow very slowly—over long periods, & with intervals in their formulation . . . .
     —HPL to Alvin Earl Perry, 4 October 1935 (*SL* 5.204)

I have a whole book full of idea-jottings which I could never write up if I lived to be a thousand . . .
—HPL to Robert E. Howard, 30 January 1931 (*MF* 1.144, *SL* 3.284)

Perhaps one of the chief reasons the body of work left behind by H. P. Lovecraft is still so highly regarded today is its relative slenderness and the consequent concentration of creative power into a few major landmarks of weird literature. Although the same unique aura pervades his lesser tales, and his marginalia too is worthy of attention, even taking them into account his fiction, written over just two decades, does not fill many volumes. In a way, this very paucity of material may have ensured that what he had to say was not spread over too many works, and accordingly he has taken his place as arguably the only figure and innovator in the history of supernatural literature who can claim an equally eminent and influential position as Edgar Allan Poe. And yet, who of us who has been enchanted by Lovecraft's imagination has not wished that he would have written at least a few more stories? It is not difficult to contemplate a slightly different version of the history: what if Farnsworth Wright, the editor of *Weird Tales*, had been just a little less "capricious" and had accepted Lovecraft's longer and more ambitious stories; one book publisher had been just a little more foresighted; Lovecraft just a little less prone to self-depreciation and doubt—there is no end to such conjectures.

Lovecraft's letters provide ample and valuable information on the sources for the main themes and ideas, as well as more incidental details, of his extant fiction. Not only do they allow us to gain important insights into how he crafted his unique stories and novellas, and aid in setting them into the context of his life—for instance, we can learn how his exploration of the "ancient" town of Marblehead was ultimately transformed into "The Festival," and how the discovery of Pluto in early 1930 was woven into a tale then in progress, "The Whisperer in Darkness"—but a study of his correspondence also reveals how particular stories were either essentially elaborations of certain extraordinary dreams (or, perhaps more properly, nightmares), or incorporated important features from them. Of course, nowhere near all the recorded peculiar nocturnal visions that might have lent themselves to fictional use were so utilized, and many surviving letters contain several and at times lengthy descriptions of such dreams; but in some cases Lovecraft indicates that he did intend to use them later, or their nuclei can be found recorded in his famous commonplace book. Still other letters provide occasional and tantalizing allusions to planned stories that either were never actually set down on paper or were ultimately abandoned and destroyed. Relatively few written narrative fragments survive among the Lovecraft papers in the John Hay Library of Brown University in Providence, yet for the last years of his life we can find almost constant mentions of unsatisfactory "experiments" that seem to have been completely discarded. It is well known that "The Shadow over Innsmouth" and "The Shadow out of Time" evolved through several successive and discarded drafts, and their finished versions might easily have been likewise destroyed; but a careful reading of the available correspondence reveals that apart from these there were also other, separate and largely unidentified tales that were never completed and are now irrevocably lost. It is regrettable that Lovecraft, disillusioned as he

THE LOVECRAFT ANNUAL

Edited by S. T. Joshi   No. 5 (2011)

Contents

Abbreviations used in the text and notes:

AT   *The Ancient Track* (Night Shade Books, 2001)
CE   *Collected Essays* (Hippocampus Press, 2004–06; 5 vols.)
D   *Dagon and Other Macabre Tales* (Arkham House, 1986)
DH   *The Dunwich Horror and Others* (Arkham House, 1984)
HM   *The Horror in the Museum and Other Revisions* (Arkham House, 1989)
LL   *Lovecraft's Library: A Catalogue* (Hippocampus Press, 2002)
MM   *At the Mountains of Madness and Other Novels* (Arkham House, 1985)
MW   *Miscellaneous Writings* (Arkham House, 1995)
SL   *Selected Letters* (Arkham House, 1965–76; 5 vols.)

Copyright © 2011 by Hippocampus Press

Published by Hippocampus Press, P.O. Box 641, New York, NY 10156
http://www.hippocampuspress.com

Cover illustration by Allen Koszowski. Hippocampus Press logo designed by Anastasia Damianakos. Cover design by Barbara Briggs Silbert.

Lovecraft Annual is published once a year, in Fall. Articles and letters should be sent to the editor, S. T. Joshi, c/o Hippocampus Press, and must be accompanied by a self-addressed stamped envelope if return is desired. All reviews are assigned. Literary rights for articles and reviews will reside with *Lovecraft Annual* for one year after publication, whereupon they will revert to their respective authors. Payment is in contributor's copies.

ISSN 1935-6102
ISBN13: 978-0-9844802-5-8

was with his success as a writer at this stage, did not consider such perceived failures worth preserving, if only as "sort of quarr[ies] of imagery & incidents for possible future tales" (*WD* 44).

In the following more or less chronological account I will try to summarize what is currently known of various such "lost stories" spanning the whole of Lovecraft's life. It is important to note that I intend this somewhat nebulous categorization to be understood in a very wide sense, encompassing both completed narratives that are lost in the sense that their texts have yet to be located (or cannot, being known to have been destroyed), as well as at the other extreme stories that were little more than conceived of, yet could in other circumstances have borne fruit. I do not claim to have made account of all such latter items, but instead will try to draw attention to certain notable cases where the available evidence—scant though it may be—allows some room for speculation on Lovecraft's intentions. Falling within these bounds, there exist about half a dozen actual fragments of abortive story attempts or notes for such that still survive in manuscript; a division to which the more numerous jottings in his commonplace book can also be added for inquiry. To be sure, I by no means aim to examine each and every memorandum contained in that invaluable document, but it will be useful to cite certain selected entries from it in the course of this investigation, even if the identification of their purpose, measured against other available evidence, can often be only very tentative due to their rather terse and obscure nature.

I. Infantile Efforts: 1897–1918

Regrettably little of Lovecraft's early juvenile fiction survives. Judging from the scattered comments made in the course of his vast correspondence about various now non-extant works, it almost seems that the stories that do survive might well be the least interesting specimens. Purely from an aesthetic standpoint, the loss of the bulk of the young Howard's fictional attempts is not a great one; nevertheless, we would still very much like to have them in order to be better able to trace his development as an author. As it is, "The Beast in the Cave" (1905) emerges from virtually nowhere. Compared to the ambitious verse Lovecraft was writing at this time—or indeed, even earlier, beginning with the very early "Poem of Ulysses"—the relative lack of distinction exhibited by his prose work is somewhat anomalous.

The very first of Lovecraft's stories has itself been lost. Its basic premise is, however, known to us as recorded by him in a letter to J. Vernon Shea years later: it concerned "a boy who overheard some horrible conclave of subterranean beings in a cave" (*Life* 31). The autobiographical sketch "Some Notes on a Nonentity" (1933) adds a little more: "About this period the weird illustrations of Gustave Doré—met in editions of Dante, Milton, and the Ancient Mariner—affected me powerfully. For the first time I began to attempt writing—the earliest piece I can recall being a tale of a hideous cave perpetrated at the age of seven and entitled 'The Noble Eavesdropper'" (*CE* 5.208). Interestingly, this might lead us to think the story supernatural, although in another letter this is not suggested, as it is there described as "something about a cave of robbers called 'The Noble Eavesdropper'" (*SL* 4.380)—perhaps a natural explanation to a supernatural premise is being implied. S. T. Joshi has speculated on a possible influence of the *Arabian Nights* (cf. *Life* 31), and this may very well be a correct assumption.[1]

A few insignificant items of slightly later date have come down to us: "The Little Glass Bottle," "The Secret Cave or John Lees Adventure," "The Mystery of the Grave-Yard; or 'A Dead Man's Revenge,'" and "The Mysterious Ship"; all of them except the last (1902) apparently date to around 1898–99,[2] and none of them is at all remarkable. "The Mystery of the Grave-Yard" is manifestly influenced by Lovecraft's early reading of the popular dime-novel adventures, and its hero, detective King John, was doubtless also featured in a further non-extant piece belonging to the same period, "John, the Detective," which perhaps antedated the former story. As far as I am aware, Lovecraft never mentions the latter in any correspondence, but its existence is revealed by the fiction

---

1. A letter to Bernard Austin Dwyer fixes the year of writing as 1897: "In 1898 I began my prose career, (no—the first was still in 1897, though it was pre-Poe)" (*SL* 2.109).
2. A later note on the autograph manuscript of "The Mystery of the Grave-Yard" reads "evidently written in late 1898 or 1899."

section of a catalogue of his works, purportedly listed "for sale" and found at the back of the compilation of juvenile poetry *Poemata Minora: Volume II* (1902):

The Mysterious Ship	0.25
The Noble Eavesdropper	0.10
The Haunted House	0.10
The Secret of the Grave	0.25
John, the Detective	0.10

In addition to the information directly provided by this catalogue, it is also of some interest for what it *does not* contain. Of the intriguingly titled "The Haunted House," nothing further is known, but judging from the price of 10 cents affixed to it—the same as for the very early "The Noble Eavesdropper"—it could scarcely have been a very substantial work, much less a true anticipation of the author's later weird stories. The price of 25 cents given for "The Mysterious Ship" is, on the other hand, odd as the *two* versions of it that survive (one of them only as an Arkham House transcript, however) are both less than 1000 words long; the explanation likely is that this item had been prepared as a booklet (issued by "The Royal Press" and explicitly dated to 1902).

Something of a mystery is presented by the fact that, aside from "The Mysterious Ship," the three other extant early works of fiction—"The Little Glass Bottle," "The Secret Cave," and "The Mystery of the Grave-Yard"—all fail to be listed in this 1902 catalogue, inasmuch as Lovecraft has apparently taken care to note all his other works composed so far in the other departments. In more than one letter Lovecraft speaks of the "Secret of the Grave" as if that still existed, and I am inclined to accept Joshi's proposition that it is merely an alternate title or error for "The Mystery of the Grave-Yard"—it can be postulated that the title in the catalogue is an accidental fusion of both that and the likewise unlisted "The Secret Cave." Following this line of thought, the non-appearance of "The Little Glass Bottle" might be explained by the fact that it was prepared as a special booklet presented to Lovecraft's mother. In any case, the relative shortness of this fictional catalogue leads one to doubt what he elsewhere gives as the dates of lost juvenile tales.

The hints of what must have been many more stories than are

known even by title only are scant and tantalizing—perhaps unjustifiably so, if "The Mysterious Ship" is any indication. In one letter, occasioned by a discussion of W. Clark Russell's adventure novel *The Frozen Pirate* (1887), the following information is revealed: "I read it in extreme youth—when 8 or 9—& was utterly fascinated by it . . . writing several yarns of my own under its influence" (*RFS* 34). But as we have already seen, no such "yarns" are listed in *Poemata Minora*. Actually, I think that these stories were only composed contemporaneously with Lovecraft's scientific writing on the Antarctica, around the winter of 1902–03. He variously dated the commencement of his interest in the polar continent to 1900 or 1902, and the remarkable early autobiographical letter to Rheinhart Kleiner (of 16 November 1916) states that:

> About 1900 I became a passionate devotee of geography & history, & an intense fanatic on the subject of Antarctic exploration. The Borchgrevink expedition, which had just made a new record of South Polar achievement, greatly stimulated this study. I wrote many fanciful tales about the Antarctic Continent, besides composing "learned" treatises on the real facts. (*RK* 71, *SL* 1.37)

Although S. T. Joshi is willing to accept this dating (cf. *Life* 47), there is some reason to doubt that Lovecraft did any actual writing on the Antarctic region as early as 1900. It is suspicious that, in addition to the lack of any supporting evidence in the 1902 catalogue, the treatises that Lovecraft mentions in other letters do not in fact expound on Borchgrevink's achievements, but are instead accounts of the much earlier polar explorations of Charles Wilkes and James Clark Ross (of 1838–43). These works, *Voyages of Capt. Ross, R. N.* (1902) and *Wilkes's Explorations* (1902), as well as an *Antarctic Atlas* (1903), were evidently still extant at the time of Lovecraft's death—C. L. Moore was actually lent the Wilkes treatise in late 1936 (cf. *Life* 659n62)—although their current whereabouts are unknown. The names of the treatises are cited in a 1932 letter to Maurice W. Moe (*SL* 4.67), while another still later letter (*SL* 5.237) supplies the dates of composition, which presumably were looked up by Lovecraft from the "Royal Atlas Company" manuscripts, as it is otherwise difficult to account for the specifically later date given for the

Atlas. Furthermore, a letter to Bernard Austin Dwyer precisely pinpoints the period for this study: "In 1902 geography displaced chemistry in my affections, and the lure of far places was upon me. The *Antarctic* was my favourite region." (*SL* 2.109). My guess is, then, that it was indeed the Borchgrevink expedition of 1899–1900 as well as the reading of *The Frozen Pirate* that sparked Lovecraft's interest in the southern continent, yet only the deepening of that interest in 1902 in the aftermath of Robert Scott's expedition led him to delve more into the history of the polar voyages and to write these lost "fanciful tales."

In any case, whether these efforts date to 1900 or 1902, it was after the latter date that a new compelling scientific interest dawned in Lovecraft's horizon, for it was in 1903 that he discovered astronomy. He dived into its study with gusto and by the autumn of that year started to produce juvenile treatises on various subjects, in addition to the well-known periodical the *Rhode Island Journal of Astronomy*—how on earth he initially managed to produce it on a weekly basis on top of his other activities is beyond me, although not attending school formally at the time must have helped. It would also appear that these studies inspired some fictional works as well as the better-known purely scientific ones, for in a 1916 letter to Rheinhart Kleiner Lovecraft writes:

> When I was about twelve I became greatly interested in science, specialising in geography, (later to be displaced by astronomy), and being a Verne enthusiast.[3] In those days I used to write fiction, and many of my tales showed the literary influence of the immortal Jules. I wrote one story about that side of the moon which is forever turned away from us—using, for fictional purposes—the Hansen theory that air and water still exist there as the result of an abnormal centre of gravity in the moon. I hardly need to add that the theory is really exploded—I even was aware of that fact at the time—but I desired to compose a "thriller". (*RK* 29, *SL* 1.19)

It is to be regretted that nothing more is known of these tales. But in addition to such solitary pursuits, the years 1902 and 1903 were also the period of the "Providence Detective Agency" that Love-

---

3. Note the additional implication here that it was in 1902 when HPL's geographical interest in the Antarctic arose.

craft had organized with some of his Slater Avenue school friends:

> I read every Sherlock Holmes story published, and even organised a
> detective agency when I was thirteen, arrogating to myself the
> proud pseudonym of S.H. This P.D.A.—whose members ranged
> between nine & fourteen years, was a most wonderful thing—how
> many murders & robberies we unravelled! Our headquarters were
> in a deserted house just out of the thickly settled area, and we there
> enacted, and "solved", many a gruesome tragedy. (*AG* 19)

Although he himself dates it earlier, a yet another fleetingly
glimpsed lost juvenile story (touched on in a 1916 letter) may
perhaps be associated with this period of detective interest:

> I used to write detective stories very often, the works of A. Co-
> nan Doyle being my model so far as plot was concerned. But Poe
> was my God of Fiction. . . . One long destroyed tale was of twin
> brothers—one murders the other, but conceals the body and tries
> to live the life of both—appearing in one place as himself, and
> elsewhere as his victim. (Resemblance had been remarkable.) He
> meets sudden death (lightning) when posing as the dead man—is
> identified by a scar, and the secret finally revealed by his diary.
> This, I think, antedates my 11th year. . . . (*RK* 30, *SL* 1.20)

The idyllic and opulent life of Lovecraft's childhood became to
a sudden end by the tragic death of his beloved grandfather
Whipple Phillips on 28 March 1904. The financial disasters that
followed his passing eventually forced Howard and his mother to
abandon the birthplace at 454 and move into rented quarters at
598 Angell Street, sharing the apartment with another family. For
a time Lovecraft claims to have contemplated suicide, but eventually his thirst for knowledge happily won. It was then on 21 April
1905 (as dated on the still extant manuscript) that he—perhaps
working under the gloom of the previous year's loss—penned
what is his earlier surviving fictional work that can be said to be
recognizably "Lovecraftian," and perhaps more important, horrific.
Much later he would remark that it had already been drafted or
planned a year earlier, in the spring of 1904,[4] but whether this

---

4. Cf. postcard to Lillian D. Clark, 15 July 1928 (ms., JHL; cited in *Life* 660n75).

would have been before or after Whipple's death is not clear.

It is woeful that the only other story of this adolescent period that survives is the last of them: "The Alchemist," written around the fall 1908, just before all the stories composed in between were destroyed when Lovecraft despaired of his abilities as a writer and abandoned original fiction until 1917. It is doubly unfortunate that the manuscript of this latter tale is not known to survive, as the final page of that for "The Beast in the Cave" carries this note:

> Tales of Terror
>   1. The Beast in the Cave
> By H. P. Lovecraft
>   (Period—Modern)

As it is, we can again only turn to the occasional but rather meager allusions in letters for any hints of the intervening "Tales of Terror" that must have been written between 1905 and 1908. Possibly the earliest of these would have been the one for which the title if nothing else is known:

> Whilst rearranging files, I tapp'd a box containing stuff undisturb'd since the Middle 598 [Angell Street] Period—and found therein the most astonishing array of tail ends of writing materials—composition books with a few blank pages, incomplete pads, and the like. One composition book of 1905 bears the title of a story about which I had completely forgotten—"Gone—But Whither"? I'll bet it was a hell-raiser! The title expresses the fate of the tale itself. (*SL* 5.140)

A little more is known of another horror story which is first encountered in an early note in Lovecraft's commonplace book: "[19] Revise 1907 tale—painting of ultimate horror."[5] A chance discussion of Robert Bloch's story "Lucian Grey" elicited the following comment, providing the title and some details of what is surely the same tale:

> It reminds me amazingly of one of the juvenile tales I destroyed—"The Picture", written in 1907. That is, the theme reminds me.

---

5. I will not cite page references for individual commonplace book entries; the whole of it is now best found in *CE* 5.219–37 and *MW* 87–103.

The tale itself is much better than mine. I had a man in a Paris garret paint a mysterious canvas embodying the quintessential essence of all horror. He is found clawed & mangled one morning before his easel. The picture is destroyed, as in a titanic struggle—but in one corner of the frame a bit of canvas remains . . . . & on it the coroner finds to his horror the painted counterpart of the sort of claw which evidently killed the artist. The idea was good, but the style was so poor that I don't regret having destroyed it a year after its composition. (*RB* 15)

Clearly Lovecraft was now beginning to find his calling as a horror writer, even if it would take more than a decade before he would come to acknowledge the fact and largely abandon poetry as a medium of artistic expression. Pictorial arts would always exert a strong influence on him, and in what we know of "The Picture" a trace can perhaps be found surviving in "Pickman's Model." But not all the tales written during this period were necessarily strictly weird or supernatural, as this casual remark to his aunt Lillian D. Clark reveals: "The idea of a Roman settlement in America is something which occurred to me years ago—in fact, I began a story with that theme (only it was about Central America & not U.S.) in 1906 or 1907, tho' I never finished it." (*Life* 75) Elsewhere Lovecraft elaborates engagingly on the matter, disclosing that several tales with such a theme were set down, and then describes one at length:

Half of the stories I wrote during that research period (when I was 14, 15, and 16) had to do with strange survivals of Roman civilisation in Africa, Asia, the Antarctic, the Amazon Valley, and even pre-Columbian North America. They are all destroyed now, but I wish I had kept the one (based on an actual dream of 1904) about Roman Providence, with its familiar hills crowned with many-columned temples and its forum near the site of the Great Bridge. (I had a marble bridge there—the Pons Æbutii, named from L. Æbutius, the founder of the colony of B.C. 45, which was tragically cut off from the mother respublica whence the colonising fleet of six quinquiremes had sailed.) I had Roman wars with the Narragansetts, Wampanoags, and Pequots, a gradual blood mixture which have the whole mass of Eastern Indians their still-unexplained (in view of the known Mongoloid basis of the whole race) aquiline features, and a final destruction of MOTIATICUM (2nd Moshassuck) by an earthquake. I had the story begin with the exhumation of a Roman column on the ancient hill during the digging of a sewer-main—the universal perplexity aroused, and the dreams it inspired in one lone student. My native highway Angell Street (actually the Wampanoag Trail, older than English colonisation, and naturally determined as the shortest line between the ford at the head of the bay and the narrow ferrying-place in the Seekonk River) was a Roman road, line with tombs as it stretched beyond the marble temples and brick-and-plaster houses or urban Motiaticum. (*SL* 4.336)

It is a pity that this particular early effort does not survive! It probably was these juvenile stories that Lovecraft was thinking of when toward the end of his life he wrote to Fritz Leiber: "Just as you think of Vikings in the Hellenistic-Roman world, so do I think of Roman navigators in strange and distant parts—washed across the Western Ocean to unknown shores, camping on the future site of Providence and fighting the coppery predecessors of the Narragansetts and Wampanoags, or captured by the soldiers of the Mayas and forced to escape from ornately carven dungeons in Guatemalan jungles" (*WD* 47, *SL* 5.374–75). As can be seen, the Roman world would always elicit a powerful fascination and a sense of familiarity in Lovecraft, and he would later often contemplate writing a story in or connected to a Roman setting, but unfortunately in the end it never quite came to pass. In 1929 he makes mention of more or less the same premise as used in the early tales:

The cuttings you enclosed are all interesting. That Roman coin in the Indian grave could be used fictionally to sustain a notion which I have been ruminating for years—a forgotten colony of Rome on American soil, including a city of Roman architecture with temple-crowned citadel, columned forum, & marble arenas & baths. I would have it come in conflict with the representatives of some native civilisation—Maya, Aztec, &c.—& perhaps suffer extirpation in a desperate battle, or sink amidst an earthquake. (*SL* 3.27)

In 1933 he would also again bring up the notion of Roman explorers cast away in Central America which had been the subject of the unfinished juvenile story, noting an obstacle to actually utilizing it:

It is possible, though, that I may use a Roman setting in certain weird tales—probably some in which a character covers long time-intervals. The thing which I would probably enjoy most in connexion with history would be bringing utterly separate culture-streams into anomalous contact—as in having a Roman washed across the ocean on a derelict galley and land amidst the Mayas, or having a Greek cross the great deserts to China. But the scholarship needed to write a really good historical tale is utterly dizzifying in its extent. (*MF* 2.656, *SL* 4.297)

With the loss of the early stories, the most tangible fictional proof of the imaginative stimulus the Ancient Rome gave to him is thus preserved in the remarkable descriptions of the long "Roman dream" he experienced on the Halloween night of 1927; I will have more to say of this fragment subsequently when we reach its proper chronological place, but it is of some interest that Lovecraft above says that the lost juvenile story set in Roman Providence was inspired by a dream as well. When discussing that of 1927 with Donald Wandrei he would note that nocturnal adventures like this were in his youth common fare to him, writing that "in my youth I dreamed nearly every night of Rome or the flash of the republick's aquilae & vexilla against the barbarick sunsets of far frontiers" (*MTS* 187, *SL* 2.200). Elsewhere he elaborates on the topic:

But my real dreams are less often filled with the decadent East than with the barbaric West; and it is with the legions in Spain and Gaul and Britain, and on the Rhine and Danube frontiers, that my spirit has most frequently seen service. I am also quite often a private citizen or civil official, either in Rome or some Italian municipium, or in one of the towns of the western provinces. These dreams were most numerous in 1905 or 1906, but have recurred off and on since then. (*SL* 2.189)

My image of myself in all these dreams is of a man of early middle age and typical Roman physiognomy—the image having never varied from boyhood to the present day. My name, however, does vary widely ... (*MF* 1.142)

Only scenes of the eighteenth century would surpass the Roman world in vividness in Lovecraft's remarkable dream life.

*   *   *

After the conflagration in which all the fiction written between 1902 and 1908 except "The Beast in the Cave" and "The Alchemist" perished—in 1923 he noted that their "number was infinite" (*SL* 1.202)—we must then skip ahead almost a decade to 1917 for the proper inauguration of Lovecraft's career as a fictionist with the writing of the short stories "The Tomb" and "Dagon" in the summer of that year. Even then, this career only began in a series of fits and starts. As early as 1915 (scarcely a year after his joining the United Amateur Press Association) he had answered to the fellow amateur G. W. Macauley's persuasions that "I wish I could write fiction, but it seems almost an impossibility" (cited in Macauley 3). This did not lead to anything at the time, but Macauley's encouragement may have contributed to the eventual printing of "The Alchemist" in the amateur press in 1916. (Lovecraft had submitted the story in 1914 as his credential, but for reasons that are not entirely clear to me it took its time in appearing.) A quite remarkable piece of information related to the association of Lovecraft and Macauley has recently come to light as part of a letter that surfaced in an online auction. In the course of this letter, written in 1934 to Macauley when the latter had again initiated contact with Lovecraft after a lapse of several years, it is revealed that instead of merely extensively commenting on a story Macauley had enclosed for review—as his allusions to the matter in an article on their correspondence have so far led us to believe[6]—Lovecraft appears to have revised it wholesale:

> Going to an old cabinet which has never, despite many moves, been unpacked or rearranged since the old days, I found at once (as if I had placed it there but yesterday) the manuscript of your medieval tale "When Swords Were Bold", which (you'll perhaps recall) I touched up a bit & meant to publish or place sooner or later. Alas for my negligence! It seemed very fresh to me, & only when I observed the yellowed paper & the long-vanished twists of

---

6. ". . . a February letter of 1915 protests, at my urging of Lovecraft to turn his pen from poetry to story writing . . . About this time I had occasion to send Lovecraft a long story I had written asking for his criticisms. On receipt of the lengthy and much elaborated criticisms I knew at once that he, the critic, should have written my story" (Macauley 2).

my 1915 handwriting could I fully appreciate the abyss of years separating its writing & its exhumation. Curious how my script has changed—retaining only its basic characteristic of discouraging illegibility! I think I'll enclose the story for your perusal (if you can peruse such writing!), since it cannot but give you a feeling of picturesque linkage with the past. Really—we ought to get it published somehow![7]

It is not clear if Lovecraft actually did in the event enclose the manuscript, but even if he did, it does not appear to have been published in the amateur press. Macauley's Mayhew Press seems to have issued a few individual stories as pamphlets later on, but none of these (e.g., "Eight Dead Men on a Live Man's Chest: A Tale of Truth" [1954], "Little Wisconsin Town: Saratoga of the West" [1956], "The Man of Forty Crowns" [1952]—the last apparently a translation of Voltaire's fable) seems to match "When Swords Were Bold" even vaguely. The possibility that the revision still survives to this day is then somewhat remote, but if ultimately located, an extremely important and hitherto unknown step in Lovecraft's path to a weird fantasist would be available for study. In its absence, we can only speculate just how much Lovecraftian prose it would contain: my guess is that it might count as a 50/50 collaboration. A careful reading of the letter seems to indicate that he was forced to prepare a new autograph manuscript, rather than writing interlinear emendations and comments on Macauley's draft, as "touched up a bit" likely is merely an instance of the customary downplaying of his role in the revised result. Just how genuinely interesting as a story this lost medieval tale would be is, of course, another matter. In his "Department of Public Criticism" column for the June 1916 *United Amateur* Lovecraft commented on Macauley's work that he "is less at ease in stories of contemporary life than in historical fiction, particularly mediaeval and Oriental tales" (*CE* 1.115), and I wonder if there are any other stories by Macauley that Lovecraft touched up to lesser or greater degree, besides "When Swords Were Bold."

    After the relatively quick writing of "The Tomb" and "Dagon," no more original prose fiction in the strictest sense would follow

---

7. HPL to George W. Macauley, 12 August 1934 (ms., private collection).

until 1919. For 1917 we have also the comic piece "A Reminiscence of Dr. Samuel Johnson" (published in the November 1917 issue of the *United Amateur* and thus conceivably even preceding the two weird stories in composition); later that year, after the enthusiastic reaction of W. Paul Cook to these tales, Lovecraft began work on "Psychopompos," a narrative poem in form because he was "as yet unable to cast off my beloved heroics altogether, even in fiction."[8] Taking inspiration from a vivid dream and written around the June of that year, the only original entry for 1918 is "Polaris." A somewhat more anomalous, collaborative (or round-robin) work from this period has, however, yet to surface, if it indeed even survives. The first mention of Lovecraft's part in this bit of fun is encountered in a letter to Rheinhart Kleiner dated 27 June 1918:

> My Hesperia will be critical & educational in object, though I am "sugar-coating" the first number by "printing" a conclusion of the serial "The Mystery of Murdon Grange". . . . It is outwardly done on the same patchwork plan as before—each chapter bears one of my different aliases—Ward Phillips—Ames Dorrance Rowley— L. Theobald, &c. It was a rather good diversion to write it. Really, I think I could have been a passable dime novelist if I had been trained in that noble calling! (*RK* 145, *SL* 1.68)

A slightly later letter offers an additional comment: "It is a typical dime novel—with all the time-worn appurtenances of its type!" (*RK* 149). From other correspondence of the period it can be inferred that *Hesperia* was a typescript amateur "magazine" circulated on both sides of the Atlantic; there may have been carbon copies, but it has still most likely perished. A letter to Alfred Galpin dated 21 August 1918 (*AG* 33) reveals that Lovecraft was still struggling with the typing at that time, so that his conclusion of "Murdon Grange" may have been lengthy. Based solely on this information we might be forgiven to think that the whole of the dime novel serial was written by Lovecraft, but this was in fact not the case, as his reviews of the earlier portions of the novel attributed to other amateurs (not pseudonyms) in the "Department of Public Criticism" columns for the early 1918 make clear:

---

8. It would, however, be completed only the following summer. Cf. HPL to the Gallomo, April 1920 (*AG* 82).

[The November 1917] issue closes with the first instalment of a "follow-my-leader" serial, "The Mystery of Murdon Grange", contributed by Joseph Parks. Naturally this type of tale is more liable to develop interest than literary finesse, but Mr. Parks acquits himself very creditably in the opening. The United will watch with interest the progress of this fictional mosaic, and will be anxious to see what the various storytellers of amateurdom will make of the fertile theme presented them. (January 1918; *CE* 1.180)

"The Mystery of Murdon Grange" receives its second instalment from the not unpracticed hand of Miss Beryl Mappin, and continues in the pleasantly conventional channel mapped out by Mr. Parks in the preceding chapter. The plot thickens! (January 1918; *CE* 1.180)

Mr. Benjamin Winskill continues "The Mystery of Murdon Grange" with much cleverness, carrying us back into the past for the source of a strange curse. (March 1918; *CE* 1.188)

"The Mystery of Murdon Grange" this month falls into the hands of Editor [Ernest Lionel] McKeag, who furnishes one of the best chapters we have so far perused; possibly the very best. It is exasperating to be cut off abruptly in the midst of the exciting narrative, with the admonition to wait for page 47! (May 1918; *CE* 1.195)

These reviewed portions appeared in the British amateur journal *Spindrift*, and only one of the segments has so far come to light. It is perhaps thus not impossible that Lovecraft's portions were also printed in that magazine and might yet surface by a careful search of amateur journal collections in British institutions, although the fact that he took the trouble of typing up (always a hateful task for him) the conclusion for *Hesperia* would seem to indicate the opposite. The last portion reviewed by Lovecraft appeared in the January 1918 issue of *Spindrift*, and the notes on the February issue in the same column make it clear that the serial was not continued there, and as Lovecraft does not mention the journal in any further amateur writings it may well have ceased publication then. As far as I am aware, Lovecraft never refers to the novel in his correspondence after 1918, and he never considered it as one of his avowed stories. Nevertheless, it would be a fascinating item to have, and we must lament that it was not printed in some less elusive journal.

II. Incessant Scribbling: 1919–26

Discounting the tentative attempts of 1917 and 1918, Lovecraft's fictional career most properly begins with his discovery of the Anglo-Irish fantasist Lord Dunsany in late 1919. True enough, few more tales had already been composed earlier that year—"Beyond the Wall of Sleep" and the very short prose poem "Memory" in the spring, and "The Transition of Juan Romero" in mid-September—but it was only after reading Dunsany and seeing him in person in October during his lecture tour of the United States that Lovecraft's muse got into full swing, initially heavily under the Irish writer's influence. In a quick fashion would be composed first "The White Ship" (likely soon after the October lecture), then "The Street" (around late November), "The Doom That Came to Sarnath" (early December), and others perhaps less directly dominated by Dunsany's example. It is not a coincidence that around this time Lovecraft also began taking down notes for future stories in what is now known as his "commonplace book," a notebook that, as he in 1934 described it, consisted of "ideas, images, & quotations hastily jotted down for possible future use in weird fiction. Very few are actually developed plots—for the most part they are merely suggestions or random impressions designed to set the memory or imagination working. Their sources are various—dreams, things read, casual incidents, idle conceptions, & so on."[9]

Exactly when the keeping of these notes commenced is not certain, but we can probably make a good guess for January 1920. Years later, when R. H. Barlow prepared a typed copy of the book, Lovecraft tried to assign dates to the entries and "1919" has thus been affixed next to the early ones numbered 24 and 25; but clearly many of these dates were given rather tentatively, even if the ones closer to 1934 are probably more or less correct.[10] The first mention of the notebook in extant correspondence is encountered in a letter to Rheinhart Kleiner dated 23 January 1920:

---

9. Note on the AMS version presented to R. H. Barlow.
10. For example, the year 1923 occurs two times, as does 1922, the latter actually queried by HPL himself.

I have lately—by the way—been collecting ideas and images for subsequent use in fiction. For the first time in my life, I am keeping a "commonplace book"—if that term can be applied to a repository of gruesome & fantastick thoughts. (*RK* 178, *SL* 1.106)

The next available letter to Kleiner, of 10 February (*RK* 180–81, *SL* 1.107–8), quotes the early entries 8, 13, and 21, attesting that at least this many had already been set down by that date. Entries 6 and 24 are in fact explicitly derived from two specific stories by Lord Dunsany ("Idle Days on the Yann" and "A Shop on the Go-By Street," respectively), which may be why Lovecraft later assigned to them the year "1919," of his first reading of Dunsany; but as S. T. Joshi has pointed out (*Life* 233), they were more likely written down when Lovecraft was reading them in *Tales of the Three Hemispheres* in early 1920.

One early entry that may be worth examining is the one that rather opaquely reads "[9] Dr. Eben Spencer plot." This is by itself not very helpful, but fortunately more information is provided by contemporary letters. The first relevant discussion is found in the same 23 January letter to Kleiner in which the commonplace book itself is described:

I had a vivid dream a few nights ago—involving the possession of another distinct personality. The period was 1864, & the crux of the dream was a horror in a doctor's secret laboratory. I think the dream-doctor was going to shew me an artificial man like M. Frankenstein's uncomely creation, but premature waking robbed the dream of its climax. In this dream I was Dr. Eben Spencer, an army surgeon home on a furlough. The sinister experimenter was a colleague of mine, Dr. Chester. Some dream! (*RK* 180)

Just how vivid the dream must have been is driven home by a lengthy description that has been preserved in a letter to the Gallomo correspondence cycle (between Lovecraft and his fellow amateurs Maurice W. Moe and Alfred Galpin), dating to around April 1920 (*AG* 71–73, *SL* 1.100–103). Here the account has been considerably fleshed out, and I suspect that Lovecraft, as in the case of "The Statement of Randolph Carter," which likewise was initially recounted to Gallomo at length before being written out as an actual short story, must have after waking up recorded the details of the dream in synoptic notes while the impression was still fresh.[11] The course of the dream can be summarized as follows: It began with Lovecraft occupying the personality of one Dr. Eben Spencer, getting dressed in his room in a New York village. Spencer is an army surgeon on furlough, and after dressing up and entering the street he is persuaded by an acquaintance to meet a colleague of his, Dr. Chester. Chester has for two years been conducting secret experiments behind a locked door, and the acquaintance (Chester's brother) wishes that Dr. Spencer would try to speak to him. Agreeing to do this, Spencer (or Lovecraft) finds Dr. Chester uncannily aged and reluctant to talk of his experiments—"Better not ask Spencer! Better not ask!"—but after Spencer persists in his queries, Chester finally leads the way to his locked laboratory and shows Spencer two severed human arms, which, however, do not appear to belong to "any living thing." But just as Spencer feels that a great revelation is coming, the dream evaporates as Lovecraft woke up. In the letter he offered an analysis of the motivation for the nocturnal experience: "The cause of the whole is clear—I had a few days before laid out Mrs. Shelley's 'Frankenstein' for re-reading. As to details—Ambrose Bierce supplied the Civil War atmosphere, no doubt, whilst it's easy to trace in Dr. Chester and his brother—facially, I mean—the likeness of my boyhood friends *Chester* and Harold Munroe" (*AG* 73).

In this account to the Gallomo Lovecraft may have already begun to enrich the original experience with an eventual transformation into a story in mind, but even so, with details such as a calendar giving the date "Friday, July 8, 1864," the strange odor in Dr. Chester's laboratory—not to mention the persona of Dr. Spencer—it must have been a very vivid and extraordinary dream indeed. But no more of it is heard in any subsequent letters, and although the commonplace book entry has been crossed out as if having been used, it does not seem that Lovecraft actually tried to weave this germ into a story; perhaps one reason for this was that,

---

11. That he did so for "The Statement of Randolph Carter" is confirmed by a letter to Robert Bloch (22 July 1933; *RB* 27): "The dream gave me such a punch that I jumped at once, lit the gas, & made a set of synoptic notes before the first keen edge of the impression wore off. Then later I wrote the story."

unlike the dream that furnished the genesis for "The Case of Randolph Carter," there was no ready-made climax.

But is the contemplated story of "Dr. Eben Spencer plot" actually lost? Perhaps not in a sense, for although the setting has been transformed from that of a Civil War–era New York village to contemporary Providence and there is no trace of Dr. Spencer himself, the basic scenario may have been incorporated into "From Beyond," written in November of the same year. In both that tale and the dream account we have an old friend of the protagonist who has been making secret experiments in his locked laboratory and who has become sinisterly aged or transformed when met again. The revelation that Crawford Tillinghast makes in "From Beyond" is of course something quite different from the "artificial man" who Lovecraft thought was about to appear in the dream. But the basic premise may still have been fused into the later story, combined with ideas probably derived, as S. T. Joshi has conjectured (*Life* 238–39; *Primal Sources* 167–71), from a reading of Hugh Elliot's *Modern Science and Materialism* (1919). In addition, the artificial man concept may later in part eventually have influenced the "Herbert West—Reanimator" serial (September 1921–Spring 1922).

Slightly later in the commonplace book there is an enigmatic entry that has tortured many Lovecraft scholars:

Life and Death
Death—its desolation and horror—bleak spaces—sea-bottom—dead cities. But Life—the greater horror! Vast unheard-of reptiles and leviathans—hideous beasts of prehistoric jungle—rank slimy vegetation—evil instincts of primal man—Life is more horrible than death.

This entry is the one just previous to that recording the germ of "The Cats of Ulthar" (28), and like that is the only one bearing a title in the book. The latter story was written out on 15 June 1920,[12] but the gist of "The Cats of Ulthar" as set down in the commonplace book had been already recounted to Kleiner in a letter of 21 May 1920 (*RK* 190–91, *SL* 1.116–17); some time thus

---

12. As dated on a fair copy autograph manuscript given to Rheinhart Kleiner, formerly in the Grill–Binkin collection (#554).

elapsed between the conception and composition. This letter also describes the dream concerning a bas-relief and a museum that was (much) later incorporated into "The Call of Cthulhu" and which has itself been preserved as entry 25 in the book. On the other hand, the bas-relief dream is also described in the same April 1920 letter to the Gallomo in which we have encountered the long account of the "Dr. Eben Spencer" dream, so that it seems very likely that the whole group 25–28 was put down at more or less the same time, shortly before if not actually on 21 May 1920.

But the crucial question of course is, was "Life and Death" actually ever written out as a story as "The Cats of Ulthar" was, near this date or later? The evidence is inconclusive. Lovecraft himself never mentions it (as far as we can now tell), although admittedly this is also true for certain other minor items from the same period, so that perhaps a letter noting it has simply been lost. It is unfortunate—and perhaps significant—that neither in the letter to Kleiner nor in the one to the Gallomo does he say a word about this story idea, even though a number of further dream experiences jotted down in the commonplace book are recounted. It is first listed as an actual story in the Laney–Evans Lovecraft bibliography of 1943, but the compilers may well have derived their information simply from the commonplace book itself, as it had already been published in 1938 in an edition by the Futile Press, edited by Lovecraft's literary executor R. H. Barlow.[13] In the bibliography the story is dated as "c. 1920," clearly on account of the commonplace book. Probably because of its inclusion in this work, August Derleth queried Barlow in 1944 about "Life and Death" and other tales not then located; Barlow's reply was that "As for the sort [of] pieces you ask about, I can be of no help . . . THE STREET I saw once, I think, and LIFE AND DEATH"[14] (*Life* 246). If Barlow in fact had once seen it, that would surely have been in some amateur journal appearance that has yet to come to light, but it seems inconceivable that he would then have

---

13. Barlow may, however, have provided additional information to Laney and Evans; his assistance is acknowledged in their bibliography. I am grateful to Christopher O'Brien for this observation.

14. R. H. Barlow to August Derleth, 14 June 1944 (ms., State Historical Society of Wisconsin).

failed to copy the item. W. Paul Cook suggested to Derleth the *United Amateur* as the place of possible publication (see *Encyclopedia* 148), but this at any rate is not where it was printed, if the story (or perhaps a prose poem) ever did appear in an amateur magazine. George T. Wetzel, who did pioneering early bibliographical work on Lovecraft's amateur appearances, claimed in his article "Research of a Biblio" to have located the purported publication during his research at the Fossils Collection:

> The exorbitant price asked for what few copies of the Lovecraft books *The Outsider and Others* and *Beyond the Wall of Sleep* were available, plus the fact that not all his stories were procurable in moderately priced copies of *Weird Tales* magazine, had long caused me to be on the look-out for other appearances of his work. When I heard that certain Lovecraft items were to be found in some amateur press papers I was exceptionally interested. . . . Not only to see and read HPL items unobtainable in the few available "pocket editions", but also for the prestige of compiling a bibliography of his amateur works is what made me decide to go to the Franklin Institute in Philadelphia and research these items. . . . While in Philadelphia I showed some of my initial compilation to Oswald Train who immediately decided he would collaborate with me on the project; since that time he has apparently done nothing, since he has never written me. The Lovecraft story "Life and Death" was found by me at this time, but the amateur paper and date were on one page of my biblio which vanished while I was visiting at Train's home. I attempted to re-locate this item on a later trip, but I feel I've not back-tracked enough. Suffice it to say that it exists in those files and may one day be uncovered by some one more blessed with funds for research expenses than myself. (41)

But needless to say, posterity has yet to vindicate Wetzel's prediction, as searches in the Fossils and other amateur journalism repositories have not uncovered the story. We may then reasonably ask whether "Life and Death" was actually ever written at all: it would seem more likely that Wetzel's memory was simply muddled, and that Barlow may likewise have been simply thinking of the commonplace book note. S. T. Joshi has more recently put forth the proposition that the alleged existence of the story may be explained by confusion with the extant "Ex Oblivione," which seems to be vaguely similar in conception to the commonplace book note.

After writing "The Cats of Ulthar," and just possibly "Life and Death", new stories continued to flow from Lovecraft's pen at steady rate: at least "The Temple," "Facts concerning the Late Arthur Jermyn and His Family," "Celephaïs," "From Beyond," "Nyarlathotep," and "The Crawling Chaos" were all probably composed between June and December 1920. "The Nameless City" followed by the end of January 1921 (see *SL* 1.122), establishing that the commonplace book had reached entry number 47 by this time, as it cites a description of the fabled city of Irem from *Encyclopaedia Britannica* which was incorporated into that story. But on 24 May 1921 a disaster struck when Lovecraft's beloved mother Sarah Susan died unexpectedly as the result of a botched gall-bladder operation. For a short time the effect of this bereavement must have been devastating, but before long Lovecraft began to take an increasing part in amateur activities, and as soon as 8 and 9 June of that year Lovecraft was visiting Myrta Alice Little and C. W. "Tryout" Smith in Westville and Haverhill in New Hampshire. Other amateur meetings then followed, including another trip to Haverhill toward the end of August. In the commonplace book we find a mysterious entry that is probably contemporaneous with one of these visits:

> [56] Book or MS. too horrible to be read—warned against reading it—someone read and is found dead. Haverhill incident.

The central idea of this jotting is manifestly derived from Ambrose Bierce's "Suitable Surroundings," read by Lovecraft in the collection *In the Midst of Life* in 1919 (see *SL* 1.89).[15] But there seems to be no clue as to the significance of the "Haverhill incident." I suppose, however, that it may have been something that C. W. Smith had related to Lovecraft, rather than anything he himself experienced during either of the visits.[16] But if nothing

---

15. The previous entry may likewise have been derived from Bierce, in this case from "The Damned Thing."

16. In a letter to Alfred Galpin (31 August 1921), while relating the second Haverhill excursion, HPL briefly mentions a climb "through the spectral wood" attempted in order to make astronomical observations and which he thought might "perhaps furnish an idea or two for a story" (*AG* 100), but this took place

else, this enigmatic note allows us to date this portion of the commonplace book to around this time with good certainty.[17]

During the 1920–22 period in particular Lovecraft seems to have been bursting with fiction ideas, and although 1920 records the greatest number of stories composed by him for a single year, only a handful of all the conceptions occurring to him were actually developed, at the time in any case. It is now that we first begin to hear of nebulous ideas for actual novels instead of short stories. Although mainstream publishers would in the 1930s more than once request a novel-length work from him, Lovecraft in the end would never truly write one, perhaps partly because the actual length of his existing novellas was dictated more by accident than design and he felt that attempting a novel consciously would be tantamount to writing to order, something that was anathema to him. Quite frankly, Lovecraft was in 1920 probably nowhere near the stage of actually composing a full-scale novel, but there of course would have been no obstacle to merely daydreaming about writing one.

The first mention of such a notion comes in a letter to Rheinhart Kleiner of 7 March 1920, in the context of discussing weird fiction: "I am at present full of various ideas, including a hideous novel to be entitled 'The Club of Seven Dreamers'" (*RK* 183, *SL* 1.110). This is the only known reference by Lovecraft to this planned, intriguingly titled work in surviving correspondence, and in view of the lack of further information it is perhaps futile to speculate on what kind of novel it might have been; yet the hypothesis by S. T. Joshi and David E. Schultz (cf. *Life* 233, *Encyclopedia* 40) that it might have been an episodic narrative of linked stories told by the eponymous "seven dreamers" is plausible enough. Perhaps it can be also guessed that this kind of framework would have allowed Lovecraft to incorporate and develop some of the

during the Hampstead part of the August 1921 trip, not in Haverhill.

17. The writing of "The Outsider" may also date to near this time, as in the same letter to Galpin HPL tells of reading it aloud, along with "The Other Gods," apparently indicating that it was then not very old. Another letter to Frank Belknap Long of 17 July (*SL* 1.141) says that "I have written nothing for aeons," supporting a hypothesis that "The Outsider" was written between this date and the second Haverhill visit, perhaps in early August 1921 before "The Other Gods" (the manuscript of which is dated 14 August).

dream-nuclei noted down in the commonplace book. Working merely from the title, it has been further suggested (ibid.) that the example of Poe's abortive collection *Tales of the Folio Club*—which likewise was supposed to utilize a framework of a club narrating (previously written) otherwise unconnected stories—as well as that of John Osborne Austin's *More Seven Club Tales* (1900) may have been influential; but such a theory is of course impossible to verify. The latter volume, a sort of a sequel to the author's earlier *The Journal of William Jefferay* (1899), relates seven strange accounts purportedly sent by historical New England (mostly Rhode Island) figures to Jefferay "with a desire that they be read unto the Seven Club." (Austin was a genealogist of note and a friend of Lovecraft's uncle F. C. Clark, which is no doubt why he had both volumes in his library.) As for Poe's planned collection, Lovecraft may conceivably have learned of it from James A. Harrison's edition of the *Complete Works* (1902), where a manuscript of the preface to the original incarnation of the unissued collection was included[18]— Lovecraft did not own this edition, but could have consulted it in a library. Only an influence of a very general sort can here be postulated, however. But until some further mention of *The Club of Seven Dreamers* surfaces in a hitherto unknown letter, we are left very much in the dark for what designs he might have had for this novel, which probably was never actually begun.

Somewhat more is known of another abandoned novel conceived slightly later. Unlike perhaps *The Club of Seven Dreamers*, this would presumably have been a true book-length narrative, and although only a short fragment of less than 500 words now survives—in all likelihood all that was ever set down on paper— Lovecraft seems to have carried the idea for a long time in his mind, as an offhand remark to the *Weird Tales* editor Edwin Baird, written more than three years after the earliest adumbrations of the work are encountered, reveals: "All this apart from my big novel idea—Azathoth—which will be exotic and highbrow,

---

18. See Mabbott (ed.), *Tales and Sketches*, 1.200–207. A little more information of Poe's intentions for the *Folio Club* is revealed in a letter (2 September 1836) to the publisher Harrison Hall, but HPL could not possibly have known of this, as the letter was first printed by T. O. Mabbott in his essay in the *Suwanee Review* (April 1928); cf. ibid. 1.202, where the letter is again quoted.

and wholly unsuited to Weird Tales" (*SL* 1.295). The name
Azathoth itself occurs in a jotting found in the commonplace
book that probably dates to around the first half of 1921: "[49]
AZATHOTH—hideous name."[19] A bit later an actual plot germ
has been recorded: "[61] A terrible pilgrimage to seek the knighted
throne of the far daemon-sultan Azathoth." The note is possibly
contemporary with a letter to Winifred V. Jackson of 7 October
1921, where Lovecraft speaks of a planned "weird Eastern tale in
the 18th century manner; a tale perhaps too long for publication
in amateurdom" (*Life* 286). This appears to reveal a direct influence of a fantastic work in the eighteenth-century manner and
with an Eastern setting that he had first read only a short time before: William Beckford's *The History of Caliph Vathek* (1786),
which Rheinhart Kleiner had lent to him in the July 1921 N.A.P.A.
convention (cf. *RK* 209). Lovecraft in fact confirms that this is so in
a letter written to Frank Belknap Long on 9 June of the next year:

> *Imagination* is the great refuge. That is the theme of the weird
> Vathek-like novel *Azathoth*, on whose opening pages I have been
> experimenting. I planned it long ago, but only began work—or
> play—on it a few days ago. Probably I'll never finish it—possibly
> I'll never even get a chapter written—but it amuses me just now
> to pretend to myself that I'm going to write it. (*SL* 1.185)

He then proceeds to quote the entire extant fragment; probably
no more of it was indeed afterwards ever set down. The continuation of the letter is interesting:

> The rest—for which this introduction prepares the reader, will be
> material of the Arabian Nights type. I shall defer to no modern
> critical canon, but shall frankly slip back through the centuries and
> become a myth-maker with that childish sincerity which no one
> but earlier Dunsany has tried to achieve nowadays. I shall go out of
> the world when I write, with mind centred not in literary usage,

---

19. As we have seen, entry 47 was incorporated into "The Nameless City," so it
cannot be later than late January 1921 when that story was composed, and entry
56 is the "Haverhill incident," probably of August 1921. R. H. Barlow has recorded that HPL later stated that the name—like Nyarlathotep—had come to
him in a dream ("[Memories of H. P. Lovecraft (1934)]," *FF* 404).

> but in the dreams I dreamed when I was six years old or less—the
> dreams which followed my first knowledge of Sinbad, of Agib, of
> Baba-Abdallah, and of Sidi-Nonman. (*Life* 286 [omitted in *SL*])

From this is seems that he perhaps had no very clear idea of just
what kind of "material of the *Arabian Nights* type" the narrative
would exactly have contained, which may be why no more of it
was written. But it is possible that it was *Azathoth* that Lovecraft
was still in part thinking of when he wrote from New York to his
aunt Lillian D. Clark on 30–31 July 1925 that he intended "yet to
give several of my contemplated phantasies an Eastern—probably
Baghdad—setting" (*NY* 159). But if this is so, the intention was
evidently never taken up, unless the hypothesis is correct that
something of the novel survives mutated into *The Dream-Quest of
the Unknown Kadath*.

　　In the same letter to Edwin Baird quoted above and where
Lovecraft was still presenting *Azathoth* as a going concern, a third
lost novel is fleetingly mentioned:

> I should hardly say that [Henneberger] made me any "proposi-
> tion", as he intimated to you he might. The only part of his letter
> that brought me in was a request for a novel of 25,000 words or
> over, which I shall be happy to send when I finish it. I've nothing
> of that length complete, but after trying serial stuff for Home
> Brew I experimented a bit with the novel form, and an idea partly
> shaped which will probably suit Mr. Henneberger's requirements.
> It is a hideous thing whose provisional title (subject to change) is
> *The House of the Worm*. (*SL* 1.295)

A few days later he writes of the prospect in much the same
words to Long:

> Henneberger wants a novel or novelette from me—something un-
> speakably terrible, and over 25,000 words in length. I think I shall
> comply with his request, developing a monstrous and noxious idea
> which has been simmering unwholesomely in my consciousness—a
> ghastly thing to be intitul'd *The House of the Worm*. (*SL* 1.304)

Apart from this, I am not aware of any other references by Lovecraft to this projected work. What is notable here is that he says
to actually have "experimented a bit with the novel form"; the

reference to the *Home Brew* serials would apparently date this to no earlier than late 1922, "The Lurking Fear" having been written in November of that year—and the following separate mention of *Azathoth* in the letter to Baird indicates that it was not that fragment to which Lovecraft was referring. Perhaps this experimentation in part accounts for the gap between that second serial story and "The Rats in the Walls," written in August 1923. But what does he in fact mean by "experimented": had he actually prepared some kind of plan or synopsis and begun work on it? In the absence of anything else we can only speculate, but from the two passages above it can be surmised that he at least had the idea fairly well developed in his mind in February 1924, even if pen was never put down on paper. The title itself may indicate that two entries in the commonplace book could be relevant:

[80] Shapeless living thing forming nucleus of ancient building.

[117] A secret living thing kept and fed in an old house.

After the second entry Lovecraft has later added the date "1924"; it may have been inspired by his reading of Bram Stoker's *The Lair of the White Worm*, which had been lent to him by W. Paul Cook in early October 1923, and of which Lovecraft thought that its "plot idea is colossal, but the development so childish that I cannot imagine how the thing ever got into print" (*SL* 1.255). Soon after writing to Baird Lovecraft would, after first completing the rush-job of ghost-writing "Under the Pyramids" under Houdini's name (and by J. C. Henneberger's request) for *Weird Tales*, marry Sonia H. Greene and move to New York. In the immediate aftermath of all this, other literary prospects (which ultimately came to naught) seem to have kept him busy for a while, and the notion of writing *The House of the Worm* must eventually have fallen by the wayside by the collapse of Henneberger's business plans during the spring.

But was the idea for the story utterly lost? William Fulwiler originally proposed (59) that it may have been a "working title" for "The Shunned House," and there may be some truth to this. "The Shunned House" (written in October 1924) was the first tale written by Lovecraft in New York after "Under the Pyramids," and it can be plausibly conjectured that *The House of the Worm* would also have revolved around a house to which a hideous "living thing" of some sort is attached. The gradual beginning of "The Shunned House" may also indicate that Lovecraft would have been ready to develop that story at considerable length. But even so, there can be little doubt that had the novel been written as planned instead of the extant story, the development would have been very different from what was set out in "The Shunned House," which for one thing is tightly tied to its Providence setting, the immediate impetus for the writing of the story having been a view of "a terrible old house" glimpsed during a visit to Elizabeth that reminded Lovecraft of the house on Benefit Street in Providence. We can again only hope that in the future some further letters will eventually surface and reveal just what that "monstrous and noxious idea" was that *The House of the Worm* was supposed to have embodied.

A puzzling aspect of Lovecraft's two-year New York stay is how little fiction he wrote during it, considering his acute need of income and the relatively lucrative venue that *Weird Tales* now offered. The simple explanation for this is that he simply felt unable to attempt composition most of the time, outside the familiar soil of Providence, but other factors came into play as well. Until about the middle of 1925 he had to attend to amateur matters, and even then once his responsibilities were theoretically over, requests for assistance continued to come in from the new officials. In November W. Paul Cook would request that he write an article "on the element of terror & weirdness in literature" (*NY* 249), and Lovecraft threw himself into the work with zest, devoting much of his time to the necessary research, eventually producing the landmark historical treatise "Supernatural Horror in Literature." In fact, there was no overriding need to compose new fiction at all, as for the time being Lovecraft could simply keep *Weird Tales* stocked by submitting older stories from the backlog he had accumulated between 1917 and 1924.

But in addition to the tales that he did manage to write after "The Shunned House" during this difficult period—"The Horror at Red Hook" and "He" in August 1925, "In the Vault" in September, and "Cool Air" in February 1926—there is one lost work that Lovecraft mentions several times in the letters to his aunt Lillian

D. Clark. Unfortunately, at no point does he seem to expound on any of the details, although the first mention of the tale suggests that Lillian was already familiar with the basic idea:

> Very shortly I shall start some businesslike writing—copying more stories for *Weird Tales* & beginning some new ones whose ideas are clamouring for expression—notably that novel or novelette of Salem Horrors which I may be able to cast in a sufficiently 'detectivish' mould to sell to Edwin Baird for *Detective Tales*—which rejected the "Shunned House". (*NY* 155)

Slightly later, after having composed "The Horror at Red Hook" on 1–2 August, he would write that "I think I shall try my new story on *Detective Tales*," adding a note against the name of the magazine: "where also I shall send my Salem novel—if I ever get the undisturbed leisure to write it. That, if accepted, would bring in a goodly sum of cash" (*NY* 167). There is not much else to go by in the correspondence, but from these remarks it can still be gauged that the novel had been planned to some degree of completeness, even if none of it was ever set down. Were it not for the second mention, one could actually be forgiven to think that the Salem setting was morphed into the New York slums of "The Horror at Red Hook" (which is in a "detectivish mould"), but the fact that it is also alluded to subsequent to the completion of that story makes clear that this is not the case. Perhaps the newly arisen idea for "The Call of Cthulhu," for which a synopsis was written on 12 August (cf. *NY* 172), displaced the "Salem novel" in Lovecraft's imagination, for in early November he would assure Clark Ashton Smith that this "tale of the sunken continent will probably be written during the coming week, and you shall certainly be the first to see it";[20] in the event, that task would itself not be accomplished until nearly a year later, after he had returned to Providence.

But even if little information is revealed by the surviving letters of the New York period, we can perhaps speculate on the sources for this another lost novel. A hint is provided by the Salem location, and in the commonplace book this note is found:

---

20. 4 November 1925 (ms., JHL).

[99] Salem story—the cottage of an aged witch—wherein after her death are found sundry terrible things.

This entry can probably be dated to around early 1923; at any rate it must be later than 17 December 1922, for it was on this date Lovecraft first saw Marblehead, an event that must be contemporary with the entry numbered 81. It was during this same trip that he also visited Salem (see *RK* 226, *SL* 1.203–4), and another visit there followed in February (*AG* 128, *SL* 1.213), but a description of the Rebecca Nurse house from a letter recounting an April 1923 excursion to the nearby Danvers (originally named Salem Village) seems quite suggestive as a possible source:

Beyond a low crest a thick group of spectral boughs bespoke some kind of grove or orchard—and in the midst of this group I suddenly descry'd the rising outline of a massive and ancient chimney. Presently, as I advanced, I saw the top of a grey, drear, sloping roof— sinister in its distant setting of bleak hillside and leafless grove, and unmistakably belonging to the haunted edifice I sought. Another turn—a gradual ascent—and I beheld in full view the sprawling, tree-shadow'd house which had for nearly three hundred years brooded over those hills and held such secrets as men ay only guess. . . . Everything about that place is ancient—even the tiny-paned lattice windows which open outward on hinges. The atmosphere of witchcraft days broods heavily on that low hilltop.

Entering, I found myself in a low, dark passage whose massive beams almost touched my head; and passing on, I travers'd the two immense rooms on the ground floor—sombre, barren, panell'd apartments with colossal fireplaces in the vast central chimney . . . In these wide, low-pitched rooms a spectral menace broods—for to my imagination the seventeenth century is as full of macabre mystery, repression and ghoulish adumbrations as the eighteenth century is full of taste, gayety, grace, and beauty. . . . After exploring the ground-floor I crept up the black crooked stairs and examin'd the bleak chambers above. . . . And the sunset wind whistled in the colossal chimney, and the ghouls rattled ghastly skeletons from unseen attic rafters overhead. Though it was not suppos'd to be open to the publick, I persuaded the caretaker to let me ascend to that hideous garret of century'd secrets. Thick dust covered everything, and unnatural shapes loom'd on

every hand as the evening twilight oozed through the little blear'd
panes of the ancient windows. I saw something hanging from the
wormy ridge-pole—something that sway'd as if in unison with
the vesper breeze outside, though that breeze had no access to
this funeral and forgotten place—shadows . . . . . shadows . . . . .
shadows . . . . . And I descended from that accursed garret of pa-
laeogean arcane, and left that portentous abode of antiquity; left it
and went down the hill the graveyard under the shocking pines,
where twilight show'd sinister slabs and rusty bits of fallen iron
fence, and where something squatted in shadow on a monu-
ment—something that made me climb the hill again, hurry shud-
deringly past the venerable house, and descend the opposite slope
to Tapleyville as night came. (*AG* 141–43, *SL* 1.221–23)

But even if scenes like this and the atmosphere of Salem in general
with its suggestion of the witchcraft-trial days set Lovecraft's mind
to work, there is now no telling what kind of a plot he had spun
from such materials. S. T. Joshi has pointed out (*Life* 416) that just
before finishing *The Dream-Quest of Unknown Kadath* and beginning writing *The Case of Charles Dexter Ward* Lovecraft evidently
still referred to the Salem novel of 1925 when he on 21 January 1927
remarked to Clark Ashton Smith that "sometime I wish to write a
novel of more naturalistic setting, in which some hideous threads of
witchcraft trail down the centuries against the sombre & memory-
haunted background of ancient Salem" (*SL* 2.99), and based on this
Joshi has proposed that the novel idea may have been transferred to
Providence as *The Case of Charles Dexter Ward*. There is probably
some truth to this—the 1927 work is in a fashion a kind of a detective story—but supposing that this is the case, I cannot help thinking that if the tale had been written out in a Salem setting the end
result would have been a very different work from what we now
have, seeing how tightly the locale and history of Providence have
been integrated into *Charles Dexter Ward*.

Another lost story whose nucleus was devised during the New
York period was what is now known as "Cassius" by Lovecraft's
colleague and correspondent Henry S. Whitehead. The basic idea
has again been recorded in the commonplace book: "[133] Man has
miniature shapeless Siamese twin—exhib. in circus—twin surgically detached—disappears—does hideous things with malign life

of his own." Lovecraft has later dated this and the surrounding entries as "1925," and this would seem reasonable, given that entry 139 (apparently the last set down in New York)[21] records the citation from Delrio that was incorporated into "The Horror at Red Hook," written 1–2 August 1925. An interesting fact about this note is that it was derived from an actual person whom Lovecraft had seen in New York. Years later, he would tell to Duane W. Rimel:

> [M]y idea came from seeing an actual case of the undeveloped-twin anomaly in a freak show (Hubert's Museum in W. 42nd St.) in New York. The man in question—an intelligent Italian who for some reason billed himself under the French name of "Jean Libera"—had a little anthropoid excrescence growing out of his abdomen which looked hellishly gruesome when uncovered. Clothed he looked merely like a somewhat "pot-bellied" individual. So far as I know, he is still living and on exhibition. He looked so essentially refined and high-grade that I wondered at his willingness to be exploited as a freak, and speculated as to what he would do if a stroke of luck removed him from the need of such an ignominious occupation. The first thing he would do, I argued, would be to have the excrescence cut off—and then and there the idea of the story came. This was in 1924 or 1925. (*SL* 5.34–35)

Lovecraft has throughout the letter given the name of this person as Jean Libera, but his surname was actually *Libbera*. Jean, or rather Giovanni Libbera was born in Rome, Italy in 1884. According to the pamphlet *Life Story and Facts about Jean and Jacques Libbera, Joined Together Twins*:

> Of all the many millions of people inhabiting the earth the counterpart of Jean Libbera can not be found. . . . The father, mother, brothers and sisters with one exception, are ordinary appearing people, nothing unusual in their personal appearance or physical characteristics. Like most Italian families, there are many children in the family, thirteen altogether. Jean is the fourth child; strange to say the third child was the same as Jean, but died immediately

---

21. The commonplace book seems to have been continued only about October 1927, as entry 141 is an extract from H. Rider Haggard and Andrew Lang's *The World's Desire* (1890), which HPL read at that time; see HPL to August Derleth, 1 October 1927 (*ES* 1.106).

after its birth. . . . In Jean Libbera we are confronted with the un-
paralleled spectacle of a handsome, normal young man, out of
whose body there grows a second body diminutive in size, but
perfect so far is it goes; arms, hands, fingers, even down to the
nails upon the fingers, hips, thighs, shins, feet, toes and nails upon
the toes. The circulation of the blood comes from the normal
body and that same body furnishes the nourishment for the two
bodies. The second body is as well developed as the normal body,
but for its size it possesses a strong bone structure. The feelings of
both bodies are the same, and the various changes of the weather
and temperature; also the touching of one body is immediately
felt by the other. As to the cause of this most wonderful birth
there can be no doubt that it was originally intended to be double
birth or twins, but owing to some incident or influence an amal-
gamation was made and so the mother supplied the world by present to it "not one child and not two children, but more than one,
yet not two". The scientific explanation is the fusion of two living
germs in the one ovum. Jean Libbera has been examined by the
leading Medical and surgical Experts of both Europe and American. In Paris, Professor Ponier presented him to the Surgical Society and he was pronounced to be the greatest anomaly of nature
ever known. In Cologne, Prof. Berdenheimer made a very thor-
ough and complete examination, using the X-ray, and in his report he declares there is embedded in the normal body a
formation that resembles a rudimentary head; this he claims has a
circumference of about 15 centimeters. Recently Prof. Van Dayse
of the University of Gand, Belgium, has given to this phenomena
[sic] the term of Epigastric Parasite.[22]

Several photographs of Libbera survive, and they verify the description given in the pamphlet. It would seem that he had originally
been exhibited in France where the name Jean was picked up; in
one French photograph taken at the age of twenty-eight, as well as
in the title of the booklet cited above, the parasitic twin is identified by the name "Jacques." There is some uncertainty as to when
he died, as I have seen it given both as 1934 and 1936, but in any
case he was "happily married and the father of four children, per-

---

22. Quoted at http://www.phreeque.com/jean_libbera.html to which I am indebted.

fectly normal in every respect."
When uncovered, "Jacques" is, however, displayed in the photographs as
indeed quite hideous, and it is not
difficult to see how Lovecraft's mind
could have been set to work on a
story based on this encounter.

I am not sure just exactly when
Lovecraft would have seen Libbera—the letters to his aunts from
the period, published in *Letters from
New York*, do not appear to record
it—but perhaps he would not have
wished to tell them of attending a
freak show. Probably he visited
Hubert's Museum on Times Square
with one or more of his Kalem Club
friends during one of their late-night
peregrinations around the metropolis after a club meeting. The
existing diary for 1925 records for 15 July a "walk [to] Times Sq."
(*CE* 5.163), which at least fits the period. It is possible that it was
Arthur Leeds of the Kalem Club who had shown him the
Hubert's Museum in 1925, as in 1934 Lovecraft would note a surprising development:

> Years afterward . . . I chanced to mention the matter to my old
> friend Arthur Leeds of New York, who has had extensive deal-
> ings with freaks and other amusement enterprises. Fancy my sur-
> prise when he told me[23] that he knows Libera well . . . that he is
> interested in everything *weird*, and that he (believe this or not—
> it's actual truth!) he is especially fond of *my* work in *Weird
> Tales!!!!* Talk about coincidence! Leeds was going to tell him
> about "Cassius", but I told him not to, since he might feel some
> delicacy (despite his occupation) about being used that way. At
> the time (1930) Leeds was going to introduce me to Libera; but

---

23. In fact HPL may have learned of the fact indirectly from Frank Belknap Long,
as he seems to reply to this information conveyed by Long in a letter dating to
April 1931 (Arkham House transcripts): "About that dual Hubert's Museum
freak—what a coincidence that good old Arturo shou'd know him!"

something prevented, so the meeting never came off. It certainly would have seemed odd to meet one of my plot-germs in the flesh . . . . the flesh of two bodies, or a body and a half at that! (*SL* 5.35)

F. Lee Baldwin perhaps somewhat indiscreetly copied these remarks in his brief "H. P. Lovecraft: A Biographical Sketch,"[24] although there is little reason to think that Libbera ever saw this article, even if he did live until 1936.

The story idea was not developed by Lovecraft in New York or later, and it lay dormant in the commonplace book for several years, but after coming in touch with the fellow *Weird Tales* author Henry S. Whitehead around October 1930 a cordial correspondence ensued, as a result of which Lovecraft would lend Whitehead the book in late January 1931 (see *MF* 1.144, *SL* 3.284). Whitehead then soon began a work on the entry 133 in it:

> Whitehead . . . has just started a tale from an idea of mine which he is suggesting that I finish as a collaborated work—but I may pass it up because of inability to do justice to the West Indian locale he has seen fit to choose. I am the sworn enemy of armchair exoticism, & believe in writing about things one personally knows—except of course in the case of Dunsanian phantasy of cosmic infinity. I hope I can get to a few tales of my own before long. (*ES* 1.320)

Whitehead kept urging him to accept the offer for collaboration through at least February, but Lovecraft could not get very enthusiastic about the prospect:

> Whether I do anything with that Whitehead tale depends on how eager he is about it—for I hate being churlish and uncivil. He says he has it all started, & that he has prepared some guiding notes on the chosen West-Indian background. His spontaneous affability is disarming—just now I am vastly indebted to him for the generous & wholly unexpected gift of Cline's "Dark Chamber." (*ES* 1.321–22)

> As for collaboration—though I've done it in scores of ghostwriting cases, I think I'll dispose of the Whitehead case by keep-

---

24. Published in *Fantasy Magazine* 4, No. 5 (Spring 1935); rpt. in S. T. Joshi, ed., *Caverns Measureless to Man* 11–15.

ing things in the air till he writes the whole thing himself. (*ES* 1.324)

It is probably just as well that Lovecraft did not choose to cooperate with Whitehead on the story but concentrated instead on the writing of *At the Mountains of Madness*. Whitehead went on to complete the tale by himself, and it was eventually published later that year as "Cassius" in the November 1931 issue of *Strange Tales*.[25] In his version the locale has been transferred to Whitehead's familiar West Indies, the tale made one of his Gerald Canevin cycle of stories, and the man with the parasitic twin as one of Canevin's servants: "Whitehead made his tale so typical of his own style and milieu that I told him to finish it himself . . . He has the foetal twin very tiny, and possessed of a crude intelligence. African atavism (it is a West Indian nigger) appears, and it torments the normal and liberated twin. Finally a cat kills it—for it is no larger than a rat and moves with ratlike silence and rapidity. Nice old Felis!"[26] Lovecraft commented on the story's success—or lack of it—to August Derleth:

> About "Cassius"—it is hard for me to give an unbiased judgement, since the development is so antithetical to that which I had in mind when offering the central idea. To me it seems that a vast number of atmospheric & other horror-possibilities have been left unrealised, & that the typically bland, urbane, & almost unctuous style (the stereotyped Kipling tradition) wrecks the sort of hideous tensity really needed. Yet on the other hand I can see where Whitehead has used a fertile cleverness in incident-devising that I could never have approached. The chief scientific objection is, of course, the part played by "hereditary memory"—a thing wholly repudiated by responsible biologists, though still favoured by weird writers. I'd call "Cassius" a typical anthology item—for "sophisticated" professionals love that unctuous urbanity which to me is so markedly unsatisfying. (*ES* 1.404–5)

But how Lovecraft would himself have envisioned writing the

---

25. Collected in Whitehead's posthumous Arkham House collection *Jumbee and Other Uncanny Tales* (1944); also in *Tales of the Jumbee and Other Wonders of the West Indies* (Wildside Press, 2009).
26. HPL to Frank Belknap Long, Arkham House transcripts (Sun's Day April, 1931).

story? We will of course never really know, but the letters quoted earlier offer some clues:

> I was divided between two plans of development. One would have had the monster escape as Whitehead had it—but would have had it much more terrible and much less human. I would have had it grow in size, and frighten people much more terribly than *Cassius* did. Indeed, I would have tried to convey the implication that some *Outside* force or daemon had taken possession of the brainless, twisted body—impelling it to strange acts of *apparently deliberate but plainly non-human motivation*. (SL 5.33)

> Let the man inherit money and have the twin removed . . . . . and then let the twin disappear from the hospital laboratory . . . . and then let something be found appearing to travellers at night and looking into windows . . . . . . But none of us mean to insult Leeds's cultivated friend. I shall be careful to make my hero a gentleman. Perhaps he need not even be a circus freak. Let us say he is a French Viscount, who had to have the operation postponed on account of early poor health. As he grows more robust in middle life, he decides to risk the operation. It is successful, and the patient lives . . . . . but SOMETHING ELSE lives, too, and is seiz'd upon by a sort of intelligence from Outside. [27]

> The climax would have consisted of some dramatic and unmistakable revelation of this Outside tenancy—probably connected with the spectacular destruction of the thing in one way or another. My story would have had none of the lightness, suavity, and humour of Whitehead's, but would have been grim and terrible all through. So much for *one* plot. (SL 5.33)

He then goes on to record an alternate development of the same commonplace book nucleus that he had himself had in mind:

> The other plot I had in mind was much more human—not supernatural at all, in fact. This idea was to have the connection of the man and his miniature twin *much more complex and obscure* than any doctor had suspected. The operation of separation is performed—but lo! An unforeseen horror and tragedy results. For it

---

27. HPL to Frank Belknap Long, Arkham House transcripts (Sun's Day April, 1931).

seems *that the brain of the twin-burdened man lay in the miniature twin alone . . . .* so that the operation has produced *a hideous monster only a foot tall, with the keen brain of a man, and a handsome man-like shell with the undeveloped brain of a total idiot.* From this situation I planned to develop an appropriate plot, although—from the magnitude of the task—I had not progressed very far. I had an idea of having the midget monster assume the guardianship of his hideous handsome, brainless twin and endeavour to hypnotise it in such a way that it could do his talking for him and act as a substitute in the outside world. I meant to have him succeed, so that after about a year there appears in society a handsome, brilliant man *who always carries a satchel, and who displays vast alarm when there is any danger of his being separated from it.* This, of course, is the brainless twin—who now serves as the mouthpiece and exterior façade of the intelligent monster, who rules him by hypnotism from the shelter of the satchel. From then on I had decided nothing. One idea was to have an accident destroy the satchel, causing the idiot to collapse helplessly and perhaps die. Another was to have the man gain fame—but finally to have the idiot body die in such a way that the death can hardly be concealed. The intelligent twin still lives—but how can he now keep his secret? He may be able to hide bodily, but how can he continue the work which brought him fame (say as a writer or painter or scholar) when the famous man is supposed to be dead? I had not progressed to the point of solving that problem—or even decided whether I'd have such a problem—when Whitehead began urging collaboration and I finally gave him the plot to develop in his own way. Hence "Cassius". (*SL* 5.33–34)

This idea perhaps dimly recalls the previously mentioned lost juvenile story in which a man murders his twin brother and "tries to *live the life of both*—appearing in one place as himself, and elsewhere as his victim. He meets sudden death . . . and the secret [is] finally revealed by his diary" (*RK* 30, *SL* 1.20). Perhaps Lovecraft himself remembered this, as in the course of writing the same letter a further development of the plot-germ occurred to him:

> Now—after years—*another* alternative occurs to me. I might have the death of the handsome idiot-body concealed, and have the intelligent monster embalm it and display it seated in chair—

ostensibly still alive but paralysed. He could have it appear to speak—in a feeble, alien voice supposedly due to the paralysis—through the clever practice of ventriloquism. Then some awful climax or revelation could occur—any one of a dozen hideous sorts. The embalming could be *imperfect*, so that the supposedly living man would display signs of decomposition. Or notice could be attracted by its failure to age through the passing years. In writing such a story, I'd probably *begin near the end*—that is, have the bulk of the action concern the final phase, when the supposed paralytic begins to arouse suspicion. The antecedent history—the operation etc.—would be subtly worked in as back-flashes. I would make the revelation very gradual and suspense-filled—and at the last might leave the reader in some doubt of what the truth really was. Whether I shall ever do this or not remains to be seen. It certainly wouldn't be duplicating "Cassius"—for the whole spirit and emphasis of my conception is antipodally alien to Whitehead's. Whitehead urged me to go ahead and try—but I thought some time had better elapse in any case. (*SL* 5.34)

Lovecraft does not at the moment seem to have been aware that this also in part very much brings to mind the climax of "The Whisperer in Darkness," as well as the gist of "The Cool Air"—or for the failure to age, the similar notice Curwen attracts in *The Case of Charles Dexter Ward*, for that matter. Unfortunately, he would never attempt his own take of the "Cassius" idea; when the preceding was written Lovecraft was just about to commence experimenting with "The Shadow out of Time"—another story whose elements had then been percolating in his mind for years—and the only other strictly original piece of fiction he would live to compose after that would be "The Haunter of the Dark."

After the writing of "Cassius" Lovecraft would eventually relent to collaboration with Whitehead, by helping the latter with "The Trap," probably during his Florida visit of the latter's home in Dunedin in the summer of 1931. Lovecraft likely wrote at least half of the story as it now stands, but refused a joint byline. The next year he would again lend assistance to Whitehead, this time by plotting around spring 1932 what probably was an extensive synopsis for a new version of a rejected story "The Bruise" (published posthumously as "Bothon").[28] And from what Lovecraft once mentions in correspondence to R. H. Barlow, it appears that there is also another commonplace book entry that Whitehead had planned to write out:

> As for the cat & brain operation—I had told Whitehead about a plot-idea of mine, wherein a strange scholar transfer his personality to the brain of cat which has been his constant companion—& which is the only living thing available when he feels death overtaking his original body. Whitehead thought I implied a *surgical* brain-transfer (which I didn't)—hence the reference in his letter. (*FF* 65)

This clearly refers to entry 88: "Lonely philosopher fond of cat. Hypnotises it—as I were—by repeatedly talking to it & looking at it. After his death the cat evinces signs of possessing his personality. N.B. He has trained cat, & leaves it to a friend, with instructions as to fitting a pen to its right fore paw by means of a harness. Later writes with deceased's own handwriting." Barlow had evidently come upon the matter while collecting Whitehead's letters for a planned memorial publication that was to have been titled *Caneviniana*. (Like many of Barlow's ambitious projects, this pamphlet never appeared.) But if this had been Whitehead's intention, such plans seem to have been derailed by his death. It is unfortunate that Lovecraft's letters to Whitehead do not appear to survive, as much of interest could probably be learned from them concerning their collaborative, or near-collaborative, efforts. In their absence, we will to have to do with what can be gleaned from the cited secondary sources.

III. Lovecraft Pieces: 1927–31

After the return to Providence from New York in spring 1926 Lovecraft still took his time before attempting any new stories, but when he finally did so arguably the most fruitful phase of his fiction writing would commence, an *annus mirabilis* that would bestow us "The Call of Cthulhu" (August 1926), "Pickman's Model" (Septem-

---

28. In *West India Lights* (Arkham House, 1946).

ber), "The Silver Key" (November), "The Strange High House in the Mist" (November), the novellas *The Dream-Quest of Unknown Kadath* and *The Case of Charles Dexter Ward* (fall 1926 to January 1927 and January to March 1927, respectively), and what may be his masterwork, "The Colour out of Space" (March 1927). Having accomplished all this, a long pause then followed, lasting until the writing of "The Dunwich Horror" in August 1928, as the burden of financial considerations began to lie heavily on him and he felt forced to turn his attention to poorly paying, but at least in his mind more certain, revision work. We can only regret that the inspired streak that produced the above stories did not continue longer. In early April 1927 he remarked to Donald Wandrei, who at the time was depressed by a case of writer's block:

> I have several new tales in mind—some potentially marketable, & others of too great bizarrerie for popular reception—but have just now been too busy for writing. . . . The inability to write at all times is something which you share with nearly every other writer . . . I can report many a day of blankness with ideas in my head & pen & paper in front of me; during which I have had to turn to something else & await the kindness of Fate in doling out a creative interval. . . . Today is a good case of this very thing with me. I have a notion I want to get in story form, but it simply doesn't shape itself this afternoon. . . . tonight I shall try again. If it works, all right. If not, I'll get some revision done & wait for a still later mood. (*MTS* 76–77)

Evidently this notion did not shape itself that evening either, unless it was related to the extant fragment to be discussed presently. Three days later, he would write to August Derleth:

> Just now I'm making a very careful study of *London* by means of maps, books, & pictures, in order to get background for tales involving richer antiquities than America can furnish. It is really a very fascinating pursuit, for I am doing it in a thorough, gradual way involving a minute following of the town's historic growth from a thatched Celtic village on piles. . . . If there's anything I hate, it's writing about a locality without an adequate knowledge of its history, topography, & general atmosphere; & I don't wish to make this blunder in anything I may concoct with an Old London

setting. What I write will probably begin in Roman times—
something will *survive* in one way or another. (*ES* 1.83)

But because of pressing revision jobs, the task of reading the
proofs for "Supernatural Horror in Literature" (due to appear in
W. Paul Cook's *Recluse*), teeth problems requiring several dentist
appointments in May, and Donald Wandrei's Providence visit in
July, nothing seems to have come of this research. Later in April
Lovecraft already notes to Derleth that "I have not yet begun to
use the London material, & perhaps I shan't for a long period to
come. These impressions must have time for assimilation & incubation" (*ES* 1.84). That is, unless S. T. Joshi's theory is correct that
the fragment that R. H. Barlow titled "The Descendant" was a
product of this study of London and dates to this time. Barlow has
also supplied (probably by sheer guesswork) a date of 1926 for the
fragment, but as Joshi points out (*Primal Sources* 182–84), the
fragment seems to make use of the study of London Lovecraft
undertook—such actual features of London as Gray's Inn, Chan-
dos Street, and Clare Market are mentioned—hence a date of 1927
can be conjectured. In fact, the manuscript contains not one but
two fragments, for what has in earlier editions been given as the
first paragraph—"Writing what the doctor tells is my deathbed,
my most hideous fear is that the man is wrong. I suppose I shall
seem to be buried next week, but . . ."—is actually a separate sen-
tence struck out and written upside down at the bottom of the
first page. The first-person narration alone suggests that this portion of the text is not connected with "The Descendant" itself but
is a separate false start that perhaps would have dealt with some
kind of premature burial theme; but probably it is not much earlier than the main fragment in any case.

I will not echo here each and every point made by Joshi in his
examination of "The Descendant," but it appears to me that he
has somewhat belabored the point that Lovecraft has incorrectly
referred to the Third Augustan Legion, which was never stationed
in England, as being "then stationed at Lindum" (*D* 361), when
from his reading of Arthur Machen's *Hill of Dreams* (1907) Lovecraft should have known that it was the Second Augustan Legion
that was in Roman Britain, in Isca Silurum (modern Caerleon-on-
Usk). Lovecraft's error is interesting in that the third legion is also

mentioned in "The Rats in the Walls," there camped in the
(mythical) Anchester. Actually, I am not convinced that Lovecraft
is here necessarily making a repeated error so much as deliberate
choice. Clearly he would have been aware from Machen alone
where the second legion was actually stationed, the sufficiently
well-known Caerleon location making it unavailable for his use.
This is confirmed by the fact that in November 1927, not much
later than when "The Descendant" was supposedly written, Lovecraft would have to point out to Derleth, when commenting on
the latter's story "Old Mark," that "Caerleon . . . was the headquar-
ters of the Second Augustan Legion" (*ES* 1.116). I think that he has
simply taken the next legion in the sequence, as it were, in order
to avoid using the real one already utilized by Machen. In "The
Descendant" the citation of the third legion occurs in the course of
a description of the origins of Lord Northam's line:

> . . . there were family tales of a descent from pre-Saxon times,
> when a certain Cnaeus Gabinius Capito, military tribune in the
> Third Augustan Legion then stationed at Lindum in Roman Britain,
> had been summarily expelled from his command for participation
> in certain rites unconnected with any known religion. Gabinius had,
> the rumour ran, come upon a cliffside cavern where strange folk
> met together and made the Elder Sign in the dark; strange folk
> whom the Britons knew not save in fear, and who were the last to
> survive from a great land in the west that had sunk, leaving only the
> islands with the raths and circles and shrines of which Stonehenge
> was the greatest. There was no certainty, of course, in the legend
> that Gabinius had built an impregnable fortress over the forbidden
> cave and founded a line which Pict and Saxon, Dane and Norman
> were powerless to obliterate . . . (*D* 360–61)

This very much brings to mind what is told of de la Poers and the
history of Exham Priory (which "stood on the site of a prehistoric
temple; a Druidical or ante-Druidical thing which must have been
older than Stonehenge" [*DH* 29]) in "The Rats in the Walls," and I
wonder whether this passage has been introduced as an allusion to
that story, or if the 1927 dating is actually not correct and the
whole fragment slightly predates "The Rats in the Walls" and was
intended as an exposition of the same ideas. In this case it would

need to have been composed shortly after Lovecraft first read Machen, which was in May 1923 (cf. *SL* 1.233–34). The passing mention of the "Elder Sign," however, seems to weigh against this theory, as that invention is otherwise not mentioned until *The Dream-Quest of Unknown Kadath* (*MM* 311).

As said earlier, Lovecraft would often state his intention of placing a story either purely in the Roman times or connecting to the era, and a sample passing comment where he indicates a desire "to compose a tale some day based upon Roman Britain & the dark Druid secrets preceding Roman Britain; a tale in which both are glimpsed against a background of stark cosmic *outsideness*" (*SL* 2.283) is just one of many such remarks made over the years.[29] The closest Lovecraft ever came to actually writing a story of this sort—if we discount the lost juvenile works dealing with Roman explorers and colonization—was probably a planned story that originated in a singular dream he had on Halloween night of 1927, quite likely the most extraordinary dream he ever experienced— no small feat in itself. While the dream was in the end never developed into a full narrative as Lovecraft initially intended, he did recount it at considerable length to several correspondents, and it is thus that we at least have a very notable fragment of a Roman tale that never was. Currently three extant versions (with small variations) are known, and there may well have been others that have not come to light. Let Lovecraft himself explain the background that begot the dream:

> I have myself been carried back to Roman times by my recent perusal of James Rhoades' Æneid, a translation never before read by me . . . This Virgilian diversion, together with the spectral thoughts incident to All Hallow's Eve with its Witch-Sabbaths on the hills, produced in me last Monday night a Roman dream of such supernal clearness & vividness, & such titanic adumbrations of hidden horror, that I verily believe I shall some day employ it in fiction. Roman dreams were no uncommon features of my

---

29. Another occasion is in HPL to Richard F. Searight, 2 April 1934 (*RFS* 21): "The suggestions evoked by the name 'Eltdown Shards' are to me tremendous, and I shall undoubtedly use these hellish fragments in some future tale—perhaps one dealing with Roman Britain, & with horrors trickling down from forgotten millennia before it."

youth . . . but I had so long ceased to experience them, that the present one impressed me with extraordinary force. (*MTS* 177)

A résumé of what followed can scarcely do justice to what must have been an extremely vivid dream, and even the complete letter excerpt to Donald Wandrei that has been published as "The Very Old Folk," evocative as it is, cannot wholly reproduce what it must have been like to actually experience it: "The vivid reality of that dream is impossible to describe. I lived for days as a Roman in Spain—rising, reading, talking, travelling—even after six years the memory is *disconcertingly* vivid" (*SL* 4.334). In another occasion Lovecraft stressed that his curiously lifelike Roman experiences were not limited to just this one case:

> I have always had very curious Roman dreams—invariably laid in some western *Province* rather than in Italy itself (though I am al-ways—unlike my waking self—a native Roman of the old hawk-nosed, broad-templed Italic stock . . . Latian, Sabine, Samnite, Oscan . . .), and with myself generally a minor civil or military of-ficial. The *detail* and apparent duration of some of these dreams is exceedingly singular—and their lifelike vividness is impossible to exaggerate. Perhaps the most vivid of all occurred late in October 1927, when I dreamed I was a provincial quaestor in Hispania Citerior—at some time vaguely placeable as late in the republican age . . . . say B.C. sixty or seventy. The dream seemed to cover three days in continuous succession, and had a terrific nightmare ending. (*SL* 5.181)

Let it be summarized anyway that in the dream Lovecraft occu-pied the persona of one Lucius Caelius Rufus, a quaestor in the town of Calagurris in the Roman province of Hispania Citerior. The dream began by dissolving into a conversation between Rufus and his guest, Cnaeus Balbutius. Rufus leads Balbutius into his li-brary, where minute details such as a copy of Lucretius' *De Rerum Natura* open on the table at Book V are visible. They continue the conversation there, the subject being "one of *nameless hovering horror*": a monstrous doom is brewing near the town of Pompelo in the hills where a "Strange Dark Folk" dwells. The dark folk—"Miri Nigri"—hold sabbaths with sacrifices twice a year. Each summer trading is done with this folk, but they are hated and their language is completely alien; now some of them have been slain in Pompelo, and the townspeople are fearful of revenge. Balbutius has therefore been asked to send a cohort and invade the hills before the impeding autumn ritual to *Magnum Innominandum* takes place. Balbutius has, however, rejected the request, and the messenger has thus come to Rufus, who agrees that a cohort should be sent. Balbutius has in turn come to dissuade him, arguing that such an action will not be necessary. As an agreement cannot be reached, Rufus dictates and sends "a long and explicit letter" to the proconsul of the province. He then bathes and discusses the matter with his household during the evening until retiring for the night. Rufus wakes up in the following morning— Lovecraft's dream still continuing—and Balbutius calls again after a breakfast for a repeated argument. After a dinner Rufus converses with his family about Lucretius and Epicurean philosophy, and then retires again, after which there is "*a dream within the dream*": "a nightmare [that] involved some stupendous Eastern ruin of which I had read in that frightful *Hieron Aigypton*" (a parchment seen earlier in the dream in the library). After waking to the *third day* inside the dream, Rufus reads and writes in his garden until a reply arrives from the proconsul (Publius Scribonius Libo), who agrees about sending the cohort and authorises Rufus to accompany it. He then seeks Balbutius, whom he finds reading Cato's *De Re Rustica* in the military camp. Balbutius bows to the authority of the proconsul, after which Rufus returns home and prepares for the following travel to Pompelo. He marches with the infantry for the next night and day and another night, until Pompelo is reached at the following noon (the last day of October in the dream), meeting the proconsul Libo there. They can only at length secure a local native guide, who "for an enormous offer of money" agrees to take them through the foothills "to the head of a certain ravine, but no farther," set out after the sunset, but cannot "help catching the horror of the [villagers'] whispering." A drumming, "an eldritch sound—muffled and monotonous, and hideously deliberate and persistent," begins with the dusk, and flames can be seen in the distant peaks as the night falls. The company eventually reaches the narrowing ravine, "its steepness becom[ing] almost precipitous," but they climb on in the darkness, after being forced to abandon their horses. The horses are suddenly heard to flee, "not *neighing*, but *screaming*," and they stop "half-paralysed with fright." Next a cry comes from the vanguard and a torch is lit, revealing that the local guide has slain himself. "And the drums still sounded, and the horses screamed in the gulfs below." The men begin to flee, trampling each other in the defile, a torch showing "a sea of faces convulsed with every last extreme of frenzy." Balbutius goes mad, Rufus is stunned to paralysis, and the aged Libo alone retains his poise: "I can yet see his calm Roman face in the fading light of the torch he held." The long dream then comes to a sudden end:

> From the slopes and peaks above us a crackling chorus of daemoniac laughter burst, and winds of ice swept down to engulf us all. My spirit could not endure the strain no longer, and I awaked . . . But still there rings in my ears those last calm words of the old proconsul—"*Malitia vetus—malitia vetus est—venit—tandem venit . . . .*" (*SL* 2.197)

> And then I waked. It was the most vivid dream in years, drawing upon wells of the subconscious long untouched & forgotten. Of the fate of that cohort no record exists, but the town at least was saved—for encyclopaedias tell of the survival of Pompelo to this day, under the modern Spanish name of Pampelona. I shall have to look up Pampelona in some guidebook or travel volume, & see what its ancient tales & superstitions may be. (*MTS* 182)

The correspondents to whom the dream was related—at least Donald Wandrei, Bernard Austin Dwyer, and Frank Belknap Long[30]—must have been much impressed with this extraordinary account, "exceptional in its scope, vividness, & mnemonic persistence" (*MTS* 187, *SL* 2.200), and Lovecraft soon expressed an intention to weave it into a story:

> The dream I *may* work on when—or if ever—I get the time, is

---

30. These three versions have been collected in *The H. P. Lovecraft Dream Book* 17–29. It also seems to have been described to Robert E. Howard at one point, but the letter is non-extant: see REH to HPL, January 1930 (*MF* 1.126).

the *Roman* one lately related to you. Its details & names will have to be greatly changed, & I shall introduce a motivating framework & modern sequel to furnish the necessary elements of fictional plot & climax. (*MTS* 192)

But most unfortunately Lovecraft was at this very time taxed by a vexing revision job he was doing for Adolphe de Castro—"The Last Test"—and thus could not attend to the matter immediately: "I'd like to get a chance to grind out some more junk—especially a story which my fancy has woven the Roman dream I described to you—& perhaps I shall stage some sort of revolution after I get through with the execrable story revision now weighing me down" (*MTS* 201). Such a chance would not soon arrive, but he did outline a possible framework in a letter to Dwyer:

How to handle the tale will be quite a problem. I don't think Rufus or anybody else ought to survive—and it ought somehow to be made clear that the sacrifice of the cohort saved the town. Or better still—for of course it would be foolish to follow the dream when it isn't convenient to do so—*the town had better be destroyed*; its entity being of course changed from Pompelo. The best beginning would be an archaeological one. A rusted Roman signum washed down from the Pyrenees in the spring rains and placed in the museum of some surviving town—a sensitive and contemplative traveller inexplicably and continually attached to it—his fear of the hills, but his visit to them after having been told where the Aquila was found. His camp at the base of the foothills and his discovery of the ruins. Perfect preservation of the buried town uncovered by the Spanish archaeologists whom he summons. Conclusion that the town was overwhelmed instantaneously by an avalanche in the midst of work—*but no human remains found*. Only small heaps of grey dust. Graffiti of very puzzling sort on walls—prayers scrawled everywhere, as if in fear of a terrible doom . . . Spanish archaeologists tell of fear which natives posses for the Basques of the hills, amongst whom the Evil Sabbath is still said to be celebrated— traveller determines to wait for Sabbath night and go into hills to witness horrors—interests archaeologists and persuades them to accompany him. Makes a preliminary survey of the hills alone, and finds an exceedingly strange altar and circle of monoliths on a distant peak. Meets a strange dark man, whom makes a evil sign in the

air and flees. Returns to camp an falls ill with fever. Taken to hospital in Pompelona—too ill to go into the gills Hallowe'en night. But
the Spanish archaeologists go just the same. That night the dream
ensues—exactly as previously related except for identity of town.
Horrible waking—but still more horrible news that afternoon. *The
party of Spanish archaeologists has disappeared, and the unknown
excavated village has been buried again, precisely as it had remained
for two thousand years.* The Magnum Innominandum does not forget. By Jove! That doesn't sound half bad! But it'll take a helluva lot
of care in handling. This sort of thing has to be damned adroit, or it
doesn't convince. . . . the irregularities of the [Roman] calendar
would require some explaining rather foreign to the directness and
simplicity of good fiction so I guess I'll push the date ahead to the
early Imperial age, after the calendar's reform. The province will
then be called *Hispania Terraconensis*, and the brave old man will
be *Legatus pro praetore* instead of proconsul. (*SL* 2.216–18)

As it happened, Lovecraft could not get to composing another
original work of fiction until August 1928, and the story that then
finally emerged was "The Dunwich Horror." This was itself followed by another long fictional silence, and in the February of the
next year, having slightly earlier lent his commonplace book to
Frank Belknap Long who was "complain[ing] that he's wholly run
out of ideas" (*ES* 1.181), he finally suggested that Long utilize the
dream-kernel instead:

> Glad you found the commonplace-book and cuttings of interest.
> Have you started your novel, or any short tales? Another thing you
> could use is that Hispano-Roman dream I described a year ago Oc-
> tober. I probably shan't get around to writing it up, so if you can
> find the letter containing it, you're welcome to the thing. (*SL* 2.261)

This Long eventually did, and the possibility of Lovecraft ever
writing it out himself thus passed; he later told correspondents
that Long had incorporated his letter account practically verbatim
in his novelette *The Horror from the Hills*.[31] This must be one of

---

31. See HPL to C. L. Moore, 2 July 1935 (*SL* 5.181–82): "the completed narrative
(*The Horror from the Hills*—*Weird Tales* Jan. and Feb. 1931) contains my epistolary account in the original wording . . . put into the mouth of a character"; and

the most lamentable losses in the Lovecraft canon, and while it is by no means certain that he would have eventually handled the Roman story idea himself had it not been given to Long, there is still a high probability that he would have done so.

An aspect of Lovecraft's oeuvre suitable for discussion at this point, but of which far too little is still known, is the peculiar body of his revisory work. It was a constant mystery to some of his more professionally oriented colleagues, such as August Derleth and E. Hoffmann Price, why Lovecraft continued this thankless and poorly paying enterprise, while in their minds he could have easily earned at least as much by using the same time and energy on composing original fiction, even if only a fraction of that would have sold. Much—perhaps the bulk—of this writing is likely to remain forever lost or unknown; and purely from the point of view of literary value it is no doubt a well-merited oblivion. Certainly Lovecraft himself would have been aghast at the resurrection of even the majority of the known weird revisions that have been, with a few exceptions, collected in the Arkham House volume *The Horror in the Museum.* Yet for a student of his, even the most insignificant bit of writing is worthy of some attention, and we would very much like to know—to take a single example—just what was that "80,000-word novel MS." whose revision was "loom[ing] formidably ahead" in March 1933 (*AG* 180).[32] But the fact is that Lovecraft would only rarely mention the specifics of such work in his correspondence unless a weird story was concerned, in which case his colleagues would be likely to read or had already seen the story in question.

Many of the known revisions from Lovecraft's later years are actually tales that he touched up as a favor rather than for a fee; and here the surviving letters to these youthful correspondents have of-

---

HPL to Clark Ashton Smith, 13 December 1933 (*SL* 4.334): "I told that dream in full to Belknap, and he incorporated it without any linguistic change in his Chaugnar story." In a late letter (HPL to C. L. Moore, 2 July 1935 [*SL* 5.182]) HPL suggests that it was Long who had initially requested permission to use the dream in his novelette, which was finished around June 1930 (cf. *MTS* 253).

32. The same novel is also mentioned in HPL to Elizabeth Toldridge, 25 March 1933 (*SL* 4.166).

ten led to the discovery of these stories. Of the remunerative work, that performed for David Van Bush in the earlier years is well known, and we have some scraps of information on poetry that was fixed up for other clients, but in many cases where the material that Lovecraft was revising or even ghost-writing did not come into the realm of the weird, he does not seem to have been very inclined to elaborate on its details, nor was there much reason to do so, other than explaining being "exceedingly crowded with annoying tho' doubtfully remunerative revisory tasks" (*AG* 180), "all tangled up with work" (*SL* 4.166), and so forth. To be sure, Lovecraft did once declare, in response to E. Hoffmann Price who had received a somewhat erroneous picture of extent to which ghost-written fiction by him was appearing, that "I have ghost-written all sort of junk for various clients. . . . What is more—most of the tales I have ghost-written have been weird"—but he then qualified this by adding that "a lot of this ghost-written stuff has never sold, anyhow!" (*SL* 4.244). We would probably be much wiser if the full correspondence to Samuel Loveman was available, as it seems to have been through him that many of the revision clients were directed to Lovecraft who, except for few half-hearted efforts, did not do very much to advertise his services but relied on word-of-mouth recommendation instead.

There are, however, three revision clients for whom Lovecraft may have done more work than has been so far identified and are perhaps worth examining in more detail; there may even be a slim chance that some of this fiction will be located one day. The first of these was Adolphe de Castro, who in time would threaten to turn into an almost David Van Bush–like nuisance, except that his ability to pay in advance was practically nil, so that Lovecraft seems to have tactfully averted de Castro's later overtures, even if he at least once came dangerously close to doing some work free of charge out of sheer pity for the "old codger." The work that he did do for de Castro dates to 1927–29, and it consisted mainly of the wholesale rewriting of short stories originally published in the collection *In the Confessional and the Following* (1893), which de Castro had managed to put out decades earlier, although some unspecified nonfiction revision may have been involved as well. (De Castro in vain also attempted to persuade Lovecraft to make sense of his memoir of Ambrose Bierce, but this task was eventually assigned to Frank Belknap Long.) Now two of the stories that Lovecraft rewrote are of course well-known, but there is much reason to believe that there was at least one more in addition to them, for in 1934 he would state that "I have revised several tales for de Castro" and this cannot easily refer to only two (*SL* 5.44). He never names any other stories than "The Last Test" (December 1927–January 1928)[33] and "The Electric Executioner" (July 1929), which were both published in *Weird Tales*, but there is circumstantial evidence for the existence of a third item. In an earlier letter to Long Lovecraft unequivocally says that "I did accidentally land *Yig*, and three tales of Old Dolph's" (*SL* 3.204), implying that he had also handled the placing of the stories in magazines. But no publications for de Castro outside *Weird Tales* for this period have so far come to light, and it may be that if the story was indeed accepted somewhere, the magazine ceased to appear before it could be published. The most likely juncture for its writing would seem to be in connection with "The Electric Executioner" in the summer and fall of 1929, for although Lovecraft had begun work on the latter in July, mentioning to August Derleth that "I am just now confronting a damnable revision job from old De Castro . . . who has made delay impossible by paying in advance!" (*ES* 1.200), he would in late October note that he would only tackle "The Mound" after "I finish my current De Castro quota" (*ES* 1.225)—a curiously long time to spend on just "The Electric Executioner." Furthermore, in December he would lament to Clark Ashton Smith:

> I hope to get at some more *signed* original fiction within a month. I say "signed", because the "revision" job I'm doing now is the composition of an original tale from a single paragraph of locale & subject orders . . . ["The Mound"]—& the two De Castro jobs preceding it—will tend to limber up my fictional pen for the spontaneous effusions to follow! (*SL* 3.88)

Again, "the two De Castro jobs" cannot well refer to "The Last

---

33. The revision was probably started after 19 December 1927 (see a letter of this date to Donald Wandrei, *MTS* 195) and finished between 20 and 31 January (see letters to Donald Wandrei and August Derleth of these dates, *MTS* 201 and *ES* 1.134, respectively).

Test" and "The Electric Executioner," as the former was by then almost two years old. In early March of the next year de Castro would have "the nerve to ask me to give a *free* second revision to a tale which editors didn't like—& which I warned him in the first place that they wouldn't! Did he get it? He did not!" (*ES* 1.254). "The Electric Executioner" had already been accepted at this point (see *ES* 1.249), hence cannot be the story in question, which may actually never have been placed, despite Lovecraft's later claim to the contrary. If such was the case, there may be only scant hope of it ever being seen—perhaps not an intolerable loss, considering the success of the extant *In the Confessional* rewrites—although 2 linear feet of de Castro's papers, including unspecified manuscripts, are in the American Jewish Archives of the Hebrew Union College of Cincinnati (The Jacob Marcus Rader Center, MS-348), and I wonder if these have been carefully examined by anyone.[34]

Zealia B. Bishop, or Reed as her surname still was at the time, is a similar case. Like de Castro, she initially came in touch with Lovecraft through the mediation of Samuel Loveman, and although in October 1929 Lovecraft would state that "Mrs. Reed is a client for whom Long & I have done oceans of work" (*ES* 1.222)—and let us recall that of the three known tales ghostwritten for her, only "The Curse of Yig" (c. March 1928) had by this time been composed—we do not have a very detailed idea of just how extensively he assisted Bishop in her auctorial endeavors. At the instigation of August Derleth, Bishop would later pen a memoir of Lovecraft ("H. P. Lovecraft: A Pupil's View," evidently revised by Derleth), whom she actually had once met in New York. Bishop kept all or many of her letters from Lovecraft and quotes them briefly, but the memoir is still quite suspect in places, even to the point of practically lying about the extent to which "The Curse of Yig," "The Mound" (December 1929–January 1930), and "Medusa's

---

34. A piece of evidence to the contrary may be seen, however, in R. H. Barlow's note on the de Castro stories: "L. was hired to rewrite them; and, taking the best one first ('The Last Test') 'revised' it; then came 'The Electric Executioner'—and afterwards de Castro couldn't pay him more so it stopped" ("[Memories of H. P. Lovecraft (1934)]," *FF* 403). But in light of HPL's own first-hand remarks, no great weight need be given to this.

Coil" (May–August? 1930) are really Lovecraft's work. Bishop, who still at the time of writing the memoir in 1953 appears to have been somewhat irritated over his attempt to steer her in the direction of the weird, makes clear that what she really wished to write was romantic fiction for the love-story and confessional pulps:

> Being young and romantic, I wanted to follow my own impulse for fresh, youthful stories. Lovecraft was not convinced that this course was the best. . . . After a long period of endless work and steady and ruthless direction and criticism without selling, I grew discouraged. . . . The stories I sent him always came back so revised from their basic idea that I felt I was a complete failure as a writer. (*LR* 267–68)

There is, I fear, a distinct possibility that it was the "youthful" sort of material that Lovecraft (and Long) helped to mold into more publishable state. S. T. Joshi has pointed out what may well be a reference to the onerous job revising and criticizing of Bishop's romantic fiction in a letter of May 1927, nearly a full year before the more congenial task of "The Curse of Yig": "the most deodamnate piece of Bushwork . . . the sappy, half-baked *Woman's Home Companion* stuff of a female whose pencil has hopelessly outdistanced her imagination" (*SL* 2.129). It is in fact just at this time that Lovecraft's letters to Bishop begin to appear. No doubt a good deal of his assistance was in the form of advice given in the course of this surprisingly rich correspondence—in her memoir Bishop makes an amusing note of Lovecraft telling her that "No gentleman would dare kiss a girl in that fashion," and that "No gentleman would think of knocking on a lady's bedroom door even at a house party." Nevertheless, there must have been some stories that Lovecraft actually touched up or revised for Bishop to a significant degree, and when sending her the completed "The Curse of Yig" in early March 1928 he would note that his charge of $17.50 for the untyped manuscript would "bring the total bill up to $42.50" (*SL* 2.233). This earlier $25 probably consisted of charges for at least two previous stories, and they could conceivably have numbered even more than that, depending on the degree of touching up that Lovecraft performed, especially if some of the bill had been picked up at an earlier date. The question then may

be whether Bishop actually succeeded in placing these non-weird
pieces anywhere despite the many rejections she says they gar-
nered. Only an arduous search of the type of magazines printing
this sort of fiction could provide the answer, assuming that copies
even survive. There is one piece by Bishop that I have found in
online bibliographies: "One-Man Girl," in the 26 December 1928
(52, No. 3 [156]) issue of *Cupid's Diary*. This journal, subtitled
"The Best Love Stories," appears to have been a semi-monthly that
was published by the Corte Publishing Co. from October 1923 to
April 1929, when it switched over to Dell until April 1931 before
finally lapsing (in July 1930 the title was changed to *Cupid's Best
Love Stories*). By no means have all its issues been catalogued—in
fact, for 1928 only the contents of four are available—so that it
may well have printed more than just this one story by Bishop. In
any case, I strongly suspect that if "One-Man Girl" was not
worked over by Lovecraft, then probably Long would have been
responsible for putting it into printable form. Even more so than
in the case of the lost de Castro tale, we need not mourn the per-
ishing of this side of Lovecraft's revisory work too much, but a
story for a romance pulp would still be a very curious bit of marginalia to have; and some assiduous researcher may well yet succeed in exhuming "One-Man Girl" or some similar items.[35]

Another female revision client introduced to Lovecraft via a
mutual acquaintance, but in this case other than Samuel Loveman,
was Hazel Heald. Of her very little is known, for although communicating later with August Derleth, unlike Zealia Bishop she

---

35. The task may, however, have been rendered more difficult if Bishop published this work pseudonymously. In one letter to her, HPL responds to a request
for advice on this topic (see *SL* 2.162). Bishop also writes in her memoir of showing HPL a novel dealing "with a Catholic upbringing" at some unspecified time,
quoting his enthusiastic comments: "Best of all is your description of the Catholic
school and the sense of spaciousness, of colourful activity Deon experiences in it
. . . Enthusiastic commendation is seldom a spur to creative endeavour and I was
determined at first *not* to praise your work too heartily. But . . . well, I have read
the endorsed opus twice and I really can't avoid commenting upon it! It is really
great—it has élan" (*LR* 270). Bishop does not suggest that HPL gave any revisory
assistance on the novel, although it could be imagined that such might have been
required, despite his remarks.

left no memoir of their association. Muriel Eddy, the acquaintance who introduced Heald to Lovecraft, has however left some small scraps of information, including the fact that she wished to be romantically involved with Lovecraft. Five stories that Lovecraft either ghostwrote or extensively revised for Heald have of course been long since identified, but there is a curious footnote to them that does not seem to have been much noted. In his article "Research of a Biblio," George Wetzel acknowledges at length the invaluable assistance of Jack Grill, "Lovecraft collector par excellence," and goes on to state:

> Grill was able to obtain from a certain few people connected with Lovecraft items which I had tried years before, unsuccessfully, to secure. He also has copies of two unpublished stories of Hazel Heald written in the Lovecraft idiom. Many of the experiences Grill has had in the course of gathering his collection would make interesting reading, as would—even more so—a description and commentary of each item that is in the collection. It is to be hoped he will someday catalogue it. (43)

By the time this was written the five known Heald stories had already been published, having first appeared in magazines (the last, "The Horror in the Burying-Ground," in the May 1937 issue of *Weird Tales*), and subsequently in the Arkham House Lovecraft collections. Neither Wetzel nor Grill could well have been unaware of this. Jack Grill would unfortunately never write an account of the acquiring of his collection; it was eventually catalogued after Irving Binkin purchased it after Grill's death,[36] but there was then no trace of any Heald manuscripts, unpublished or otherwise. She died in 1961, so that it is in theory at least possible that Grill could have contacted her and thus acquired the manuscripts, but for the time being the matter is likely to remain a mystery unless Lovecraft's correspondence with her somehow surfaces.

Further mystery is added to the matter of the Lovecraft revisions by certain obscure remarks in the letters. In June 1933 he corrects Robert Bloch's citation of von Juntz, the author of Robert E. Howard's mythical book *The Nameless Cults*:

---

36. As *A Catalog of Lovecraftiana* (Mirage Press, 1975).

> . . . you give Howard's von Juntz the praenomen of Conrad,
> whereas at least one printed allusion (which I put into a story I
> ghost-wrote for a revision client!) establishes it as *Friedrich*. How-
> ard himself, amusingly enough, did not give von Juntz a first name
> so far as I know. (Am I mistaken?) (*RB* 23)

This is curious, for there is no known instance of Lovecraft giving
Juntz's full name in any story. He is, however, referred by surname in "The Horror in the Museum," which had just been
printed in the July 1933 issue of the *Weird Tales*, and my guess is
that it is that revision which Lovecraft was here thinking of—
probably the typescript of this tale would have been prepared by
Hazel Heald, its nominal author, and "Friedrich" could well have
been mistakenly dropped by her in transcription. Alternatively,
Lovecraft may have failed to actually cite the first name while in-
tending to so. That a story has been lost seems to be countered by
the fact that when he a month or so later notes to Howard stories
of his referring to *The Nameless Cults*, Lovecraft only mentions
"The Horror in the Museum" and "Out of the Aeons" (*MF* 2.619).

There are, however, certain unidentified stories by other authors from the same period (the mid-1930s) when Lovecraft was
working on the Heald stories and on which he may have provided
some assistance, even if no actual prose was revised. The first of
these are mentioned in an unpublished letter to Clark Ashton
Smith (23 August 1931): "Am utterly swamped with revision—
from a rather quaint & interesting ex-westerner now living in Florida, whom Whitehead sic'd on to me. The fellow is fairly clever in
a naive, semi-illiterate way, & I really think I can make something
of one or two of his tales."[37] Unfortunately, Lovecraft does not
name this individual, and as his letters to Whitehead are not extant, the matter is currently a mystery. Another possible revision
is alluded to in an April 1932 letter to August Derleth when Lovecraft was visiting W. Paul Cook and the *Weird Tales* author H.
Warned Munn in Boston: "[Munn] has some fine plots in his head,
& it is possible that I may work one up for him to help him develop his style—about those limitations he is very sensitive" (*ES*

---

37. Ms., private collection.

1.473). I am not aware of any other references to this matter; it may not have come to pass. But a second story clearly was written, even if it no longer survives. This too comes up in the course of the correspondence between Lovecraft and Derleth:

> Congrats on the 50-buck prize. Not long ago the local writer—or ex-writer—C. M. Eddy Jr. sought my assistance on a mystery-ending for some contest—I wonder if it was this one? Was the story about a haunted mill with mysterious deaths by strangulation? I fixed up a long synopsis for Eddy—attributing the strangulation to the victims themselves, who raised their hands to their throats to tear away the imagined talons of others when a certain drug (as mentioned in the story) in the air produced the illusory sensation of strangulation. The yarn was a fearsome piece of crap. (*ES* 1.530)

Again, I do not know of any other letters bearing on this, but perhaps someone more familiar with Eddy's writings will be able to verify whether the description above matches any extant story.

The exhausting revision work Lovecraft was doing seems to be largely responsible for the low amount of purely original fiction he was composing between 1927 and 1931. After "The Dunwich Horror," the latter half of 1928 and the entire year 1929 are blank. There is an intriguing note in the commonplace book dating to around late 1930, on which a postcard to Clark Ashton Smith elaborates briefly and tantalizingly, commenting upon the similarity of the central conception to Smith's story "The Beast of Averoigne":

> [It] makes me think of something I was going to write—albeit in a very different way—one of the notes in my commonplace book reads: "A very ancient tomb a deep wood where a 17th century Virginia manor-house once stood. The bloated, undecayed thing found inside it." My tale would probably be of Randolph Carterish sort—but quasi-realistic, & contemporary in period! There would be an historic antecedent, harking back to the earliest days Jamestown, & a moldy document found & perused with nightmare trepidation.[38]

---

38. Undated, c. October 1930; private collection. The actual commonplace book

The reference to Randolph Carter is particularly interesting here, but raises more questions than it answers about the story kernel. Nothing seems to have come of this, and only in February 1931 would Lovecraft again have enough leisure to work on the novelette "The Whisperer in Darkness," and after this tale had been revised in August,[39] another unspecified ghostwriting job kept him sufficiently busy until early 1931, when he began to work on *At the Mountains of Madness* (February–March 1931).[40] There is, however, another evidently planned story of which not much is known, and which I would tentatively like to place into this period, say sometime in 1928 or 1929 after "The Dunwich Horror." The story in question is the one contained in the set of memoranda known as "The Round Tower"; I will explain the reasons for this conjecture presently.

After the publication of the Derleth's "posthumous collaboration" *The Lurker at the Threshold* (1945), and the subsequent printing of the authentic Lovecraft notes from which the work was in part "evoked" by Derleth,[41] Lovecraft's Providence friend C. M. Eddy, Jr., made the following statement in his brief memoir "Walks with H. P. Lovecraft" (1966):

> That nocturnal journey to Poe Street prompted Lovecraft to ask me to accompany him on a series of exploratory trips in and around Providence . . . The second of these trips was to Newport, to view the old stone tower, said to have been constructed before Columbus by the Norsemen, though its reason for being has been a puzzle through the years since then. . . . Lovecraft saw in it all the elements for a weird tale, and he spent most of the afternoon jotting down ideas while I watched the pigeons that seemed to

wording for the entry (178) differs slightly from that given by HPL in the postcard.

39. HPL at one time considered writing a sequel to this story; see HPL to R. H. Barlow, 13 July 1931 (*FF* 4): "I had thought of some possible later story dealing with Yuggoth, Akeley, & the Outer Ones, but may never get around to it. There are so many ideas to write out, & so little time to write them in!"

40. Cf. HPL to August Derleth, 16 October 1930 (*ES* 1.280): "Now I am finishing up one more 'ghosting job'—after which I hope to snatch time for several short tales of my own, Pegāna willing."

41. In *Some Notes on H. P. Lovecraft* (Arkham House, 1959): rpt. as "Final Notes" in *DB*.

have adopted the ancient structure as their home. Some of his notes were subsequently utilized in "The Lurker at the Threshold" . . . (*LR* 66–67)

I am not sure when this trip would have taken place, although Eddy perhaps implies September 1923. Lovecraft would later make several further, almost yearly visits to Newport, often accompanied by friends to whom he wished to show the town, and of which he would write to Robert E. Howard that he "almost wish[ed he] could live there" (*MF* 1.63). Several correspondents would over the years also receive postcards from the town, some of them no doubt depicting the tower, which is commonly believed to have been a seventeenth-century windmill, fanciful theories of Viking and other pre-Columbian origins notwithstanding. My belief is, however, that the brief story notes that we do have are not what Eddy remembered Lovecraft writing down in Newport. This single paragraph is short enough to be cited in full:

> S. of Arkham is cylindrical tower of stone with conical roof—perhaps 12 feet across & 20 ft. high. There has been a great arched opening quarter way up, but it is sealed with masonry. The thing rises from the bottom of a densely wooded ravine once the bed of an extinct tributary of the Miskatonic. Whole region feared & shunned by rustics. Tales of fate of persons climbing into tower before opening was sealed. Indian legends speak of it as existing as long as they could remember—supposed to be older than mankind. Legend that it was built by Old Ones (shapeless & gigantic amphibia) & that it was once under water. Dressed stone masonry shew odd & unknown technique. Geometrical designs on large stone above sealed opening utterly baffling. Supposed to house a treasure or something which Old Ones value highly. Possibly nothing of interest to human beings. Rumours that it connects with hidden caverns where water still exists. Perhaps old ones still alive. Base seems to extend indefinitely downward—ground level having somewhat risen. Has not been seen for ages, since everyone shuns the ravine. (*CE* 5.253)

Now manifestly these extant notes, whenever they were written, aside from simply concerning a tower, have little to do with the one standing in Newport and known as "The Old Stone Mill." There is no reason to doubt the kernel of Eddy's recollection—that Lovecraft jotted down some ideas during their Newport trip—but there is likewise no independent evidence to suggest that "The Round Tower" has anything to do with them, and they could just as well have treated some altogether different subject. For one thing, Lovecraft's tower does not much resemble the Newport one, which, while circular, is roughly 23 feet in diameter and 28 feet in height, but without a conical roof and certainly not sealed shut; nor is it situated in a wooded ravine but on a hill in the town itself.

In the editorial notes to the most recent appearance in *Collected Essays* (volume five), together with other sets of notes (of which more later) left behind but never used by Lovecraft, S. T. Joshi has tentatively dated "The Round Tower" to the mid-1930s, possibly contemporary with the spate of fictional experimentation attempted toward the end of 1933 and of which the only surviving completed story is "The Thing on the Doorstep" (August 1933). This is plausible enough, but there is also another possible juncture that, based on internal evidence, I would like to suggest. For it is my guess that in these notes we have an early adumbration of a feature that was *later* incorporated into *At the Mountains of Madness* (February–March 1931). Let us recall that the first appearance of shoggoths in a finished story occurs, as Will Murray has pointed out, not in that novelette, but in the ghostwritten "The Mound" over a year earlier:

> . . . when the men of K'n-yan went down into N'kai's black abyss with their great atom-power searchlights they found living things—living things that oozed along stone channels and worshipped onyx and basalt images of Tsathoggua. But they were not toads like Tsathoggua himself. Far worse—they were amorphous lumps of viscous black slime that took temporary shapes for various purposes. (*HM* 141)

The name *shoggoth* itself is cited at almost the same time in the sonnet "Night-Gaunts" in *Fungi from Yuggoth* (27 December 1929–4 January 1930), although it is by no means clear if the same entities are intended there—it is perhaps significant that the name is not used in the synoptic notes for *At the Mountains of Madness*, where their description is highly reminiscent of "The Mound," so that the connection may only have arisen during the composition of the former tale:

> slaves of *submarine* things . . . Eyeless Things stave off hideous giant luminous savagely intelligent protoplasm—masses composed of plastic jet black—reflectively iridescent bubbles & capable of forming temporary organs adaptable for any medium . . . Spawn of inner earth . . . viscous like Tsathoggua (*CE* 5.247)

But regardless of when the name and the image were connected, it seems unlikely to me that the passage "built by Old Ones (*shapeless & gigantic amphibia*) & that it was once *under water*" (*emphasis mine*) in "The Round Tower" notes could have been made after the writing of the Antarctic novelette, especially in these exact words, as it seems to contain a reference to the shoggoths with an apparent conflation with the star-headed Old Ones of Antarctica. Also somewhat suggestive of *At the Mountains of Madness* is the mention of alien masonry work and stone carvings. It therefore seems to me that the gist of that work is here contained in a very primitive form. But this is by no means an affirmed conclusion, and I can only offer the theory for consideration.

Much of Lovecraft's time in the 1930s was taken up by extensive travels, particularly in the southern states of the United States during the summers. The one for 1931 commenced on 2 May, just after he had completed the typescript for *At the Mountains of Madness*, and much of the time was spent in Charleston, Dunedin, and St. Augustine. A letter written to his aunt Lillian D. Clark on 22 June from the latter city contains an intriguing passing remark stating that he had there done "quite a bit on a new story yesterday" (*Life* 511). But "The Shadow over Innsmouth" was begun only in November of that year, so what was this story? The answer seems to be provided by letters written to August Derleth. In May Lovecraft had made an extended visit to Dunedin as a guest of Henry S. Whitehead, and a postcard sent to Derleth testifies how captivated by he was by the Floridian scenery:

> Well—this place may not look much like your beloved hill, but I'll wager it would set your aesthetic apparatus working if you ever get down here—especially if you saw it under the guidance

of an host as ideal as my present one! Last night we saw the white
tropic moon making a magical path on the westward-stretching
gulf that lapped at a gleaming, deserted beach on a remote key.
Boy! What a sight! It took one's breath away! (*ES* 1.342–43)

Scenes such as this seem to have soon set Lovecraft's imaginative
faculties at work, for a few weeks later, and just five days before
the remark to Lillian, he reveals that "I have had an idea of starting a
new story down here, but have not found any time so far. If I use
the tropic setting for any kind of a tale, it will be one involving
brooding mysteries on one of those low coral keys which lie in
spectral desertion just off the shore" (*ES* 1.349). It is impossible to
tell exactly what Lovecraft meant by having done "quit a bit" of this
story in St. Augustine, but however far it went, no more may have
been composed, as that same evening he began his journey back
toward Providence, from which he wrote on 18 August to Derleth
that "I've abandoned the Florida story, at least for the present.
Doubt if it would have amounted to much. For the time being, revision has me engulfed" (*ES* 1.363). Derleth then urged him not to
abandon the story, but Lovecraft ignored commenting on this in his
reply. In the annotations to the appearance of these letters in *Essential Solitude*, the editors have noted (*ES* 1.350n1) that the image of
mysterious reef lying off the shore has been carried over into "The
Shadow over Innsmouth," thus making it possible that this "Florida
story" was some kind of a precursor of the other story. But on careful inspection, the matter seems to be more complex than this. The
direct impetus for "The Shadow over Innsmouth" came from a pair
of visits to Newburyport in early October and November, following which Lovecraft wrote to Clark Ashton Smith:

> [Newburyport] has started me off on a new story idea . . . How-
> ever, this story may not see the light, since that Putnam rebuff has
> caused me to pause for a general stock-taking . . . I am using the
> new idea as a basis for what might be called laboratory experimen-
> tation—writing it out in different manners, one after the other, in
> an effort to determine the mood and tempo best suited to the
> theme. . . . My latest move is to destroy all three versions written
> to date, preparatory to embarking on a fourth. (*SL* 3.435–36)

These "laboratory" versions constitute kinds of lost stories in themselves, and it would be fascinating to have them, despite the existence of the final attempt. But more importantly, while explaining the matter to Derleth, Lovecraft describes the earlier story as a distinct entity from "The Shadow over Innsmouth":

> My present experiment has gone back to zero—since I've torn up the last of the consciously modelled versions & am slowly writing the thing out just as I would have written it in the first place. . . . You can see it if you like—that is, if it gets as far as a legible copy. The coral key idea doesn't seem to pan out—largely, perhaps, because I cannot readily associate the macabre with the South. Somehow, my idea of the sinister seems basically bound up with northern cold. (*ES* 1.418)

It would seem clear, then, that whatever concept lay behind it, it had not been preempted by the Innsmouth story. Some years later, Lovecraft would remark cryptically to E. Hoffmann Price that "I have vainly tried to lay weird tales in the south" (*SL* 5.337), a statement that perhaps becomes more easily interpretable when we see that he had actually started and destroyed one set in Florida in 1931.

IV. Diverse Experimentation: 1932–37

After the completion of "The Shadow over Innsmouth," self-doubt continued to plague Lovecraft for the rest of his life, and he would never write another story with which he was thoroughly satisfied. So disillusioned was he about the lack of merit in the few tales that did fitfully emerge that he neglected to prepare typescripts of them himself and refused to submit them to *Weird Tales*. In letters he often complains of the "very discouraging influence" of the "contemptuous" rejection (*ES* 2.717) of *At the Mountains of Madness* by that magazine, a puzzling statement considering how low an opinion Lovecraft professed to have of the periodical's literary value:

> . . . its hostile reception by Wright and others to whom it was shown probably did more than anything else to end my effective fictional career. The feeling that I had failed to crystallise the

mood I was trying to crystallised robbed me in some subtle fashion of the ability to approach this kind of problem in the same way . . . (*SL* 5.224)

The *Weird Tales* editor Farnsworth Wright may, however, have been something of a scapegoat in these complaints, and a more important source of frustration can perhaps be found in the repeated failure of a book collection of his work to materialize, coupled with the lukewarm reaction some of his correspondents and colleagues (particularly W. Paul Cook) displayed toward his later work. Over January and February 1932 Lovecraft did manage to write a new story, "The Dreams in the Witch House," but expressed dissatisfaction with it as soon as the autograph draft had been finished: "I don't believe I'll send it around for a long spell, but will merely hold on to it as I used to do—perhaps attempting other things in the meantime. The only thing that sets me writing is complete freedom from all restrictions & from all thoughts of any critical standards or readers other than myself" (*ES* 2.458). A few days later he adds that "Whether it's any good or not, I have not the faintest notion—but I shall let it rest unread & unattacked, & presently experiment with another story" (*ES* 2.460). There does not seem to be any indication what this was; in April there is a letter to Clark Ashton Smith in which it is mentioned that "There's another story I want to write, but I don't believe I can till this tooth business is over,"[42] but after that nothing more is heard of it. Later that year E. Hoffmann Price, to whom he had been introduced during his New Orleans visit in June, began to badger Lovecraft about collaborating on a sequel to "The Silver Key," the Randolph Carter story of 1926. Against his better judgment Lovecraft eventually grudgingly agreed to revise Price's draft (titled "The Lord of Illusion"), although it does not seem as if he did any concrete work on it until March of the next year, when in the middle of revision work he rewrote it in a relatively quick fashion as "Through the Gates of the Silver Key." Not counting the Carter sequel, a long time would elapse before he again had the courage to attempt another original work of fiction, although in January

---

42. HPL to Clark Ashton Smith, 4 April 1932 (ms., private collection).

1933 he does express a hope "to get time for some more fictional experimentation before 1933 is over" (*MF* 2.533) This hope was in the event not fulfilled until months later, and in March Lovecraft notes being "in a sort of impasse again. I'm dissatisfied with my stuff, but can't agree just what to do about it. If I ever get time to write any more original tales, I'll probably do quite a bit of diverse experimenting" (*MF* 2.582).

A good deal of such experimentation duly followed between August and the end of the year. From the letters of that time it appears that a veritable flood of different works were attempted during this period, although only one completed tale, "The Thing on the Doorstep" (written 21–24 August), survives; the rest evidently having either been abandoned or destroyed. Exasperatingly, he never really identifies any of the other attempts, and a few days after finishing "The Thing on the Doorstep" there is merely a laconic comment: "Experimenting with new tales—don't know how they'll turn out" (*SL* 4.239). It was, however, clear to him that drastic improvements were necessary if he were to succeed in writing anything of value, and with a view to this practice work Lovecraft had for some time been keeping notes on the classic weird stories he had been re-reading:

> I don't think much of the new story. Revision & excessive correspondence have interfered with my writing—as has also my too close contact with 'pulp' stuff. I must have more unhurried leisure, & must think less of magazines & editors, if I am ever to write anything worth reading. For the present, I'm letting "The Thing on the Doorstep" rest untyped, & am meanwhile trying to figure out just where I am weakest. As a possible restorative of incident-handling faulty I am re-reading some of the standard weird classics & forming analyses of their basic plots & motivations. As it is, I tend to fail in everything but the weaving of atmosphere. (*ES* 2.604)

That this exercise continued over the following months is made clear by a letter written to Robert E. Howard in early November, where he reveals that "I am at a sort of standstill in writing— disgusted at much of my older work, & uncertain as to avenues of improvement. In recent weeks I have done a tremendous amount of experimenting in different styles & perspectives, but have destroyed most of the results" (*MF* 2.656, *SL* 4.297). In a slightly later letter to J. Vernon Shea Lovecraft elaborated a bit on the nature of these efforts:

> As for my recent fictional experimentation & its nature—it primarily concerns the type of perspective, atmosphere, & language to use in capturing & crystallising the moods forming the subject-matter. I am trying to see which of several possible types of handling best fits certain conceptions—what tales ought to start abruptly on a note of feverish tension, when a semi-poetic style ought to be employed, how intricate explanations are best camouflaged when they are necessary to a story, what subjects demand an utterly bizarre angle of approach, what the length of a given type of tale ought to be, & how the various modulations ought to be proportioned, &c, &c., &c. So far I have torn up everything I have written, & I may decide that further writing is impossible. (*SL* 4.310)

While the notes on weird fiction themselves, as well as an essay distilled from them,[43] are extant, it can be little more than guessed what the actual story attempts might have been. In the letters quoted above Lovecraft claims to have discarded either most or all of them; in another written to Clark Ashton Smith toward the end of November he says that "All my recent attempts have so been so unsatisfactory that I've destroyed them after three or four pages" (*SL* 4.328), so that we might be persuaded to believe the latter statement.

Is it possible to pinpoint some of the experiments? I think that certain tentative identifications can at least be presented. S. T. Joshi has already observed that the three-page fragment on which R. H. Barlow bestowed the title "The Book" could date to this time (*Primal Sources* 190–94), and I think that this is highly likely. By this date it scarcely needs to be pointed out that this work is very much an attempt by Lovecraft to write out in prose his *Fungi from Yuggoth*—or at any rate the first three sonnets thereof[44]—but

---

43. "[Notes on Weird Fiction]" and "Notes on Writing Weird Fiction," respectively (in *CE* 5).

44. Which are based on entries in the commonplace book: "[144] Hideous book

it is worth noting again that he had indicated such a design already directly after the sonnet sequence had been composed: "Some of the themes are really more adapted to fiction—so that I shall probably make stories of them whenever I get that constantly-deferred creative opportunity I am always waiting for" (*SL* 3.116–17). Any narrative structure in *Fungi from Yuggoth* effectively evaporates, however, after the first three sonnets, and it appears that Lovecraft had much difficulty in deciding how to weave "The Book" into a part of a coherent whole. The very beginning of the fragment seems to hint as much:

> My memories are very confused. . . . I am not even certain how I am communicating this message. While I know I am speaking, I have a vague impression that some strange and perhaps terrible mediation will be needed to bear what I say to the points where I wish to be heard. My identity, too, is bewilderingly cloudy. (*D* 362)

But perhaps Lovecraft was here merely following the advice he had set out in the notes on weird fiction he had put down:

> In certain cases it is advisable to begin writing a story without either a synopsis or even an idea of how it shall be developed and ended. This is when one feels a need of recording and exploiting some especially powerful or suggestive mood or picture to the full. In such a procedure the beginning thus produced may be regarded as a problem to be motivated and explained. . . . Once in a while, when a writer has a marked style with rhythms and cadences closely linked with imaginative associations, it is possible to begin *weaving a mood* with characteristic paragraphs and letting this mood dictate much of the tale. ("[Notes on Weird Fiction]," *CE* 2.170)

In any case, "The Book" went nowhere, but whether or not it dates to precisely this time, it is worth pondering why Lovecraft still kept what was written when so much else was discarded.

Another manuscript that I am inclined to place here is a set of memoranda, not so much a synopsis for a story but a record of

---

glimpsed in ancient shop—never seen again"; "[171] Hideous old book discovered—directions for shocking evocation." T. R. Livesey (6) has also made the acute observation that these images may ultimately derive from HPL's obtaining a copy of Charles A. Young's *Lessons in Astronomy* (1891).

thoughts captured as they arose, and now known (somewhat mis-
leadingly) as "The Rose Window" (*CE* 5.253–54). These concern a
"very ancient house on Central Hill, Kingsport" built by one Edward Crane around 1700, "a very early classical specimen" with
"thick walls" and "labyrinthine plan." The current owner of the
house has always felt an odd sense of fear, "especially in high-oak-
panelled library" of the house, and during renovations the dis-
placement of a wooden panel of its north wall reveals a "strangely
carved surface with convex glass circle 7" diameter in centre":

> Carving very baffling. Possibly just classical conventional designs,
> possibly something else. Disquieting resemblance under certain
> lights to huge octopus-like thing—yet not like anything of
> earth—of which glass circle is a huge, single central eye. Signs in
> corners of pediment uncomfortably familiar. Glass itself also baf-
> fling. Opaque—evidently convex mirror like many in old
> houses—but curiously devoid of reflective power. Also too high
> up to reflect anything but top of room. What one sees in it is gen-
> erally only cloudy light. This light seems to shift oddly, and one
> acquires a perverse tendency to keep staring at the thing as if one
> expected something to appear. Suggestion of self-luminousness at
> night. Cleaning does no good.

Lovecraft then jots down further thoughts for the mirror's *raison
d'être*:

> Stimulates hereditary memory. Is lens, prism, or mirror reflecting
> vision from other dimension or dimensions—time or space. Or
> rather, reflecting obscure rays not of vision but operating on ves-
> tigial and forgotten extra senses. Constructed by outside Entities
> in effort to inspect human world—or rather const. by elder wiz-
> ard under their direction.

> Outer beings peer through it. Influence humans by opening up
> other senses and dimension-perceptions possibly including heredi-
> tary memory. Explains odd dreams of strange horror. Also works
> through dreams.

> Principal effect, perhaps, to hold the attention and make mind
> susceptible to outside influence.

Steven J. Mariconda has pointed out ("Some Antecedents of the Shining Trapezohedron" 70) what seems like an antecedent to these notes in a commonplace book entry that evidently dates to some time in 1933:[45]

> [195] Pane of peculiar-looking glass from a ruined monastery reputed to have harboured devil-worship set up in modern house at edge of wild country. Landscape looks vaguely and unplaceably *wrong* through it. It has some unknown time-distorting quality, and comes from a primal, lost *civilisation*. Finally, hideous things in other world seen through it.

While there is little in "The Rose Window" to suggest where it was ultimately going—the notes merely supply the most meager of hints, "Supply details of effect on occupant / hered. mem.? / going for door now closed. / Discovering books in attic / shadowy companion? / wanders around tower / final denouement"—the intriguing Kingsport setting raises the question of whether Lovecraft had some particular house in the real-world analogy of that town in mind as inspiration. The Central Hill location perhaps points to a house on or near the Old Burial Hill in Marblehead, but not having visited the town myself, I can only suggest as a candidate the "Old Brig" on Orne Street, "where Old Diamond the witch-man liv'd, and where his hideous granddaughter, the witch Moll Pitcher, was born" (*SL* 1.236).

As for the evidence of placing "The Rose Window" notes to late 1933, consider the following passage in a letter written to Clark Ashton Smith in mid-December:

> . . . at present I am haunted by the cloudy notion of brooding, elder forces surrounding or pervading an ancient house and seeking to achieve some sort of bodily formation. Well and good. But when I sit down and try to think up the suitable elements—the nature of the elder forces, the reason for their concentration in this spot, the precise manner of their manifestation, their motive in seeking embodiment, and their procedure when embodied—I find that every

---

45. Mariconda also identifies a still earlier adumbration in "The Window" in *Fungi from Yuggoth*, and a possible ultimate source of the mirror/trapezehedron concept in H. G. Wells's story "The Crystal Egg."

idea occurring to me is hackneyed and commonplace. What I get is a mere catalogue of stock paraphernalia too crude and derivative to have any convincingness or adult significance. What I wanted to say remains unsaid—and the mystery of an old, shadowy house's suggestions remain unexplained. (SL 4.329)

The identification of this notion with the extant set of story notes is by no means certain, but I think it is still a hypothesis worth considering.

A third piece that can perhaps be associated with the experiments of late 1933 is the interesting fragment titled by Lovecraft "Of Evill Sorceries Done in New-England, of Daemons in No Humane Shape," apparently purported to be an extract from an imaginary work named *Thaumaturgicall Prodigies in the New-English Canaan,* by the Rev. Ward Phillips, Pastor of the Second Church in Arkham, in the Massachusetts-Bay—Boston, 1697." This carefully constructed text is in the late seventeenth-century style and relates certain events that are said to have taken place in or near the (New) Plymouth colony during William Bradford's governorship; S. T. Joshi has again made a valuable observation, suggesting the model of Cotton Mather's *Magnalia Christi Americana,*[46] but Bradford's own writings may also have been equally influential.[47] The manuscript mainly concerns the dealings of certain Richard Billington, who

being instructed partly by evill Books, and partly by an antient Wonder-Worker amongst the *Indian* Salvages, so fell away from good *Christian* Practice that he not only lay'd claim to Immortality in the Flesh, but sett up in the Woods a Place of Dagon, namely [a] great Ring of Stones, inside which he say'd Prayers to the Divell, and sung certain Rites of Magick abominable by Scripture. This being brought unto the Notice of the Magistrates, he deny'd all blasphemous Dealings; but not long after he privately shew'd great Fear about some Thing he had call'd out of the Sky

---

46. See the editor's note in CE 5.256.

47. Although it has not been catalogued, HPL may still have had Bradford's *History of the Plymouth Plantation* in his library, as he quotes from the work in a letter to Robert E. Howard (*MF* 1.67, *SL* 3.175). In any case, he would surely have been well familiar with it.

at Night. There were in that year seven slayings in the Woods near to *Richard Billington's* Stones, those slain being crushed and half-melted in a Fashion outside all Experience. Upon Talk of a Tryall, *Billington* dropt out of Sight, nor was any clear Word of him ever after heard. (*CE* 5.255)

Two months later, the leader of the Wampanaug Indians, Misquamacus ("that same antient Wonder-Worker of whom Billington had learnt some of his Sorceries"), comes to Plymouth to tell Governor Bradford that Billington has called from the sky a "worse Evill than cou'd be well repair'd," and while this thing could not be sent back to where it was summoned from, the Indians have imprisoned it in a pit in the ring of stones, covered with a flat stone inscribed with the Elder Sign, and a mound. Misquamacus also tells that the daemon "had the Name *Ossadagowah*, which signifys the child of *Sadogowah*," and "saying it was sometimes small and solid, like a great Toad the Bigness of a Ground-Hog, but sometimes big and cloudy, without any Shape at all"—clearly a reference to the entity invented by Clark Ashton Smith and frequently cited by Lovecraft elsewhere, Tsathoggua. "This much the antient Wizard Misquamacus told to Mr. Bradford, and ever after a great Mound in the Woods near the Pond southwest of New-Plymouth hath been straitly lett alone. The tall Stone is these Twenty years gone, but the Mound is mark'd by the Circumstance, that nothing, neither Grass nor Brush, will grow upon it."

While August Derleth of course made much use of this in his novel *The Lurker at the Threshold*, there is no indication at all what Lovecraft himself intended to do with the text; it can only be assumed that the quotation was intended to be placed into a story either not written or one that was started but subsequently destroyed, except for the fragment that he in that case wished to keep for future use. But perhaps an examination of the internal evidence can provide us with some clues. For it happens to be that Billington is a real surname associated with the history of the Plymouth colony, a John Billington being one of the original *Mayflower* passengers.[48] He is noted as a troublemaker by Bradford,

---

48. The possible connection to between the fictional and real Billingtons has also been pointed out by Andrew E. Rothovius (*DB* 191, 195).

and the Governor eventually sentenced him to be hanged for murder, a fact that Lovecraft was probably well acquainted with. It is also probably not a coincidence that there is a pond south-west of Plymouth, named after the real John Billington's son Francis as "Billington's Sea." It seems that Lovecraft has taken these bits of local color known to him in order to add some historical verisimilitude to his account, and a recent visit to Plymouth may well have been an impetus to the composition of the fragment. In fact, such a visit did take place on Thanksgiving Day 1933 (cf. *ES* 2.615, *FF* 89), and in the same letter that was quoted above in the context of "The Rose Window" notes he refers to it as an incentive to the recent experimentation:

> During the past week—and largely under the imaginative stimulus resulting from my trip to Plymouth's archaic lanes and bordering hills—I have been constantly attempting tales; though each one has been destroyed after a few pages because of the imaginative barrenness and cheap, concrete mechanicality revealed. . . . I shall not finish any more tales unless they are better than my previous attempts. Mean while the experimenting goes on . . . . . the quest for even half-way adequate images and incidents. (*SL* 4.329–30)

But again, this can only be a very tentative identification, until something more concrete hypothetically turns up in another letter.

We now reach the tale that may perhaps the most justifiably lay claim to the status of the lost Lovecraft story of his final decade. After the ultimately fruitless experimentation attempted in the latter half of 1933, ideas would still continue to linger in his mind and clamour for expressions, but he began to find it more and more difficult to set them down in coherent and satisfactory form, so that in the end only two more would emerge from his pen. The first of these, "The Shadow out of Time," would then only be composed after great difficulty over a period of nearly four months between 10 November 1934 and 24 February 1935 (as recorded on the autograph manuscript that finally surfaced in 1994). Even after completing it Lovecraft was—inexplicably, as the tale ranks among his finest—so disgusted with the story that he refused to type it and threatened to destroy it; it may be that only R. H. Barlow's surreptitious typing of "The Shadow out of Time" in the summer of 1935, when Lovecraft visited him for the second time in Florida, has prevented it from having become a prime topic of discussion here. But prior to embarking on the writing of this tale, and perhaps also after its completion, another much less-known work of fiction had occupied Lovecraft's thought. Indications of this began to appear in his letters around spring 1934, when he writes Richard F. Searight, one of his newer correspondents:

> I'm writing nothing at the present, though I have a rather ghoulish Arkham tale half planned in my head. Incidentally, I recently drew a map of "Arkham" embodying such casual geographical allusions as I have made in my various yarns. As such stories multiply, it becomes necessary to get their background somewhat systematised to avoid confusion & contradictions. I'll have to tackle "Kingsport" before long! (*RFS* 23)

It is perhaps surprising that he had not felt the need to draw such a map previously—in June 1933 he had noted to Robert Bloch that he may "some day" (*RB* 24) do so—as he had found it necessary to sketch one for Innsmouth during the writing of "The Shadow over Innsmouth." The map, covering "Arkham south of the Miskatonic," now exists in at least three versions, all being largely identical in intent with some minor variations that may be due to oversight. At least two of them were enclosures in letters to correspondents, and the third, reproduced in Arkham House's *Marginalia*,[49] may be the original from which these were quickly copied. In this diagram the course of the Miskatonic runs from west to east near the top edge, with a "Boston trains railroad" and station north of it, and a network of streets south. Lovecraft has taken pains to incorporate any street names cited in previous stories, such as High Street and Saltonstall Street, but several of them, for instance the Powder Mill and Senti-

---

49. Preceding p. 279. One of the apparent copies, titled "Map of the Principal Parts of Arkham, Massachusetts," was enclosed in a letter to F. Lee Baldwin (19 April 1934; ms., JHL), a facsimile of this is in *Books at Brown* 38/39 (1991–92 [1995]), and a tracing appeared in *Acolyte* 1, No. 1 (Fall 1942): 26. The other copy was enclosed in an April 1936 letter to Robert Bloch (see *RB* [supplement] 17) and has been reproduced as a frontispiece to *RB*. (I am grateful to Martin Andersson for clarifications concerning the *Marginalia* facsimile.)

nel Streets, are unique to the map. The Miskatonic University Quadrangle has naturally been included, as has St. Mary's Hospital (cited in "The Unnamable" and "The Festival") and Christ Church and Christ Church Cemetery (the latter mentioned in "Herbert West—Reanimator"), and roughly in the center a "Polish Quarter" has been defined, enclosing the Witch House. But it is not this street structure clarifying the allusions of past tales that is of interest for our discussion, but rather certain additional features not cited in any extant stories. In "The Dreams in the Witch House" a "Hangman's Brook" is once mentioned in passing (*DH* 275), and in the map this is shown to flow from "Hangman's Hill" lying to the west. This is alone not very significant, but in the northeastern section there is also a "French Hill" with a "French doctor's house" and "[garden]," and furthermore, on Hangman's Hill there is a "Wooded graveyard."

What are we to make of these features? The logical conclusion is that they intimately relate to the "ghoulish" and "half planned" tale Lovecraft was contemplating, and fortunately their importance to it can still be more or less recovered. A week or so before the letter to Searight, he had elaborated a bit on the plot he was putting together to F. Lee Baldwin, referring to these particular features of the map, perhaps just then drawn:

> I'm not working on the actual text of any story just now, but am planning a novelette of the Arkham cycle—about what happened when somebody inherited a queer old house on the top of Frenchman's Hill & obeyed an irresistible urge to dig in a certain queer, abandoned graveyard on Hangman's Hill at the other edge of the town. This story will probably not involve the actual supernatural—being more of the "Colour out of Space" type . . . greatly-stretched "scientifiction".[50]

This "queer old house on top of Frenchman's Hill" must be the "French doctor's house" on the *French Hill* of the extant maps. Unfortunately for us, Lovecraft had not begun to work on this concept before he left for his now annual trip to the South on

---

50. HPL to F. Lee Baldwin, 27 March 1934 (ms., JHL; quoted in *SOT* 10, *Encyclopedia* 50).

22 April. This is made clear by a letter written to Alfred Galpin en route from Charleston:

> My stuff dissatisfies me so badly that I am repudiating a great many of my old tales & experimenting with possible ways of eliminating certain characteristic flaws & weaknesses. Just now I have a new tale planned—but it seems puerile to me already— even before the start of actual writing! (*AG* 199)

Yet the novelette idea was not wholly abandoned at this point, for after reaching De Land in May Lovecraft seems to have related it in considerable detail to his youthful host, R. H. Barlow. For some reason Barlow failed to note this incident in the journal he was keeping during this lengthy visit (later published as "[Memories of H. P. Lovecraft (1934)]" in *FF*), nor does he mention it in his later memoir ("The Wind That is in the Grass," in *LR* and *FF*), but luckily August Derleth must have queried him about a set of notes that Lovecraft had left behind, as years later Barlow could still recall the following:

> This syllabus, pencilled on the blank portions of a newspaper car-toon, hints at plans for a last, never-written story. Lovecraft spoke of it with some fullness one afternoon in 1934, but since I ex-pected to read it in a few months or a year, I retained only casual impressions of the shape it was to have had. Inspired by an actual 17th-century house in the Quebec style which interrupts a staid New England street, the tale would have dealt with a French wiz-ard who sought to duplicate in himself the fabulous longevity of the crocodile, but who succeeded only in changing his form to a hideous extent. I remember there was to have been a scene where some one glimpsed the bent reptilian figure as it hurried across a miasmatic garden behind the strange house, to vanish in the well-mouth which its condition dictated as habitat; but I cannot estab-lish other details. (*DB* 312–13)

There is no direct link in this recollection to what we already know of the "novelette of the Arkham cycle," but other evidence I will soon present makes clear that they are the one and the same story. Derleth would later utilize this "syllabus" when constructing his posthumous collaboration "The Survivor," and while citing Barlow's explanation would note that this was "Lovecraft's own

title, it should be observed"[51] (*DB* 312). We need not concern us
with the specifics of Derleth's "collaboration" here, but fortunately
the Lovecraft notes themselves do survive, as they are of consuming interest for unravelling the particulars of this lost story:

> Jean-Francois Charriére. / Surgeon. / Studies crocodile and gavial.
> / B. 1636. Bayonne. Anci Lapurdum. / Elder secrets hinted. /
> Paris 1653. Aet. 17. / Study'd under Richd. Wiseman, Royalist ex-
> ile in France. Ante 1660. / Had been surgeon with Fr. army in In-
> dia. Pondicherry—Caromdall Coast 1674 & (1683). / Quebec
> 1691. / Arkham 1697. / House 1698-9. / Climax 1708.
>
> 1708 / 1636 / 72 / Have deteriorative evolution (toward croc.)
> occur in tomb.[52]

Let us next look into these jottings in detail. First, the year 1708
helps to establish that they are related to the same story described
in the letter to F. Lee Baldwin cited above, for the next day Lovecraft had described that idea to Donald Wandrei in slightly, but
crucially, different words:

> One thing I did lately was to construct a *map of* Arkham, so that
> allusions in any future tale I write may be consistent. As Arkham
> stories multiply, the various geographical allusions become harder
> & harder to keep track of without some guide. I have an un-
> formed idea for another possible Arkham story—a tale of a
> strange old house inherited by a man, & of the tree-overgrown
> graveyard on a distantly-visible hill which played upon that man's
> imagination till he was moved to disturb the huge boulder cover-
> ing an oddly hieroglyphed grave dug in 1708. (*MTS* 338)

Again the "French doctor's house" as well as the "Wooded grave-
yard" on the Hangman's Hill of the Arkham maps are no doubt
being referred to, and the notes identify this "French doctor" as a
surgeon named Jean-François Charriére. That he lived in Quebec
before coming to Arkham and building a house there (as is im-

---

51. It is not clear to me if the title appears in the notes themselves, or if R. H.
Barlow had supplied Derleth this information.
52. Quoted by Derleth in *DB* 313; not collected in *CE* 5 along with other story
notes.

plied by "House 1698–9") on the other hand must be significant for Barlow's recollection that the story was "inspired by an actual 17th-century house in the Quebec style which interrupts a staid New England street." I am not sure if there is such a house actually in New England that could have inspired Lovecraft or if Barlow has simply mixed up some details; in any case, Lovecraft would have been well familiar with Quebec architecture after his three visits there prior to 1934. Probably after the first of these trips in August 1930 he had added the following entry in his commonplace book:

> [185] Scene of an urban horror—Sous le Cap or Champlain Sts.—Quebec—rugged cliff-face—moss, mildew, dampness—houses half-burrowing into cliff.

This does not seem to relate to the story discussed, but it is indicative of how suggestive architectural scenes could be to Lovecraft.

As for the other points in the notes, *gavial* is a reptile of one of two species in the family of gavialidae in the order of crocodilians peculiar to India, hence probably significant in connection with Charriére having "been surgeon with Fr. army" in Pondicherry (now known as Puducherry), which is a former French colony on the southeastern coast of the peninsula of India. "Caromdall" is evidently Lovecraft's (or Derleth's) error for the actual Coromandel Coast. "Anci[ent] Lapurdum" stands for the Roman name of Charriére's birth-place, the town of Bayonne in France, and "Elder secrets hinted" together with it perhaps is meant to suggest that some elder lore going back to the Roman times (or earlier) was there available to him, although on the other hand he is noted to have been only seventeen when going to Paris. Charriére is then indicated to have studied medicine under Richard Wiseman, who was a real person and surgeon to King Charles II of England, in exile in France during Cromwell's interregnum until the restoration of 1660. A biographical study of Wiseman by Thomas Longmore (*Richard Wiseman, Surgeon and Sergeant-Surgeon to Charles II: A Biographical Study* [1891]) would theoretically have been available to Lovecraft, but I do not imagine he would have read this book, and more likely he picked up the information on him in some historical work dealing with the English Civil War; in any case,

Wiseman may not be a very important detail. I take the final notes to mean that at the age of seventy-two Charriére was buried in Arkham, but instead of being really dead he devolved into a reptilian form while trapped in the tomb—until "somebody inherited a queer old house on the top of Frenchman's Hill & obeyed an irresistible urge to dig in a certain queer, abandoned graveyard on Hangman's Hill at the other edge of the town." In connection with this, it may be pertinent to cite two much earlier entries in the commonplace book which seem at least partly relevant:

> [123] Dried up man living for centuries in cataleptic state in ancient tomb.

> [128] Individual, by some strange process, retraces the path of evolution and becomes amphibious. . . .

Putting together all this information, it appears that the plot "The Survivor" may be partially reconstructed as follows:

1. Jean-Francois Charriére is born Bayonne, France in 1636.
2. In 1653 goes to Paris to studies medicine (under the notable surgeon Richard Wiseman).
3. Between 1674 (?) and 1684 he works as a surgeon with the French army in India, in Pondicherry, and there acquires some secret knowledge—or perhaps is drawn there because already knows some "elder secrets" and has studied "crocodile and gavial."
4. He later moves first into Quebec in 1691, and then to Arkham in 1697, where a Quebec-style house is constructed (1698–99).
5. Charriére seemingly dies in 1708, but has evidently made some provisions before this, for he is buried in "an oddly hieroglyphed grave" on Hangman's Hill, which is covered by a "huge boulder." Are we to understand that the hieroglyphs (perhaps related to whatever information he came by in India) were necessary to his attainment of longevity? Does the boulder covering the grave prevent self-disinterment?
6. Longevity is indeed gained instead of death, but Charriére also devolves into a crocodile-like reptilian form in the tomb, probably as an unintended side-effect.
7. In the modern age, the person who has inherited the "strange

old house" of the "French wizard" (on what is now known as
French or Frenchman's Hill) is drawn looking from there
across the town to the "tree-overgrown graveyard on [the] dis-
tantly-visible" Hangman's Hill "at the other edge" of Arkham,
and is finally overcome by an urge to dig on the grave, and disturbs the boulder—thus releasing the now "reptilian figure"
Charriére has become.

8. The "survivor" escapes to live in the well in the garden by the
    house.

But unfortunately, neither Lovecraft's notes nor R. H. Barlow's rec-
ollections say anything of the dénouement of the story and where
all this would have led. Perhaps it can be guessed that the scene that
Barlow remembered and where a glimpse of the "bent reptilian figure" was to have been seen would have been part of a climax that
would have confirmed the information otherwise discovered and so
far related. There may also be a suggestion in the "irresistible urge"
that this is, as in the shelved *The Case of Charles Dexter Ward*, all
part of Charriére's plan to have a "one who shall come after" at
hand to release him from the tomb. I can only hope that some further letter will come to light and supply more details of what Lovecraft had in mind. But even if a good deal of the plot can so be
reconstructed, such a bald résumé can scarcely act as a replacement
for the story itself, which probably came only so close of being actually written. In fact, it is not out of the question that Lovecraft at
some point did put pen on paper after returning from Florida but
discarded the results, as in November 1936 he would refer to "the
season of 1934–5, when I wrote half a dozen things and destroyed all
save 'The Shadow out of Time'" (*SL* 5.346), even if he is there
probably at least partially thinking the 1933 experiments.

The fall of 1934 seems to have been occupied by some unspecified revision work, including a novel,[53] after which "The

---

53. Cf. HPL to Robert Bloch, c. August 1934 (*RB* 52): "Haven't written anything
lately, & don't know when I ever shall. My programme is all in chaos—& yesterday *another* heavy (but poorly-paying) job with a time-limit of Sept. 1st blew in
to complicate matters. A whole damn novel to look over, pep up, & supply with
a prologue!" A slightly later letter (HPL to Elizabeth Toldridge, 6 October 1934
[*SL* 5.43]) says, however, that "I'm shifting the worst of it on to someone else in
sheer self-defence." This someone may have been Frank Belknap Long.

Shadow out of Time" was written. While finishing it, Lovecraft hints to E. Hoffmann Price of another story that may or may not be "The Survivor": "I hope to continue my revolt against revision & extensive correspondence long enough to do something on another yarn (of possibly greater chances of favourable Pharnabazian consideration) which I have in mind" (*SOT* 17). After the extant tale's completion, a similar desire was expressed to Robert Bloch: "There is another story idea in my head which may prove less unsalable—& later on I shall try to develop this . . . getting the necessary leisure through a ruthless subordination of revisory & epistolary activities" (*RB* [supplement] 11). But it does not seem that he could arrange the leisure before setting out toward Florida. Slightly before the writing of "The Haunter of the Dark" (November 1935), another fleeting mention occurs that may indicate that the idea had still not been abandoned then: "When I get time I may try to write a plot (Arkham stuff) which I've had in my head for a couple of years" (*ES* 2.711). It is of course possible that "The Haunter of the Dark" had originally been conceived of as an Arkham story, but this does not seem very likely, given how closely its plot is tied to the Providence setting.

After November 1935 deepening financial troubles, the hospitalization of his surviving aunt, as well as the worsening state of his own health ensured that Lovecraft would never have the chance to write another purely original work of fiction. In June he had already stated to August Derleth that "More & more I am convinced that my days of writing are over" (*ES* 2.697), and in March 1936 he mused to E. Hoffmann Price that "fiction is not the medium for what I really want to do," adding:

> Just what the right medium would be, I don't know—perhaps the cheapened and hackneyed term 'prose-poem' would hint in the right direction . . . I doubt if I have the native capacity to do any first-rate work even under favourable conditions. If I had such, I would never have read pulp fiction, nor unconsciously acquired the taint of its perspective and materials—nor would I have persisted in a medium unsuited to my major (albeit unconscious) objectives. (*SL* 5.230–31)

Toward the end of the year his friend Wilfred Blanch Talman pulled some strings in a well-meaning but doomed effort to secure Lovecraft the possibility of placing a book with W. C. Morrow, but he felt it impossible to commit to writing a novel on whose contents external demands might be dictated:

> About this nebulous and doubtful book proposition—ten years ago I'd have snapped it up without thinking, but today the old man goes more slowly. While, as I said last month, I've always been vaguely toying with the idea of a full-length book, I have relatively little idea that any publisher would want anything which I could produce at this period. I haven't had time to think of original fiction for a year, and couldn't decide offhand just which of the various ideas in my notebooks I'd want to choose for a first novel-length attempt. Moreover—I could never create 15,000 words with any conclusiveness until I had finished the entire story—for I usually change rapidly as I proceed; often altering the first half of a story unrecognisably in order to reconcile it with elements unexpectedly introduced in the writing of the latter sections. What is more, I cannot write to order, and the imposition of a bunch of suggestions and limitations would kill the progress of anything I might get started. . . . The fact is, I believe I ought to get in practice with a few short stories before I try anything more substantial. . . . I have indeed been trying to get some time for fictional experiments during recent weeks, but have been defeated through the sudden turning-up of unexpected duties and obligations. (*SL* 5.338–39)

Talman somehow still got the impression that he was going to attempt the novel, generating an apologetic reply in which Lovecraft took pains to clarify his position, on the one hand giving assurances to show Morrow anything of the sort he might produce in the future, while on the other firmly backing off from any concrete promise that ambiguity might have suggested:

> I feel enormously and genuinely pained if I've unwittingly caused you to make elaborate approaches and semi-commitments on my behalf, from which a possible retreat would prove embarrassing. . . . At the present the thing I want to get at are not of novel calibre—and the only way to get around to wanting to write a novel is to get these short-story ideas off my chest first. . . . However, As I said be-

fore, I have for the last two weeks been trying to clear my programme for another season of fictional experimentation . . . and if I
do succeed in getting going it is quite possible that I might arrive at
the novel-synopsis stage—or the novel-writing stage. (*SL* 5.343–47)

In one of the last letters that Lovecraft probably wrote he still
feels sorry for having given Talman the wrong impression initially
(*SL* 5.419–20). There is, however, a curious postscript to Lovecraft's fiction career that makes one wonder whether the Morrow
proposition had after all set him to ponder a book-length work,
for in his memoir "Idiosyncrasies of H.P.L." E. A. Edkins made the
following surprising statement:

> Just before his death, Lovecraft spoke to me of an ambitious pro-
> ject reserved for some period of greater leisure, a sort of dynastic
> chronicle in fictional form, dealing with the hereditary mysteries
> and destinies of ancient New England family, tainted and accursed
> down the diminishing generations with some grewsome variant of
> lycanthropy. It was to be his *magnum opus*, embodying the results
> of his profound researches in the occult legends of that grim and
> secret country which he knew so well, but apparently the outline
> was just beginning to crystallise in his mind, and I doubt if he left
> even a rough draft of his plan. (*LR* 94–95)

There is no reference to this matter in anywhere else—and Lovecraft's side of the correspondence has most unfortunately been
lost—but if accurately recalled by Edkins, it seems that one final
tale could be added to the roll of the lost stories. Or perhaps almost final, as one further piece of fiction that he is known to have
attended to in early 1937 can also be mentioned: Incredible as it
may appear, Lovecraft performed one last act of literary kindness,
as he lay virtually on his deathbed in the agony of the terminal
stage of his intestinal cancer, as a note for 28 January in the so-
called "death diary" records: "Finish Rimel revision" (*CE* 5.241).
Letters reveal this to have been a story titled "From the Sea," and
Lovecraft returned it to Rimel in February in a heroic ultimate effort to coordinate his correspondence, "with such minor changes
as I think are needed" (*Life* 630). But the story was evidently not
published and seems to have been subsequently destroyed.

*   *   *

The history of literature is, in large part, a history of loss. Of the works of antiquity, only a slender remnant has been preserved, and much of this through the most precarious of circumstances: the Beowulf epic has come down to us in only a single text, and even that just narrowly escaped destruction in an eighteenth-century fire, and the transmission of what exists of the *Annales* and *Historiae* of Tacitus can be traced to merely two incomplete medieval manuscripts. Such a fate could easily have fallen on the bulk of Lovecraft's minor work, to say nothing of his correspondence, leaving much more than just "The Mystery of Murdon Grange" and "Life and Death" as enigmatic footnotes to his bibliography, with all copies of the ephemeral amateur journals in which they appeared long since crumbled and perished. Yet the research of historians and archeologists slowly continues to turn up fragments from the dust of the centuries, and more recently discoveries made in the ruins of the villa of Calpurnius Piso, Julius Caesar's father-in-law, in Pompeii have raised a glimmer of hope for the recovery of millennia-old masterpieces thought to have been lost forever. Is there any justification to anticipate similar future additions to the Lovecraft canon? Such a question must be approached with grave reservations, but there may still be a rationale for such wishes, however minor.

The lost stories discussed previously can be divided into four rough categories: First, there are those that appear to have remained only in the conceptual stage, but for which some information is available, chiefly in the letters, and in few cases in written notes. If any of these—the "Dr. Eben Spencer plot," *The Club of Seven Dreamers, The House of the Worm*, the "Salem novel," "Cassius," "The Round Tower," and so on—were ever actually attempted (and not just remolded into other works), they were almost certainly discarded by Lovecraft in his lifetime, and if we are ever to know more of them the information must come from currently unknown but extant letters where they may be discussed; this latter being not at all an unlikely prospect. Second, there are the stories that once existed but were likewise destroyed: the great majority of the juvenile fiction, the abandoned "Florida story," the drafts of "The Shadow over Innsmouth" and "The Shadow out of Time," and the various experiments of the mid-1930s.[54] Then there are also the fragments that Lovecraft for one reason or another did not discard; of these and the previous category we can too probably learn more only if more correspondence touching them surfaces.

There is, however, a fourth class into which certain items can segregated instead of the first three—the tales that are lost in the sense that they are known to have been composed and perhaps even published, and that may yet come to light even though they have so far not been located. There is a slim possibility that the conclusion of "The Mystery of Murdon Grange," "Life and Death," and "When Swords Were Bold" will some day be unearthed, but a greater chance of success perhaps lies in the discovery of some of the revisory work of the late 1920s and the 1930s that is currently not well known; and I would even hazard to predict that at least one such story, whether it be something done for Zealia B. Bishop, Adolphe de Castro, or someone else, will be uncovered in the not too distant future. Quite likely this prospect is itself more alluring than the eventual reward—like the plays of Menander, their ghost may prove more powerful than the reality—but this should not discourage us from looking for clues toward their exhumation. In the meantime, we can always imagine what was and what might have been, and thus capture at least a fleeting glimpse of those "locked dimensions . . . out of reach," even if in the end for the stories of H. P. Lovecraft "the unfinished window in Aladdin's palace unfinished must remain."

Works Cited

Barlow, R. H. "[Memories of H. P. Lovecraft (1934)]." In *FF*.

Bishop, Zealia. "H. P. Lovecraft: A Pupil's View." In *LR*.

Cannon, Peter, ed. *Lovecraft Remembered*. Sauk City, WI: Arkham House, 1998. [Abbreviated in the text as *LR*.]

Fulwiler, William. "Letter to the editor." *Crypt of Cthulhu* No. 19 (Candlemas 1984): 59.

---

54. Just possibly there may also have been some scrapped stories of the early stage of which nothing is currently known. On 29 February 1928 HPL writes perplexingly to Donald Wandrei that "of my newer [i.e. post-"Alchemist"] stories I have repudiated & *destroyed* only two so far" (MTS 210, *emphasis mine*).

Joshi, S. T. *H. P. Lovecraft: A Life*. West Warwick, RI: Ne-cronomicon Press, 1996. [Abbreviated in the text as *Life*.]

———. *Primal Sources: Essays on H. P. Lovecraft*. New York: Hippocampus Press, 2003.

Joshi, S. T., and Schultz, David E. *An H. P. Lovecraft Encyclopedia*. 2001. New York: Hippocampus Press, 2004.

Leiber, Fritz, and Lovecraft, H. P. *Fritz Leiber and H. P. Lovecraft: Writers of the Dark*. Ed. Ben J. S. Szumskyj and S.T. Joshi. Holi-cong, PA: Wildside Press, 2003. [Abbreviated in the text as *WD*.]

Livesey, T. R. "Dispatches from the Providence Observatory: As-tronomical Motifs and Sources in the Writings of H. P. Love-craft." *Lovecraft Annual* 2 (2008): 3–87.

Lovecraft, H. P. *The H. P. Lovecraft Dream Book*. Ed. S. T. Joshi, Will Murray, and David E. Schultz. West Warwick, RI: Ne-cronomicon Press, 1994.

———. *Letters from New York*. Ed. S. T. Joshi and David E. Schultz. San Francisco: Night Shade Books, 2005. [Abbreviated in the text as *NY*.]

———. *Letters to Alfred Galpin*. Ed. S. T. Joshi and David E. Schultz. New York: Hippocampus Press, 2003. [Abbreviated in the text as *AG*.]

———. *Letters to Rheinhart Kleiner*. Ed. S. T. Joshi and David E. Schultz. New York: Hippocampus Press, 2005. [Abbreviated in the text as *RK*.]

———. *Letters to Richard F. Searight*. Ed. David E. Schultz and S. T. Joshi with Franklyn Searight. West Warwick, RI: Ne-cronomicon Press, 1992. [Abbreviated in the text as *RFS*.]

———. *Letters to Robert Bloch*. Ed. David E. Schultz and S. T. Joshi. West Warwick, RI: Necronomicon Press, 1993 (also supplement). [Abbreviated in the text as *RB*.]

———. *O Fortunate Floridian: H.P. Lovecraft's Letters to R.H. Barlow*. Ed. S. T. Joshi and David E. Schultz. Tampa, FL: Uni-versity of Tampa Press, 2007. [Abbreviated in the text as *FF*.]

———. *The Shadow out of Time: The Corrected Text*. Ed. S. T. Joshi and David E. Schultz. New York: Hippocampus Press, 2001. [Abbreviated in the text as *SOT*.]

Lovecraft, H. P. (et al.). *The Dark Brotherhood and Other Pieces*. Ed. August Derleth. Sauk City, WI: Arkham House, 1966. [Abbreviated in the text as *DB*.]

Lovecraft, H. P., and Derleth, August. *Essential Solitude: The Letters of H.P. Lovecraft and August Derleth.* Ed. David E. Schultz and S. T. Joshi. New York: Hippocampus Press, 2008. [Abbreviated in the text as *ES.*]

Lovecraft, H. P., and Howard, Robert E. *A Means to Freedom: The Letters of H. P. Lovecraft and Robert E. Howard.* Ed. S. T. Joshi, David E. Schultz, and Rusty Burke. New York: Hippocampus Press, 2009. [Abbreviated in the text as *MF.*]

Lovecraft, H. P., and Donald Wandrei. *Mysteries of Time and Spirit: The Letters of H.P. Lovecraft and Donald Wandrei.* Ed. S. T. Joshi and David E. Schultz. San Francisco: Night Shade, 2003. [Abbreviated in the text as *MTS.*]

Macauley, George. "Extracts from H. P. Lovecraft's Letters to G. W. Macauley." *O-Wash-Ta-Nong* 3, No. 2 (Spring 1938): 1–4.

Mariconda, Steven J. *On the Emergence of "Cthulhu" and Other Observations.* West Warwick, RI: Necronomicon Press, 1995.

Murray, Will. "The Trouble with Shoggoths." *Crypt of Cthulhu* No. 32 (St. John's Eve): 35–38, 41.

Rothovius, Andrew E. "Lovecraft and the New England Megaliths." In *DB.*

Wetzel, George. "Research of a Biblio." In George Wetzel, ed. *Howard Phillips Lovecraft: Memoirs, Critiques, and Bibliographies.* North Tonawanda, NY: SSR Publications, 1951.

Cosmic Maenads and the Music of Madness: Lovecraft's Borrowings from the Greeks

John Salonia

Frenzied cultists writhing mindlessly to madness-inducing music that symbolizes the terrifying tumult of ultimate chaos . . . the evocative writing of H. P. Lovecraft brings them powerfully to life. Yet vivid as these images are, they did not arise spontaneously from his fertile imagination. Lovecraft based them on solid classical models.

Lovecraft's fiction deals with the loss of sanity; the surrender of the higher, finer things of consciousness to "the mindless primitive," as it is called in *Forbidden Planet*, a film that features a very Lovecraftian protagonist.[1] "Dagon," "The Call of Cthulhu," "The Rats in the Walls," *The Dream-Quest of Unknown Kadath*, "The Dunwich Horror," "The Dreams in the Witch House" and other tales and poems hold forth the threat of madness. But, to paraphrase Pilate, "what is madness?"

---

1. HPL's influence pervades this film. The Krel are a scaled-down version of the cone-shaped Great Race of Yith in "The Shadow out of Time." Using architecture to characterize an alien race (the functional form of the Krel doorways demonstrates their conical shape) is a staple of HPL's; see "The Shadow out of Time," "The Call of Cthulhu," and *At the Mountains of Madness*. Dr. Morbius's awakening of an ancient monster through his investigations into the culture of an extinct alien race is a direct borrowing from *At the Mountains of Madness*. Morbius' *Id* materializing as a roaring bestial entity that tears apart the helpless crewmen is quintessentially Lovecraftian, given HPL's view of man's animal origins and nature. Finally, Morbius learns of the rampaging of his *Id*-monster through his dreams, like Nathaniel Wingate Peaslee in "The Shadow out of Time."

To Lovecraft, madness is a reversion to the ancestral type of howling savagery, whether caused by brain-cell degeneration ("Herbert West—Reanimator") or by monstrous ancestral genes overpowering both mind and body ("The Rats in the Walls," "The Shadow over Innsmouth," "Facts concerning the Late Arthur Jermyn and His Family"). Old Castro, the captured member of the murderously Dionysian cult in "The Call of Cthulhu," offers a chilling prophecy that the Great Old Ones will reduce all humanity to the cultists' degraded level. Lovecraftian insanity thus can be caused by one's ancestry, or by membership in a corrupt cult, or by exposure to terrible shocks that violate a once-stable world-view. In Lovecraft's work, madness can be personal, social, or cosmic.

Lovecraft characterizes insanity in manifold ways. The variations include the shock-induced "brain fever" Henry Armitage suffers in "The Dunwich Horror"; the childish, semi-infantile sniveling of Edward Pickman Derby in "The Thing on the Doorstep"; the paranoid delusions of monstrous pursuit that drive the narrator of "Dagon" to suicide; and the paralyzing phobias against underground places, chilly drafts, and brick buildings that afflict, respectively, the narrators of "Pickman's Model" and "Cool Air," and the protagonist of "The Horror at Red Hook." It is a measure of Lovecraft's considerable literary skill that his doomed protagonists each go mad in his own particular fashion, adding to the credibility of his body of work. There is no standardized cliché of madness here; Lovecraft was too careful (and imaginative) a writer to fall into this pulp trap.

The truth shall set you free—and the despair of ultimate truth frees Lovecraft's protagonists from the comforting illusions that keep the rest of mankind sane. The humanoid gods of earth in *The Dream-Quest of Unknown Kadath* are weak things, powerless against the shattering truth of the Outer Gods. The keystone of the Gothic arch of Lovecraft's universe is the psychic trauma of discovering the truth.

This trauma afflicts not only the individual but also the cosmos itself. In many tales and poems, Lovecraft evocatively symbolized cosmic madness in the music of ultimate chaos. This haunting image resonates because it is part of our cultural inheritance from ancient Greece.

Lovecraft depicts thunderous pounding drums and wailing, accursed flutes to characterize supreme chaos. There, past the ordered cosmos, the boundless daemon-sultan Azathoth "gnaws hungrily in inconceivable, unlighted chambers beyond time" (*MM* 308) surrounded by "the gigantic ultimate gods, the blind, voiceless, tenebrous, mindless Outer Gods whose soul and messenger is the crawling chaos Nyarlathotep" (*MM* 308). Since the daemon-sultan's realm is lightless, the primary senses through which any luckless human visitor would experience the horrors of chaos are *touch*[2] and *sound*. It is worth noting that sight and sound are the primary senses experienced in dreams. Dreams are a constant theme of Lovecraft's work and often formed a direct inspiration for it. It is needless to add that Lovecraft's fictional alter ego Randolph Carter seeks both the world of dreams and the world of the past (in *The Dream-Quest* and in "The Silver Key," respectively).

The dream-senses of sight and sound also are the only two senses left to the surgically extracted brains in "The Whisperer in Darkness." In "The Shadow out of Time," the cone-shaped Yithians "had but two of the senses we recognize—sight and hearing" (*DH* 398)—and the narrator first learns of the Yithians' existence in his dreams. Dreams and the senses through which they are made manifest are inextricably linked in Lovecraft.

In the form of dance, music affects both vision and hearing. Lovecraft employed the device of maddening music throughout his life, in stories as diverse as "The Other Gods," *The Dream-Quest of Unknown Kadath*, and "The Dreams in the Witch House." This sinister music also echoes from the hills in his great

---

2. Cf. *The Dream-Quest of Unknown Kadath*: "Unswerving and obedient to the foul legate's orders, that hellish bird plunged onward through shoals of shapeless lurkers and caperers in darkness, and vacuous herds of drifting entities that pawed and groped and groped and pawed; the nameless larvae of the Other Gods, that are like them blind and without mind, and possessed of singular hungers and thirsts . . . Onward—onward—dizzily onward to ultimate doom through the blackness where sightless feelers pawed and slimy snouts jostled" (*MM* 404–5). The suffocating presence and touch of these nameless spawn—the maddening knowledge that supposedly empty space is crawling with hellish entities—is also effectively utilized in "From Beyond." There is room for fruitful speculation on the germlike or protozoalike imagery of these creatures that pervade both the air and outer space, which I will explore in a future article.

"Roman dream" of 1927, one letter variant of which was embodied almost verbatim in Frank Belknap Long's novel *The Horror from the Hills* (and which formed the best part of the book). Music that compels irrational dancing—and plain irrationality—is endemic in Lovecraft's work. It is always a very specific music. Even when it begins as a sweet allurement, as in *Dream-Quest*, the music quickly mutates into horror as the mask of comforting human illusions is stripped away.

Characteristically, music in Lovecraft takes the form of shrill piping; e.g., the half-musical whistling of the Elder Things that infest the ancient ruins in "The Shadow out of Time."[3] "The Music of Erich Zann" symbolizes both the descent into madness and the music's linkage with alien spheres of existence. Wild, orgiastic music figures also in "The Horror at Red Hook," although here Lovecraft mordantly links the licentious cult-music with the strident brassiness of jazz, which he detested.

Lovecraft repeatedly claimed he had "no true musical taste" (*SL* 1.9) and was "a poor judge of music" (*SL* 3.195). Despite this typically caustic self-appraisal, Lovecraft was an inveterate music lover, although he preferred simple popular tunes later in life.[4] "My early plea for a violin was granted before I was seven years of age" (*SL* 1.29), and his musical studies progressed far enough for him to play "a solo from Mozart before an audience of considerable size" (*SL* 2.30). Despite his customary self-deprecation, Lovecraft was sensitive enough to the power of music to use it as an effective fictional gateway to forbidden worlds, both cosmic and mental.

It is possible that Lovecraft intended the drums-and-pipes imagery to portray a sort of musical migraine. The throbbing thunder of the *basso profundo* drums of the other-dimensional gulfs (a brief exposure to which bursts both of Walter Gilman's eardrums in

---

3. Also note the shoggoths' eerie, musical whistling and piping in *At the Mountains of Madness*.

4. "Yes, We Have No Bananas" is a song HPL frequently named as a favorite when the subject of music came up. These references are sprinkled throughout his correspondence. In passing, it is also amusing to note that the fife and drum were the emblematic instruments of the American Revolution, which HPL always half-humorously professed to detest. It is as though he took sardonic pleasure in assigning these instruments to the forces of chaos.

"The Dreams in the Witch House") mixed with the razor-keen, ear-piercing shriek of those unbearably shrill flutes clutched in nameless paws forms a vivid depiction of hellish cranial agonies. Unbearably high and low notes conjoined in agonizing juxtaposition scrape almost palpably at the reader's nerves. It is true that Lovecraft inherited a propensity for migraines: "My grandfather had frightful blind headaches, and my mother could run him a close second . . . My own headaches . . . began as early as my existence itself . . ." (*SL* 3.368).

The physical discomfort of migraine likely was Lovecraft's original inspiration. However, there is evidence that Lovecraft, the consummate literary craftsman, with his painstaking methods of composition and revision, amplified the simple memory of physical distress through his widespread knowledge of the ancient world. He compounded sense-memory and cultural history into a conception so meaningful that he returned to it repeatedly throughout his life.

Let us grant that Lovecraft employed his migraines as a conscious artistic choice. To embody them, he selected a cacophonous, maddening music from Greek mythology. These myths were lifelong interests from his earliest childhood, and therein he found the proper symbols to characterize and convey the terrifying state of absolute chaos. As in most of his artistic endeavors, Lovecraft found his chief inspiration in the past.

Lovecraft's overwhelming sense of the past led him to take great pains to invest his horrors with a shadowy omnipresence throughout history and in a variety of cultures, lending his fictional creations verisimilitude by subtly weaving them into known chronologies. He also sought inspiration in actual legends, to give his fiction reflected believability by imitating the forms of real myths handed down from preliterate cultures. He invested his creations with all the trappings of ritual—and he did not neglect music.

"Music is part of the universal language of ritual, and without it ritual must always be impoverished" (Sharpe 1910). Ritual music has formed an essential part of religious worship for as long as humanity has existed. In concocting his fictional rites, Lovecraft made effective use of music's emotional effects and its deep historic (and prehistoric) roots.

To Lovecraft, the arch-traditionalist and supreme rationalist, the horror of formlessness was very real, and he succeeded admirably in transforming his personal dread into artistic form and communicating it with breath-stopping potency to his readers. Music was a key element in portraying this fear. What better place to find the proper music than in the classical world he so thoroughly admired? The image of the maenad springs immediately to mind.

Maenads (Ancient Greek: μαινάδες, *mainádes*) were the orgiastic female devotees of Dionysus; the name literally translates as "raving ones." Their god inspired them into a state of ecstatic frenzy through a combination of dancing, drunkenness, and drugs. In this altered state of consciousness, the maenads lost all inhibitions and indulged in violent and licentious behavior: wild screaming, indiscriminate sex, and ritualistically hunting down and tearing animals (even men and children) to pieces, devouring the raw flesh as a sacrament of their god. The maenads considered this a communion with Dionysus through devouring him by proxy. And to what music did the maenads dance?

E. R. Dodds's *The Greeks and the Irrational* provides strong evidence that Lovecraft had excellent reasons for choosing the shrill shrieking of flutes and the hypnotic throbbing of drums. Dodds's treatise is a fascinating and sometimes chilling portrayal of the Hellenic rise from primitive superstition to supreme reason, and then the decline back into archaic irrationality. (This Spenglerian cycle of decay, of course, is one of the basic themes of the Lovecraftian canon.)

Dodds's eminently readable monograph, based on a course of lectures he delivered at Berkeley in 1949, provides an explanation of what triggered Lovecraft's fertile imagination. In Appendix One, which deals with "Maenadism," Dodds writes:

> In the extraordinary dancing madness which periodically invaded Europe from the fourteenth to the seventeenth century, people danced until they dropped . . . Also, the thing is highly infectious . . . the will to dance takes possession of people *without the consent of the conscious mind* [emphasis added] . . .
>
> There are, further, certain resemblances in points of detail between the orgiastic religion of the *Bacchae* and orgiastic religion

elsewhere, which are worth noticing because they tend to establish that the "maenad" is a real, not a conventional figure, and one that has existed under different names at widely different times and places. The first concerns the flutes and tympana or kettledrums which accompany the maenad dance in the *Bacchae* [Euripides' play] and on Greek vases. To the Greeks these were the "orgiastic" instruments *par excellence*. They were used in all the great dancing cults, those of the Asiatic Cybele and the Cretan Rhea as well as those of Dionysus. *They could cause madness* [emphasis added] . . . And 2,000 years later, in the year 1518, when the crazy dancers of St. Vitus were going through Alsace, a similar music—the music of pipe and drum—was used again for the same ambiguous purpose, to provoke the madness . . . We still have the minute of the Strassburg Town Council on the subject. (272–73)

At this point it is worth quoting again from Sharpe's article on "Music":

In some cases, the apparently monotonous repetition of short musical phrases in the context of the dance can lead to trance and catalepsy, and the object of the exercise was to make contact with the spirit world. Cataleptic trance was the clearest sign of this contact . . . In Greece, certain instruments were condemned in some quarters on the grounds of their capacity for arousing the baser passions, largely because they had traditionally been used in the ecstatic cults of Dionysus, Cybele[5] and other deities . . . (1911)

Such baser passions arise from the deepest wells of the human mind. Possession by the unconscious mind would have struck Lovecraft as a fearful thing: the overpowering recrudescence of primal instinct that he dramatized as actual physical devolution in tales like "The Lurking Fear" and "Arthur Jermyn." Throughout his life, Lovecraft by *conscious* preference embraced coolly cerebral rationalism over instinctive emotionalism ("Apollonianism" over "Dionysianism").

Intriguing suggestions of the relation between maenadism and anthropophagy[6] and the sort of orgiastic cults Lovecraft portrayed

---

5. The worship of Cybele is part of the ancestral cannibal cult in "The Rats in the Walls."

6. Cf. "The Picture in the House," "The Rats in the Walls," "The Lurking Fear," and

in "The Call of Cthulhu" can be seen in a further extract from Appendix One of Dodds's study:

> A second point is the carriage of the head in Dionysiac ecstasy. This is repeatedly stressed in the *Bacchae:* [line] 150, "flinging his long hair to the sky"; 241, "I will stop you tossing back your hair"; 930, "tossing my head forwards and backwards like a bacchanal" . . . the same trait appears in Aristophanes . . . the maenads still "toss their heads" in Catullus, in Ovid, in Tacitus . . . But the gesture is not simply a convention of Greek poetry and art; at all times and everywhere it characterizes this particular type of religious hysteria. I take three independent modern descriptions: "the continual jerking their heads back, causing their long black hair to twist about, added much to their savage appearance"; "their long hair was tossed about by the rapid to-and-fro movements of the head"; "the head was tossed from side to side or thrown far back above a swollen and bulging throat." The first phrase is from a missionary's account of a cannibal dance in British Columbia which led up to the tearing asunder and eating of a human body; the second describes a sacral dance of goat-eaters in Morocco[7]; the third is from a clinical description of possessive hysteria by a French doctor. (273–74)

This firmly links the wild dancing and orgiastic music of the maenads with historical, as opposed to purely mythological, cannibalism. "As Pentheus observes at *Bacchae* [line] 778, 'it spreads like wildfire'" (Dodds 272). The orgiastic rites of Dionysus literally swept across the ancient world. This serves as a neat model of the worldwide extent of the cults of Cthulhu and the Old Ones.

The usage of ancient cults and their music was not the first time Lovecraft had dipped into Greek mythology and sorcery for inspiration. In early tales such as "Hypnos" and "The Tree," he borrowed freely from Hellenic mythology and Neoplatonist superstition.

Nor were Lovecraft's appropriations from Greek beliefs restricted to the music of madness and the mayhem of cultists. One of the most striking of these borrowings is the "Gorgo, Mormo,

---

"Pickman's Model." Cannibalism is another persistent theme in HPL's work.

7. Cf. the typical description of a human sacrifice as "the goat without horns," a phrase often ascribed to voodoo, especially in pulp fiction. The Cthulhu cultists are initially believed to be voodooists.

thousand-faced moon" incantation Lovecraft quoted in "The Horror at Red Hook." The ritual is dramatically echoed in Nyarlathotep's threatening of Randolph Carter with "my thousand other forms" (*MM* 403) in *The Dream-Quest*, which Lovecraft began writing in the year following "Red Hook."

Lovecraft adopted this incantation from the article "Magic" by Edward Burnett Tylor, LL.D., D.C.L., F.R.S., in the Ninth Edition (1902) of the *Encyclopedia Britannica*. The incantation apostrophizes the moon as a sinister deity with a thousand faces (= appearances = forms). Surely it is no coincidence that Lovecraft centered Nyarlathotep's cult on the moon and gave the crawling chaos a thousand other forms (= appearances = faces). (The moon-beast cultists play shrill pipes in Nyarlathotep's honor.)

Evidently, the incantation struck a chord with Lovecraft, prompting him to develop it further in *Dream-Quest*. This linkage cleverly implies that Nyarlathotep is the true power invoked by ancient Greek sorcerers and cultists, granting the crawling chaos a sinister pan-historical as well as pan-cultural presence. (Lovecraft also inserted the crawling chaos into the primitive roots of Egyptian mythology in the prose-poem "Nyarlathotep" [reworked into the eponymous sonnet from the *Fungi from Yuggoth* sonnet-cycle] and his tale "The Haunter of the Dark." In his tireless efforts to make his demonic pantheon both believable and picturesque, Lovecraft was hell-bent on shadowing all human culture and history with their taint.)

It is highly significant that Lovecraft's preferred spelling of "daemon" in Azathoth's title is not merely an instance of his preference for traditional British spellings; it is also the Latin transliteration of the Greek *daimon*. Sometimes a *daimon* was a tutelary spirit (as with Socrates), neatly dovetailing with the idea that the Old Ones would teach mankind Their ways in "The Call of Cthulhu." Naturally, using the British spelling also allowed Lovecraft to bridge the gap between *daimon* and "demon."

It is clear from the body of Lovecraft's writings, including his fiction, letters, and essays, in which he is a lifelong champion of civilization over barbarism, that any return to mindless, savage bestiality was anathema to him. The erosion of the family fortunes, leading to the loss of Lovecraft's cherished childhood home, filled him early in life with a bitter and painful knowledge of the precariousness of treasured, settled things. He took refuge from this in idealized visions of past centuries when order and security were assured and unconquerable.

Many commentators have misunderstood this adoration of antiquity. They misrepresent his pose of living in the past as an affectation at the best and as proof of maladjustment—even outright insanity—at the worst. The truth is that Lovecraft idolized (and idealized) the past from a deep philosophical commitment. He believed in "the blind cosmos that grinds aimlessly on from nothing to something and from something back to nothing, neither knowing nor heeding the wishes or existence of the minds that flicker for a second now and then in the darkness" (*MM*.409).

Intellectually, Lovecraft fully accepted this mechanistic worldview, but emotionally he completely rejected it. The past became the haven of security, of ordered things; the present, the inescapable crumbling, the breaking-down; the future, the inevitable downfall into complete collapse. Out of this conflict between bleak intellectual conviction and blazing emotional rejection was born his compelling literary works. (That Lovecraft emotionally did reject the bleak cosmic machine is beyond question. Both his writings and his identification with idealized visions of Georgian England and Imperial Rome were his personal raging "against the dying of the light," as Dylan Thomas wrote in "Do Not Go Gently into That Good Night.")

The most cursory examination of the brutal beliefs and practices of the Cthulhu cult reveals Lovecraft's pessimistic view of the humanity's ultimate fate. Old Castro explains the cult's ritual torture of its sacrificial victims:

The time would be easy to know, for then mankind would have become as the Great Old Ones; free and wild and beyond good and evil, with laws and morals thrown aside and all men shouting and killing and revelling [sic] in joy. Then the liberated Old Ones would teach them new ways to shout and kill and revel and enjoy themselves, and all the earth would flame with a holocaust of ecstasy and freedom. (*DH* 141)

In this context, it is hardly coincidental that Cthulhu's race intends to wipe the earth clean of human life, and that the aim of

Yog-Sothoth's half-human spawn in "The Dunwich Horror" is that earthly life is to "cleared off," as revealed in Wilbur Whateley's diary (*DH* 184). Lovecraft used the titles "Old Ones" and "Great Old Ones" to characterize different races of alien beings in various tales, yet most of them share a desire to expunge terrestrial life, cleansing the planet for their own occupation. (In ironic contrast, the crinoid race of "Old Ones" in *At the Mountains of Madness* accidentally *creates* all earthly life. Nevertheless, another of their creations—the shape-shifting shoggoths—threatens to extirpate humanity if roused from their Antarctic lair—a threat which is further explored in "The Shadow over Innsmouth.")

Moving from the destruction of reason through the use of demonic music to the destruction of the reasoning ape (*Homo sapiens*) *in toto* through demonic intervention is a logical progression for a creator of horror fiction. It increases the stakes to the highest level of dread, increasing the reader's emotional reaction to the maximum.

Lovecraft's choice of hellish instrumentation is a potent and proven method, widely known from antiquity, of blending, blurring and degrading individual human mentalities into a bestial mass-mind. For Lovecraft, this was a sufficiently compelling image of horror for him to assign it to the throne of ultimate chaos.

Works Cited

Dodds, E. R. *The Greeks and the Irrational*. Boston: Beacon Press, 1957.

Sharpe, Eric J. "Music." In *Man, Myth & Magic: An Illustrated Encyclopedia of the Supernatural*. New York: Marshall Cavendish, 1970. 14.1910–12.

Blacks, Boxers, and Lovecraft

Gavin Callaghan

In chapter three of his 1921–22 serial, "Herbert West—Reanimator," Lovecraft's physician-narrator and his colleague, the decadent/necrophilic Dr. Herbert West, are called to a "surreptitious and ill-conducted" (*D* 146) boxing match held by a bunch of Polish mill-workers, where one of the boxers lies motionless, seemingly knocked out. The injured boxer, who in fact turns out to be dead, is a black man named "Buck Robinson, 'The Harlem Smoke'" (*D* 146), described by Lovecraft as "a loathsome, gorilla-like thing, with abnormally long arms which I could not help calling fore legs, and a face that conjured up thoughts of unspeakable Congo secrets and tom-tom poundings under an eerie moon. The body must have looked even worse in life-but the world holds many ugly things" (*D* 146). The other boxer involved in the bout is an apparent Irishman named "Kid O'Brien" (*D* 146), described, however, as "a lubberly and now quaking youth with a most un-Hibernian hooked nose" (*D* 146). As S. T. Joshi suggests in his notes to the Penguin edition of "Reanimator," this ostensibly Irish boxer "Kid O'Brien" may "not in fact [be] Irish, but perhaps Jewish, and is attempting to capitalize on the fame of the great Irish-American boxer of the 1880s, John L. Sullivan." (*Call of Cthulhu* 377). Lovecraft may also be prefiguring (albeit from an opposing polemical perspective) something of Anne Nichols's famous play *Abie's Irish Rose* (1922), a hugely popular Broadway comedy that premiered the following year, which dealt in a lighthearted way with intermarriage between Irish and Jewish families.

I think more is going on here, however, in this brief passage—and that in Lovecraft's unlikely mixture of blacks, boxing, the Irish, and apparent Semitic (or anti-Semitic) themes we can see the white supremacist Lovecraft trying, however tentatively or clumsily, to feel his way toward incorporating his racial views and polemics within the larger rubric of his weird fiction work.

As S. T. Joshi has pointed out, some critics have attempted to derive a racist meaning purely from the marked *delay* in reanimation that Lovecraft associates with the necrophilic injection of Herbert West's solution into Buck Robinson's corpse. As Lovecraft's narrator observes, Robinson's corpse at first appears "wholly unresponsive to every solution we injected in its black arm; solutions prepared from experience with white specimens only" (*D* 146–47). This passage is not, however, in any way racist in itself. There are often differences in body chemistry depending upon race, age, and gender, and doctors must necessarily take into account racial differences, especially in experimental work. And, of course, as Joshi points out in his notes on this story, "The suggestion of biological racism here is countered by the later revelation that the solution does in fact work on the African American Robinson" (*Call of Cthulhu* 377).

A similar interval of delay—what Lovecraft's narrator calls a "gruesome" period of "waiting" (*D* 137)—likewise seems to figure in all the other reanimations performed by Herbert West and his assistant upon their deceased subjects. In chapter one, for instance, West waits for "about three quarters of an hour without the least sign of life" (*D* 137) from a deceased white subject. In chapter two, Lovecraft mentions another apparent delay of about an hour, from around 2 A.M. to 3 A.M. (*D* 141), before life resumes in another white subject. As for Buck Robinson, Lovecraft does not tell us the exact interval it takes before the reanimating solution works, Robinson's resurrection occurring offstage, as it were, during the early morning hours. True, it does seem as if Robinson's delay in reanimation is particularly acute, as compared to the others—indeed, in no other previous case did West go so far as to reinter the corpse, apparently believing the case hopeless. However, there is no objective way, as Lovecraft has written his narrative, to measure the exact interval or duration of the delay—and if Lovecraft had intended to suggest a racist meaning in this way, then his handling of it is certainly tentative and at best clumsy.

Boxers and Hybridism

Lovecraft, however, may have been influenced (and no doubt in-
censed), in his association of boxers with racial intermarriage (in
the form of the un-Hibernian "Kid O'Brien"), by the marriage of
famous black boxer Jack Johnson to a white woman in 1912, an
occurrence that rapidly drew the condemnation of those elite
white circles with which Lovecraft closely identified himself. As
Sig Synnestvedt observes in *The White Response to Black Emancipation* (1972),

> A highly publicized incident heightened congressional concern for
> legal props with which to maintain two classes of citizenship. The
> marriage of the flamboyant black heavyweight champion Jack
> Johnson to a white girl precipitated the introduction of several
> congressional bills to outlaw racial intermarriage through federal
> statute. When Congressman Roddenberry of Georgia introduced
> his bill he asserted, "No brutality, no infamy, no degradation in all
> the years of southern slavery possessed such villainous character
> and such atrocities qualities as the provisions of . . . [state] laws
> which allow the marriage of the negro Jack Johnson to a woman
> of the Caucasian strain." (121)

Lovecraft concurred. Indeed, as late as 1933, Lovecraft was
writing to J. Vernon Shea that racial

> intermarriage ought to be banned in view of the vast number of
> blacks in this country. Illicit miscegenation by the white male is
> bad enough, heaven knows—but at least the hybrid offspring is
> kept below a definite colour line & kept from vitiating the main
> stock. Nothing but pain & disaster can come from the mingling of
> black & white, & the law aught to aid in checking this criminal
> folly. (*SL* 4.230)

Boxers

Lovecraft's association of boxers with degeneracy and so-called
hybridism (i.e. intermarriage) in "Herbert West—Reanimator" first
appears in his earlier short story, "Facts concerning the Late Arthur Jermyn and His Family" (1920). In this story, Arthur Jermyn's
animalistic father, Sir Alfred Jermyn, is killed after "rehearsing an

exceedingly clever boxing match" (*D* 77) with his favorite female gorilla in Chicago (the same city, Joshi notes, "where Lovecraft's father had the syphilis-related breakdown that led to his confinement at Butler Hospital" [*Call of Cthulhu* 366]). In a scene that mixes sadistic, paternal, feminine/sexual, and cannibalistic themes, Alfred Jermyn and the female gorilla bite each other, after which the female tears him to pieces. (The parallels with the murderous rites of the Magna Mater in "The Rats in the Walls," the sacrifice of men to Demeter in "The Moon Bog," and the sacrifice of Suydham to Lilith in "The Horror at Red Hook" are clear.) And if, as Joshi hints, "Arthur Jermyn" functions partially as a highly colored account of his father's illness, then perhaps Lovecraft's view of boxers reflects a reaction against Lovecraft's father's illness as well. (Lovecraft, had he lived to view the bizarre and cannibalistic Tyson-Holyfield boxing match of the 1990s, would no doubt have felt himself vindicated and justified in his integration of sadistic/cannibalistic themes with boxing.)

Interestingly, Winfield Lovecraft's symptoms, according to his case-history notes, were characterized "above all" by his overt boasting about "his great strength-asking writer to see how perfectly his muscles are developed" (Joshi, *Life* 14)—suggesting a violent manliness run amok, and perhaps akin, in Lovecraft's mind, to the exhibitionistic male athleticism of boxers. Ultimately, the thread that connects all these disparate things in Lovecraft's mind—whether it be the illness of Lovecraft's father, blacks, or so-called hybridism—is *sexuality*. Lovecraft was consciously or unconsciously rebelling against everything that, to him, represented the ungoverned sexuality of his father. In Lovecraft's poetic satire "The Nymph's Reply to the Modern Business Man" (1917), interestingly, a sexually experienced woman (the titular "nymph") tells an affectionate businessman: "But others have said things like that / —And led me to a Harlem flat!" (*AT* 224); Lovecraft's later use of the nickname the "*Harlem* Smoke" in "Reanimator" perhaps reflects or preserves an association based on usage as a sexual circumlocution.

Lovecraft's apparent dislike of boxing seemingly extended to his personal life as well. In a letter written to the young (and sexually curious) Robert H. Barlow, for example, L. Sprague de

Camp observes, "Lovecraft criticized a story that Barlow had written about an artist who develops a strong attachment to a prize-
fighter. Lovecraft found this incredible: 'There is not the slightest
reason in the world why any sane & mature artist should wish to
see or talk with a cheap & undistinguished prize fighter'" (204).

Given Lovecraft's love for and identification with ancient
Rome, his concurrent antipathy to modern boxing is even more
curious, the ancient Romans themselves being obsessed with all
manner of bloodsports and gladiatorial contests. As Keith Hopkins
explains in his *Death and Renewal* (1985), the Romans had a "cultural obsession with fighting, bloodshed, ostentation, and competition" (20)—nor was this obsession limited to the lower or plebian
classes, or solely to men. As Hopkins observes, the emperor
"Commodus was not alone" in fighting as a gladiator: "At least
seven other emperors (Caligula, Titus, Hadrian, Lucius Verus,
Didius Julianus, Caracella, Geta) practiced or fought in gladiatorial
contests. And so did senators and knights, occasionally but repeatedly." As Hopkins concludes, "Gladiatorial fighting was more
popular among the Roman upper classes than modern scholars
readily admit" (21). Of course, this was during Rome's later Imperial and "decadent" period, and not the classic period of the Republic with which Lovecraft most strongly identified. Even so,
Lovecraft himself was not averse to joking about Roman
bloodsports, observing in one letter, for instance: "In their day, I
shou'd probably have liked gladiatorial sports with real killings.
Habet! Habet! Neca, Siphax, neca! Sanguinine bibe!" (*SL* 4.14).

Admittedly, Lovecraft would invoke the specter of such sadistic public entertainments in a negative manner in his weird collaboration, "The Mound" (1929–30), referring to "the many
amphitheatres where curious sports and sensations were provided
for the weary people" (*HM* 147)—"sensations" that include "cru-
elty" and "curious sadism" (*HM* 147). This passing critique, however, has more to do with Lovecraft's larger anti-bacchanalian and
anti-orgiastic polemic than with any objection to bloodsports as
such. (Lovecraft's protagonist himself is merely inclined to object
to the bloodsports as "the first of those friendly clashes of taste"
[*HM* 147] between him and the decadent Tsathians.)

Lovecraft's apparent objection to boxing is all the more curious, given his childhood love for the Sherlock Holmes mysteries of Sir Arthur Conan Doyle. According to Lovecraft himself, he identified closely with Sherlock Holmes, forming a juvenile detective agency (in which he himself was "Holmes") and writing many mysteries in the Sherlock Holmes manner; and, as I argue elsewhere, many later aspects of both Lovecraft's personality and weird fiction were highly influenced by Conan Doyle's Sherlock Holmes stories. Both Conan Doyle and Holmes, however, were amateur *boxers*—an interest, however, that seems to have never been communicated to Lovecraft himself.

This glaring omission may have been partially the result of Lovecraft's patent dislike of athletics as a child. As his childhood friend Harold Munro later observed, "Howard had no use whatever for athletics and claimed they should be no part of a school of college education" (70). There may be a more intellectual component, however, for Lovecraft's aversion—a component that has its roots in both his sexual and his racial polemics: his recognition of *the role of boxing as a means and a symbol of black liberation*, specifically as it relates to the rise of the figure of the black boxer in the contemporary sports world during this period—a heroic symbol that Lovecraft cleverly, if not too tastefully or subtly, inverts in these stories. And if there is racism in Lovecraft's "Herbert West—Reanimator," then we must look for it here.

Blacks and Boxing

Consider, for example, the figure of black boxer Jack Johnson, whose career, as Lawrence Levine observes in his book *Black Culture and Black Consciousness* (1977), "was profoundly shaped by the fact that he was not merely a fighter but a symbol," Johnson's victories against his white opponents being seen by both blacks and whites as victories against "'Race Hatred,' 'Prejudice,' and 'Negro Persecution'" (430).

According to Levine, "Like a number of black heavyweights before him, Johnson had difficulty getting a championship fight" with the reigning white champions, although when he finally did, as in his matches with Tommy Burns in 1908 and Jim Jeffries in 1910, Johnson often triumphed against his white competition—this despite the fact that, as some newspapers at the time asserted,

while the white "Jeffries had Runnymeade and Agincourt behind
him," his black opponent "had nothing but the jungle" (430)—
language that recalls Lovecraft's "Congo moon" language in "Reanimator," quoted above. (Note, in this regard, the fact that Lovecraft's Buck Robinson has "been knocked out" [and, indeed, *killed*]
by his white opponent in "Reanimator.") Lovecraft's own rhetoric
was full of similar "Agincourt" language. In his militaristic World
War I–era poem, "To Maj.-Gen. Omar Bundy, U.S.A." (1919), for
example, he similarly invokes Bradley's long, vaunted Saxon heritage in the midst of his praise, observing how:

> . . . the past bequeaths
> A heritage of dauntless might;
> Each Saxon shade his sword unsheaths,
> To aid his children in the fight.
>
> A thousand mem'ries lend their sway
> From Eastern and from Western shore;
> Quebec, Manila, Monterey,
> And Agincourt are liv'd once more . . . (*AT* 424)

Other critics of boxer Jack Johnson's 1910 victory over Jim Jeffries were less articulate than Lovecraft, however. Whereas the
mild-mannered Lovecraft reacted with a few veiled, caricatural
passages regarding boxers and boxing in general in his horror fiction, both the "afternoon and evening" after Johnson's victory over
his white opponent saw several "deaths and injuries" being re-
ported "in every state in the South as well as in New York, Massachusetts, Ohio, Missouri, Oklahoma, Colorado, and Washington,
D.C.," apparently due to "white anger and frustration" over the
symbolic black victory. (Levine 431–32). Johnson's victory over
Jeffries apparently also apparently led, much like his later marriage, to government intervention. Film pioneer Albert E. Smith
describes how Congress "Hastily [. . .] passed a law making it a
crime to ship motion pictures of prize fights from one state to another," effectively preventing distribution of "our Jeffries-Johnson
films," and resulting, Smith wrote, in a loss of "close to two hundred thousand dollars" (222).

Nor would Lovecraft's apparent association of blacks with

boxing, and not some other sport, be accidental. As Sig Synnestvedt observed in 1972, traditional opportunities for blacks in professional team-sports had long been prohibited, sports being just
as segregated as the rest of the U.S. In such *individual* sports as
boxing, however, blacks had finally found a way to compete and
distinguish themselves during the early years of the twentieth century. As Synnestvedt writes:

> Individual sports such as boxing had sometimes given way to
> black strength. The great heavyweight champions like Jack John-
> son and Joe Louis, and some like American fight history's greatest
> boxer, Ray Robinson, demonstrated the potential of the black
> athlete. Eight blacks have been heavyweight champions of the
> world. But team sports, dominated by whites, remained off limits
> to American blacks. The situation involved a continuous affront
> to black humanity. Despite ridicule of black "firsts" the break-
> through in the world of sports served as a significant precursor to
> the black revolution of the 1950's and 1960's. (161)

Lovecraft's views on boxers and boxing have some interesting
interrelations with some of his other polemical antagonisms as
well. For example, he would associate boxers with both blacks
and his hated chaotic/rootless modernism in his satire of T. S.
Eliot's *The Waste Land*, entitled "Waste Paper" (1922–23?), in
which Lovecraft includes a reference to boxing ("I saw the Leo-
nard-Tendler fight" [*AT* 255]) at the conclusion of a humorous
medley of black and jazz-related slang ("Mah Creole, au lubs yo'
well; / Aroun' mah heart you hab cast a spell," etc. [*AT* 255]).

The conservative Lovecraft's early anti-socialist/anarchist/ Bol-
shevist orientation—as reflected in his caricatures of anarchist and
Bolshevist-type revolutions in both "The Shadow over Innsmouth"
and "The Street" in his weird fiction—may have some relation to
boxers as well. The infamous 1914 coal miners' strike against John
D. Rockefeller in Ludlow, Colorado, for example—during which
an Innsmouth-style military action was undertaken by both private
and public militias against armed and militant miners—was apparently led by "A former *boxer* named John R. Lawson" (Crain 80;
emphasis mine). If Lovecraft was aware of this battle, his sympa-
thies would no doubt have been on the side of the owners and the

masters, and not on the side of the "besotted beasts" (*D* 347), i.e. the immigrant workers, who will reappear in various degenerative and hybrid disguises throughout his weird fiction.

Conclusion

The final integration of Lovecraft's racial and sociological themes into his work, however, is not to be found in "Herbert West—Reanimator," Rather, it will have to wait until the writing of his later apocalypses, particularly "The Call of Cthulhu," "The Shadow over Innsmouth," and *At the Mountains of Madness*, stories in which his caricatural impulse and socio-racial polemics will be merged seamlessly (and, for some oblivious readers, imperceptibly) with the larger narratives of his fiction. Lovecraft's portrait of enslaved shoggoths throwing off their mental/hypnotic shackles, and over-turning the rule of the Old Ones, would thus represent a knockout punch by Buck Robinson writ large—with Robinson's resurrection at the hands of Herbert West merely prefiguring that larger re-awakening which threatens the world at the end of *At the Mountains of Madness*, in the form of those "newer and wider conquests" (*MM* 105) splashing out from all the "black lairs" and "dark, dead corners and unplumbed depths" of the world.

Works Cited

Crain, Caleb. "There Was Blood." *New Yorker* (19 January 2009): 76–81.

de Camp, L. Sprague. *Lovecraft: A Biography*. New York: Ballantine, 1976.

Hopkins, Keith. *Death and Renewal*. (Sociological Studies in Roman History, Volume 2.) Cambridge: Cambridge University Press, 1985.

Joshi, S. T. *H. P. Lovecraft: A Life*. West Warwick, RI: Necronomicon Press, 1996.

Levine, Lawrence. *Black Culture and Black Consciousness: Afro-American Folk Thought from Slavery to Freedom*. New York: Oxford University Press. 1977.

Lovecraft, H. P. *The Call of Cthulhu and Other Weird Stories*. Ed. S. T. Joshi. New York: Penguin, 1999.

Munro, Harold. "Lovecraft, My Childhood Friend." In *Lovecraft Remembered*, ed. Peter Cannon. Sauk City, WI: Arkham House, 1998.

Smith, Albert E. *Two Reels and a Crank*. Garden City, NY: Doubleday, 1952.

Synnestvedt, Sig. *The White Response to Black Emancipation: Second-Class Citizenship in the United States Since Reconstruction*. New York: Macmillan Company, 1972.

Briefly Noted

The Internet is providing researchers with a wealth of material previously unavailable, and some interesting discoveries pertaining to Lovecraft have been made. Martin Andersson has discovered a very early mention of Lovecraft in the *Amsterdam* [NY] *Evening Recorder and Daily Democrat* (5 September 1905). In the unsigned article "Long Distance Predictions," on amateur weather forecasters, it is stated: "H. P. Lovecraft, who says he forecasts for Rhode Island, writes to say that he thinks his predictions will reach over into New York and New England. ¶ "'It may interest you to know,' he writes, 'that I have one mercurial thermometer by Spooner, six maximum and minimum thermometers by Casells, one psychometrical apparatus, one rain, one hair hygrometer and a wind vane.' He spells the name of the thermometer a syllable longer than usual to indicate a superior length of column." This may in fact be the first mention of Lovecraft in print. Phillip A. Ellis has discovered that Lovecraft's letter in the *Scientific American* (25 August 1906) was reprinted in the *Liverpool* [NSW, Australia] *Herald* (24 November 1906).

On H. P. Lovecraft's "The House"

J. D. Worthington

The curious poem known as "The House" (*AT* 45–46) has been alternately praised and condemned, on occasion by the same individual. For example, S. T. Joshi, in his introduction to *The Fantastic Poetry* (Necronomicon Press, 1990), called both "The House" and "Despair" "wooden and mechanical" (9). But four years later, in *H. P. Lovecraft: A Life*, that judgment had changed, as he called the latter "one of his most powerful weird poems," adding: "Rarely has Lovecraft's 'cosmic pessimism' achieved such concentrated expression as this" (192); while he called "The House" "a finely atmospheric piece" (347). Donald R. Burleson, in his *H. P. Lovecraft: A Critical Study* (1983), refers to it as one of "at least two important poems of the period" (36), proceeding to examine it in conjunction with the later "The City" (October 1919) in light of the theme of elusive memory or memory that proves too awful to be retained (37).

That the verse suffers from a tendency to be overly melodramatic in its phrasing, especially in line 9, is undeniable; as is the charge that Lovecraft uses some stereotypical signifiers to achieve his effects. Yet, as I hope to show, these remain minor flaws in a poem that nonetheless achieves a notable degree of atmospheric tensity as well as a sense of awe and wonder.

In fact, the theme Burleson mentioned is one of the most powerful themes of this brief but memorable verse, but here it also works in combination with Lovecraft's common theme of the sentience of a place—an element that was maintained to some degree when, some five and a half years later, he came to write another piece inspired by the same building, "The Shunned House" (October 1924). That place, as has long been known, is 135 Benefit

Street in Providence, Rhode Island, where his aunt Lillian D. Clark had been staying "for a few months during the absence of the family" (*Letters to Rheinhart Kleiner* 160). As he notes in this same letter to Kleiner, the house was "over 140 years old, & has been inhabited continuously by the same family," that of the Babbits, friends of "L.D.C."

This connection raises the question of whether the reference to "the hot Junetime" (l. 28) may be to an actual visit that, for whatever reason, inspired this particular production. Certainly, the mention throughout the verse of the fecund natural growth of the scene, coupled with the mention of the "strange spirit" that "stalks" (ll. 23–24), is likely to recall the passage in "The Tomb" (June 1917)—itself inspired by an incident when visiting a cemetery with Mrs. Clark (see *Letters to Alfred Galpin* 81 and *The Thing on the Doorstep* 368)—wherein the narrator first discovers the dank sepulcher of the Hydes:

It was in mid-summer, when the alchemy of Nature transmutes the sylvan landscape to one vivid and almost homogeneous mass of green; when the senses are well-nigh intoxicated with the surging seas of moist verdure and the subtly indefinable odours of the soil and the vegetation. In such surroundings the mind loses its perspective; time and space become trivial and unreal, and echoes of a forgotten prehistoric past beat insistently upon the enthralled consciousness. (*D* 5)

Here, too, we have the sense of a forgotten memory attempting to emerge, just as we have such a "spirit" in the form of both Jervas Hyde, and the unseen sylvan presences of the grove. We also, incidentally, have a stroke of lightning ("fulgury") that plays an important part in revealing or confirming the memory, as in "The House."

In the same fashion, we have "the vines, green and cold, / By strange nourishment fed; / And no man knows the juices they suck from the depths of their dank slimy bed" (ll. 7–9), which recalls the censure Randolph Carter receives from his friend Joel Manton in "The Unnamable" (September 1923):

Looking toward the giant willow in the centre of the cemetery, whose trunk had nearly engulfed an ancient, illegible slab, I had made a fantastic remark about the spectral and unmentionable nourishment which the colossal roots must be sucking from that hoary, charnel earth; when my friend chided me for such nonsense and told me that since no internments had occurred there for over a century, nothing could possibly exist to nourish the tree in other than an ordinary manner. (*D* 200)

Manton's maintaining that "we know things [. . .] only through our five senses or our religious intuitions" (*D* 200) is also refuted not only by their experience in that tale, but also by that of the protagonist in this earlier verse.

The theme of the sentience of things (taken, as many have mentioned before, from a combination of the idea of a *genius loci* and Poe's "The Fall of the House of Usher"—cf. *The Annotated Supernatural Horror in Literature* 45), is first adumbrated in what might, in other hands, seem merely a metaphoric description:

> Where the branches are telling
>   Strange legends of ill;
> Over timbers so old
>   That they breathe of the dead (ll. 3–6)

However, as we have seen from the examples above, as well as such verse as "Mother Earth" (part of the "Cycle of Verse"; November–December 1918), and the tone and hints throughout the present poem, such comforting (if macabre) bits of poetic personification are not likely to be the case here, where the place itself seems alive and imbued with a form of consciousness, or at least sentience.

The second stanza takes us a little further into the exploration of the dichotomy between seeming and reality, with its "[t]all blossoms and fair" (l. 11) that perfume the air sweetly, but which only hide that which, in the light of the setting sun, makes "the picture loom dun / On the curious gaze" (ll. 16–17). Here, too, we have the use of a common element in Lovecraft's work, the use of twilight as a transforming or revealing factor. Yet we also find that "above the sweet scent of the blossoms rise odours of numberless days" (l. 18): the unhallowed age of the place, as with so many Lovecraftian locations, rises above the seeming healthy normalcy of the diurnal flowers and their perfume, as the shadow of the past looms over the small and insignificant present and its inhabitants, which we so often take to be of such importance.

This, when one thinks of it, is a curious sort of theme for one who was so enamoured of the antiquities of the past that he was moved to ecstasies of descriptive passion in his encounters with such relics, as seen in his accounts of Marblehead, St. Augustine, Charleston, Quebec, and the like. Yet, as Lovecraft was also quick to point out, these survivals from bygone eras were more solid, more steeped in history, tradition, and life than the parvenue architectural achievements of his own time (or ours).

The next lines (19-22) once again revert to the connection between rank herbage and such an anomalous survival or at least hint of the presence of the past:

> The rank grasses are waving
> > On terrace and lawn
> Dim memories sav'ring
> > Of things that have gone;

This, along with the other such descriptive passages earlier, not only recalls the Babbit house as it must have appeared at this time (it has since been restored; see Joshi, *H. P. Lovecraft: A Life* 347), but also oddly seems almost prescient of the structure that, combined with that house, provoked the impression resulting in "The Shunned House." This was an unnamed house in Elizabeth, New Jersey, which he described thus in a letter to his aunt Lillian of 4–6 November, 1924:

> And on the northeast corner of Bridge St. & Elizabeth Ave. is a terrible old house—a hellish place where night-black deeds must have been done in the early seventeen hundreds—with a blackish unpainted surface, unnaturally steep roof, & outside flight of steps leading to the second story, suffocatingly embowered in a tangle of ivy so dense that one cannot but imagine it accursed or corpse-fed. (*Letters from New York* 82)

Certainly, in his descriptions of the place in both verse and tale, he manages to convey an atmosphere of such lingering memories; ghosts that he more plainly evokes in the following lines:

> The stones of the walks
> > Are encrusted and wet,

> And a strange spirit stalks
> When the red sun has set,
> And the soul of the watcher is fill'd with faint pictures he fain
> would forget. (ll. 23–27)

Here we have another common motif in Lovecraft, and one inherited in part from his Gothic predecessors: the linkage of damp, encrusted stone with the incursion of the unnatural and unseen world. This is itself a manifestation of the past that will not remain buried and dead ("That is not dead which can eternal lie"), whether that be the horrific history and call of the blood of the Hydes or the de la Poers, or of an even more ancient, prehuman past such as the dank city of R'lyeh and "dead but dreaming" Cthulhu, or the sand-buried city of the Great Race, or even the icy fastness of the Old Ones in the Antarctic.

In this particular instance he has managed to invoke an immensely strong presence of the unseen, *unspecified*, and perhaps therefore, as Burleson points out (37), all the more powerful and disturbing world that surrounds us at all times but which we can only rarely perceive unless something—quite often in Lovecraft either brought on by or accompanied by a different light (cf. "From Beyond," "What the Moon Brings," "The Eidolon," "The Lamp")—breaches the barriers between it and ourselves. In this context, recall his criticism for what makes truly weird literature, as given in *Supernatural Horror in Literature:*

> The one test of the really weird is simply this—whether or not there be excited in the reader a profound sense of dread, and of conflict with unknown spheres and powers; a subtle attitude of awed listening, as if for the beating of black wings or the scratching of outside shapes and entities on the known universe's utmost rim (*Annotated Supernatural Horror in Literature* 23)

This is achieved here by the precise use of alliterative repetition of certain sounds and word-choices, one of the techniques at which Lovecraft so often excelled. Such a simple thing as the repeated susurrus sibilance of the "s" in "stones" to "strange spirit stalks" to sun . . . set" calls forth both the unconscious menace of that hissing or slithering connotation and the rustling or whispering of the rank herbage—a beautiful use almost bordering on a form of onomatopoeia. This is linked to the reaction of "the soul of the watcher" which is "fill'd with faint pictures he fain would forget," with its own labiodental fricative echo of the strictly dental fricative *s*, recalling yet rejecting or retreating from an association too overwhelming to bear. (Compare this usage to that of the *s* and *d* in the first stanza: "strange legends," "strange nourishment," "breathe of the dead," and especially the aforementioned "the juices they suck from the depths of their dank slimy bed"—an ABBA structure of "suck," "depths," "dank," "slimy" that contrasts that sibilance with the deadened hollow beat of the *d*.)

This idea, indeed, is encapsulated in the final stanza, where the same sounds (varied by the pulsation of the *b* and *p*) build on the impression, bringing it painfully near the point of total recall:

> It was in the hot Junetime
>   I stood by the scene,
> When the gold rays of noontime
>   Beat bright on the green.
> But I shiver'd with cold,
>   Groping feebly for light,
> As a picture unroll'd—
>   And my age-spanning sight
> Saw the time I had been there before flash like fulgury out of
> the night. (ll. 28–36)

Again, we have several interesting points to consider here. The "hot" June "noontime" light is contrasted with the "flash like fulgury out of the night," again recalling a change from normal diurnal light and the normal diurnal world to that of a nighttime lit by erratic or dim or unpredictable light, revealing a truth that proves as much an overwhelming "avalanche of memory" as that suffered by the Outsider, yet even more nebulous for the reader as the narrator's reticence or mental safety-mechanism causes that same memory to *just* elude explication. As Donald R. Burleson so eloquently phrased it:

> By declining to disclose what the poet so shockingly remembers, Lovecraft manages to make the reader experience the same maddening effect to remember, to know what it is, under the surface

of things, that one must—yet cannot bear to—remember. A Jungian analysis, of course, would suggest that the poet, in coming to his mysterious realization, has met the Shadow and recognized it as an unthinkable but undeniable facet of his own psyche. Whatever the interpretation, these poems show an early Lovecraftian obsession with the notion that would come to be central to several important stories later on, the notion that there is something awful that maddeningly eludes the memory but lurks ever close, ever ready to obtrude on the conscious mind and shatter one's complacency. (37)

The irony of the narrator's groping "feebly for light," only to have the true light of revelation plunge him once more into the darkness of night, *even in the midst of a noontide day*, is perhaps one of Lovecraft's most subtle yet sardonic uses of this motif. This is increased even further by the use of the term "age-spanning sight" referring, paradoxically, to that one brief glimpse of one particular memory that, nonetheless, *does* span the ages between the present and whatever obscure past holds the key to the enigma.

In addition, use of the term *fulgury* is a very interesting choice, as it is a rare noun form of the already archaic (cf. "age-spanning") *fulgor* or *fulgour*, from the Latin, meaning not only "a brilliant or flashing light" but also "*dazzling* brightness" (emphasis added) and "splendour" (*OED*), and *fulgar*, "a flash of lightning," both from the Latin *fulgare*, "to lighten" or "to shine," but also, figuratively, "to be illustrious." Thus we have a brief moment that not only spans the ages but illuminates both past and present, "flashing" briefly in the darkness of the narrator's night in the brightest day—a host of complex, contradictory impressions that nonetheless lead to that feeling of discomfort, even fear, mingled with the desire and *need* to know. Such a delicate balance is, of course, one of the hallmarks of Lovecraft's work, where he so skillfully blends terror and attraction in such seemingly contradictory (yet psychologically acute) compounds as "ecstatic fear" (*DH* 44).

This idea, of course, is a central one in Lovecraft, and found its canonical expression in the opening paragraph of "The Call of Cthulhu" (1926), a tale that has long been recognized as a watershed in his corpus:

The most merciful thing in the world, I think, is the inability of the human mind to correlate its contents. We live on a placid island of ignorance in the midst of black seas of infinity, and it was not meant that we should voyage far. The sciences, each straining in its own direction, have hitherto harmed us little; but some day the piecing together of dissociated knowledge will open up such terrifying vistas of reality, and of our frightful position therein, that we shall either go mad from the revelation or flee from the deadly light into the peace and safety of a new dark age. (*DH* 125)

Thus again, as Burleson put it, "The most characteristic Lovecraftian notions generally turn out to be products of long mental incubation" (37).

Here, in the midst of Lovecraft's beloved Providence and faced with a relic of that past with which he so identified, we once again see the central tenets of "conflict with time" (*CE* 2.176) and the idea of the past reaching forth to engulf some hapless individual—not through any fault of their own, but through sheer chance of a juxtaposition of person, place, and setting (by which I mean all the attendant incidentals of season, time, light, etc.).

While far from his most accomplished verse—a distinction reserved for *Fungi from Yuggoth* and a handful of other poems—nonetheless "The House" is a powerful evocation not only of a particular scene but of many of the key concepts of Lovecraft's work. What is sheltered inside the house, like that which lurks outside it, is the force of the past, that "single and fleeting avalanche of soul-annihilating memory (*DH* 51–52) which reduces the individual to an infinitesimal speck in the vastness of time and cosmos, yet which poignantly reinforces his link to each. Neither in the structure built by man nor that of the universe is there any safety, for at any moment we may be confronted with that past—personal or synecdochical—which we had believed left mercifully behind. In the midst of the city, surrounded by our fellow beings, and facing that which should represent our security and sinecure in the midst of chaos, we find the symbol of our fragility lies in the very symbol of our hope to endure—the house we have built for generations unborn who all unknowingly (until the moment of their own revelation) must also, perforce, live in the shadow of the past that house represents.

Works Cited

Burleson, Donald R. *H. P. Lovecraft: A Critical Study*. Westport, CT: Greenwood Press, 1983.

Joshi, S. T. *H. P. Lovecraft: A Life*. West Warwick, RI: Necronomicon Press, 1996.

Lovecraft, H. P. *The Annotated Supernatural Horror in Literature*. Edited by S. T. Joshi. New York: Hippocampus Press, 2000.

———. *The Fantastic Poetry*. Edited by S. T. Joshi. West Warwick, RI: Necronomicon Press, 1990.

———. *Letters from New York*. Edited by S. T. Joshi and David E. Schultz. San Francisco: Night Shade, 2005.

———. *Letters to Alfred Galpin*. Edited by S. T. Joshi and David E. Schultz. New York: Hippocampus Press, 2003.

———. *Letters to Rheinhart Kleiner*. Edited by S. T. Joshi and David E. Schultz. New York: Hippocampus Press, 2005.

———. *The Thing on the Doorstep and Other Weird Stories*. Edited by S. T. Joshi. New York: Penguin, 2001.

Briefly Noted

Adaptations of Lovecraft into film continue apace, and the H. P. Lovecraft Historical Society has at last released its long-awaited film of *The Whisperer in Darkness*. This 103-minute film, a black-and-white "talkie" (unlike the brilliant silent film *The Call of Cthulhu*), features Matt Foyer as Albert N. Wilmarth and Barry Lynch as Henry Akeley. Both *Whisperer* and *Call* will be shown at a film program called "Lovecraft's Visions" to be held at the Seattle Art Museum on October 7–9, along with a dozen or so other Lovecraft-related films. A German adaptation of "The Colour out of Space," entitled *Die Farbe*, has also been recently released.

From Bodily Fear to Cosmic Horror (and Back Again): The Tentacle Monster from Primordial Chaos to Hello Cthulhu

T. S. Miller

On first consideration, *The Sorrows of Young Werther* may seem many millions of German miles away from the peculiar preoccupations of Howard Phillips Lovecraft. We may find the first conjunction between the two, however, when they turn their eyes skyward: like many a tormented lover before him, Goethe's Werther inscribes his sorrow in the cosmos. Moreover, on one particularly abject August afternoon, Werther's self-martyring realignment of the heavens not only spins all existence into a cosmic tragedy—with himself, of course, at its center, the cosmic sufferer—but takes the further step of transforming the surrounding universe into an all-devouring monster, an *Ungeheuer*, a monstrous enormity: "I can see nothing but an eternally devouring, eternally regurgitating monster [*Ungeheuer*]" (Hutter 65). Although Werther stops short of literally embodying this vague devouring vastness, others of like sentiment have preferred to figure this same monstrous universe as a cosmic monstrosity, to grant it a twisted and tormented body of its own to match the perversity of the slings and arrows it directs at mankind. When the universe acquires such an immanently grim aspect, the perverse body of the resulting pantheistic deity often expands toward the tentaculate, as we see most prominently in the Cthulhu of the imagination of H. P. Lovecraft, the seemingly tentacle-obsessed writer whom Michael Moorcock has fondly dismissed as "that somewhat inadequate describer of the indescribable" (15). Indeed, indescribability, one of the oldest *topoi* in the book, nevertheless becomes fundamentally implicated in the articulation of the relationship between bodily fear and what Lovecraft would call "cosmic horror." The contemplator of ultimate fear must vacillate, in any description of it, between an unutterable, disembodied terror as impersonal as infinity, and a more visceral abomination based on the terrors he may observe daily visited upon his own flesh and upon all mortal things subject to decay: perhaps, say, a kind of all-reaching, all-clutching, all-devouring tentacle monster.[1] I should note that this crisis in no way represents a Todorovian hesitation, as it were, but an inescapably equivocal probing of the extent to which perversities of the body may be mapped onto the perversity of the universe, or rather of which of these perversities, in the end, makes for the more terrifying prospect. Regardless of the variation among their responses to such questions, many of the authors who have taken up the problem insist that the two sites of fear remain necessarily imbricated, if not interconnected: even when words fail, what we feel in the body we see in the void, and vice versa.

We may observe this crisis of representation everywhere from Goethe and Hoffmann to Poe and Browning; in the modern speculative genres as well as in the more ancient tradition of the fantastic in literature; and even in contemporaries of Lovecraft as far-flung geographically and aesthetically as H. G. Wells and Conrad Aiken.[2] Moreover, a survey of these selected non-Lovecraftian sources of cosmic horror will indeed reveal a remarkable number of tentacle monsters and their near relations: in fact, as the dragon dominates an earlier epoch in the West as the embodiment of the fearsome

---

1. Tentacles or no, the connection between bodily fear and cosmic horror has proven an endlessly fascinating motif in literature and perhaps even more so in the wider popular imagination: today, HPL maintains a higher profile than ever, with Cthulhu plush toys in constant production and the image of this tentacle-faced poster child for cosmic horror overlaid on every manner of pop culture icon. Especially representative are the "Hello Cthulhu" motif (after Sanrio's "Hello Kitty" brand) and, of course, the perennial "Cthulhu for President" campaign: "Why vote for a lesser evil?"

2. In 1926, one of Aiken's reviews for the *Atlantic Monthly* brought these two authors together, but the result was, in a word, inharmonious: "For as one looks back over Mr. Wells's long and honorable record as a novelist one fails to recall a single vivid or credible character" (275).

Unknown,[3] the twentieth century may well be called the Century of the Tentacle Monster—*pace* the inventor of Smaug, really only an Anglo-Saxon relic of a wyrm. Although today the term "tentacle monster," when not applied to Lovecraftian derivatives, perhaps most commonly evokes a certain subgenre of graphic Japanese pornography,[4] I would like to extend the scope of our understanding of this category of literary entities far beyond Lovecraft, his followers, and the rather baffling hentai phenomenon. For the very mass of writhing appendages that is the standard tentacle monster points us to that same representational crisis across the history of Western literature: the fluctuating amorphousness of the tentacle monster confronts us with the horror of distinctly bodily change, with its appendages further spiraling toward the cosmic maw that both Werther and Lovecraft place at the center of the universe and at the center of being. One may perhaps object to the apparent absurdity of my inevitable admission that, for my definition of "tentacle monster," the tentacles themselves may ultimately prove incidental, as long as the roiling, grasping entity signals an unstable site of junction between bodily fear and cosmic horror—or perhaps such latitude in form should come as no great surprise for this superclass of necessarily slippery signifiers.

Monsters, of course, always *mean*. As Paracelsus puts it, invoking the portentous sense of the original Latin designation *monstra*, "they were not born in vain, but from divine order to signify something" (Sigerist 248). Although *monstra* are never mere crea-

---

3. The origins of the literary dragon long predate Fáfnir, Beowulf's bane, and the *fyrene dracan* recorded in the *Anglo-Saxon Chronicle* as having been sighted in the sky over Northumbria in 793 C.E. (Mitchell 86). Indeed, in his book *How to Kill a Dragon*, Calvert Watkins has marshaled a formidable assemblage of texts (in a formidable number of languages) to argue for "a common Indo-European formula expressing the central act of an inherited theme, the serpent or dragon-slaying myth," not only "a central part of the symbolic culture of the speakers of Proto-Indo-European itself," but a formula that continued to shape subsequent literary expression in Indo-European languages (viii).

4. Although HPL's enormous legacy has surely insinuated itself into the contemporary genre, we fortunately cannot hold him responsible for it: the tradition has a much longer cultural history, traceable at least as far back as the notorious Edo-era woodcut by Hokusai, *The Dream of the Fisherman's Wife*.

tures, but rather signs, warnings, prodigies,[5] I am interested here in
a more particular set of these signifying things than those merely
descended from cephalopods: namely, the truly universal monster,
and something far removed from any role ever played by Boris
Karloff or Bela Lugosi. It is no accident that the phrase "cosmic
horror" does double duty in referring to both the feeling of terror
located in a human body and the physical manifestation of that
horror as an immense entity, a tremendous sign. Or, in other
words, a big giant monster, a species that has always been with us
in some form. We could, for instance, conjure up the memory of
primordial gods of chaos like Tiamat or Python, and, in our attempt to begin at the beginning, we might more profitably make a
quick stop at the end: the apocalyptic monsters of Norse mythology perhaps come closest to comprising an almost Lovecraftian
anti-pantheon, the antithesis of the one they are fated to topple at
Ragnarök. For example, we can detect a frisson of bodily revulsion
mated to cosmic power in Níðhöggr, the dragon gnawing endlessly
at the roots of the world-tree Yggdrasil, or in Jörmungandr, the
incarnation of the Ouroboros serpent who encircles all Midgard in
his coils. Both of these old wyrms have left hefty legacies in contemporary fantasy, but their purest and darkest echo likely comes
in a seemingly throwaway line of Tolkien's: "Far, far below the
deepest delvings of the Dwarves, the world is gnawed by nameless
things" (490). While the Norse tradition so meticulously deline-
ates their shapes and destinies, the "serpents" here resist not only
any taxonomic nomenclature but the simplest of physical descriptions;[6] we can perhaps expect a linguistic enthusiast like Tolkien
to have recognized that there is nothing quite so unsettling as an
unnamable signifier, the indescribable meaning thing that in this

---

5. Cf. *moneo*, to warn, foretell, presage. Note, however, that in the Roman state
religion the word *prodigium* typically had a far narrower and much more techni-
cal sense than our word "prodigy." For a concise explanation of the category, see
Warrior, *Roman Religion* 49ff.

6. Tolkien names and embodies a number of horrors—goblins, orcs, trolls, dragons, giant spiders, winged beasts, and even a tentacle monster in the form of the
enigmatic Watcher in the Water—yet Sauron, the epitome of evil in *The Lord of
the Rings*, significantly seems to have misplaced his own body, existing for the
duration of the narrative only as that lidless, draconian eye.

sense begins to gnaw at language itself.

But we cannot stop with this breed of wor(l)d-gnawing monsters—though they are fearsome indeed—for there exist yet greater ones than these, monsters that themselves *constitute* the universe after the fashion of Werther's self-devouring cosmos, or, like the members of Lovecraft's dark pantheon, embody not just the instrument of mankind's destruction or the fate of the universe, but no less than the universe's disposition or attitude toward human beings, up to and including the time of its own ending: heedless, cosmically indifferent, all-devouring. To be sure, like Cthulhu, Níðhöggr may possibly function as a herald of the end times,[7] while Jörmungandr will play his own indispensable part in the final battle by slaying Thor, but the apocalypse, in the end, can seem like proverbially diminutive potatoes next to the perpetual cosmic horror in which Lovecraft and Goethe trade. In short, the monstrosity of cosmic horror is about more than death: it encompasses all species of recoilings from and revulsions at that living, pulsing, endlessly mutating artifact that is the human body.

But what precisely is the relationship between mere human flesh—that dull matter, ready meat—and, say, the fantastical form of the dragon? I cannot presume to offer here any kind of comprehensive survey of dragons, serpents, or beasts of the apocalypse, although all these classes of horrors have variously served as representations of some aspect of the human sensation or experience of cosmic horror. I would simply note for now that the sea serpent or sea monster more generally provides the most obvious analogue or antecedent for the tentacle monster, that pinnacle of Lovecraftian cosmic horror, and indeed Tennyson's indelible importation of the kraken into modern English literature likely represents the best candidate for a kind of "missing link" between the sea monsters of old and the rise of the modern Lovecraftian

---

7. See the ending of the Eddic poem Völuspá; Marijane Osborn has recently upheld Ólafur Briem's interpretation that in the poem "the seeress is saying that this dragon is coming now, as a harbinger of Ragnarök" (64). In this understanding, "the Eddic dragon is a shining, winged creature of serpentine shape evoking universal apocalypse" (64). Finally, while I am concerned with a particular type of cosmic horror, HPL himself, I should note, grants it of the Eddas in the general: "The Scandinavian Eddas and Sagas thunder with cosmic horror" (*ASHL* 25).

tentacle-form.[8] Yet, in "The Call of Cthulhu" at least, Lovecraft depicts the underwater deity as a fusion of precisely those three aforementioned types—an apocalyptic sea-monster dragon—but with the significant addition of the human figure: "If I say that my somewhat extravagant imagination yielded simultaneous pictures of an octopus, a dragon, and a human caricature, I shall not be unfaithful to the spirit of the thing" (*DH* 127).[9] We must keep in mind that the narrator can keep his wits about him to relate his story only because he experiences Cthulhu but secondhand: this most lucid description of the entity in all of Lovecraft's corpus comes at this moment precisely because the narrator is only describing a graven image of Cthulhu, itself an inadequate representation. Even so, as the narrative unfolds and the veils begin to lift from the narrator's eyes, his status as uninvolved observer can no longer protect him from the cosmic horror that consumes him: "I shall never sleep calmly again when I think of the horrors that lurk ceaselessly behind life in time and in space, and of those unhallowed blasphemies from elder stars which dream beneath the sea" (*DH* 149).[10] Cthulhu, then, represents a paradoxical admixture of the chthonic and the cosmic, the local and the foreign: here is a *thing* as alien as any extraterrestrial visitor from across the

---

8. Philip A. Shreffler, for one, maintains that HPL "could hardly have missed" Tennyson's version of an apocalyptic tentacle monster slumbering beneath the sea (see 43–44). Before Tennyson, the idea of such a great sea monster was the merest footnote to the Christian eschaton, even if we take into account Milton's own prodigious but more or less cosmically inconsequential Leviathan. For a recent discussion of Tennyson's tentacle monster and Cthulhu, see Maxwell, "Unnumbered Polypi." Finally, for some suggestive studies of HPL's relationship with Melville's quite different but decidedly universal sea monster, see Cannon, "Call Me Wizard Whateley"; Cerasini, "Thematic Links"; and Burleson, "Strange High Houses."

9. Cf. the descriptions of the half-human spawn of Yog-Sothoth in "The Dunwich Horror": "*It was a octopus, centipede, spider sort o' thing, but they was a haff-shaped man's face on top of it*" (*DH* 197).

10. In the lyrics to his song "Lovecraft in Brooklyn," John Darnielle of the musical project The Mountain Goats has perhaps best distilled the essence of Lovecraftian cosmic horror as well as the master plot arc of the so-called "Cthulhu Mythos," by way of a conflation of foundational tales like "The Call of Cthulhu" and "The Whisperer in Darkness": "Someday something's coming / from way out beyond the stars / to kill us while we stand here / it'll store our brains in mason jars."

unfathomable distances of deep space, yet as human as ourselves. Since Lovecraft stresses Cthulhu's deep connection to the human body, rather than, say, to the intellect, we must always remember that his horrors are as much horrors of time and space as of feeling and flesh: "I now felt gnawing at my vitals that dark terror which will never leave me till I, too, am at rest" (*DH* 149). That nameless gnawing thing no longer lies simply at the center of the earth or the cosmos—after the fashion of Lovecraft's Azathoth, "the monstrous nuclear chaos beyond angled space" ("The Whisperer in Darkness," *DH* 256)—but rather within the body itself.

We seem to have run up against a paradox here, since Mack Knopf rightly points to an oft-excerpted passage from "Supernatural Horror in Literature" as evidence that cosmic horror, for Lovecraft, is "not the same as mere bodily fear": "A certain atmosphere of breathless and unexplainable dread of outer, unknown forces must be present" (*ASHL* 23). And, while Lovecraft earlier notes that "this type of fear-literature must not be confounded with a type externally similar but psychologically widely different; the literature of mere physical fear and the mundanely gruesome" (*ASHL* 22), his essay perhaps does not fully account for way in which "physical fear" necessarily persists in the most cosmic of (his) horrors. Indeed, in making a humanoid entity like Cthulhu the focal point of the narrator's visceral terror, not only has Lovecraft recentered in the human body the cosmic horror he had removed from it, but, in doing the latter, he has given a body, a face, and arms—several—to what Werther experiences only as an indescribable *Ungeheuer*, a word that, especially in its adjectival form, connotes "tremendousness" or "enormity" (concepts more precisely specified by the term *Ungeheure*), but that usually denotes simply "monster" or "monstrosity":[11]

My heart is undermined by the consuming power that lies hidden in the Allness of nature, which has created nothing, formed nothing, which has destroyed neither neighbor nor itself. Surrounded by the heavens and the earth and the powerful web they weave between them, I reel with dread. I can see nothing but an

---

11. The word *Ungeheuer* can also refer specifically to dragons, serpents, or other serpentine beings: consider, for example, *Das Ungeheuer von Loch Ness*.

eternally devouring, eternally regurgitating monster [*Ungeheuer*]. (Hutter 65)

This single word *Ungeheuer*, the culmination and conclusion of Werther's entire August 18 letter, contains within its own range of meaning and resonance the same kind of oscillation we see in Lovecraft's desire to estrange cosmic horror from the individual and anchor it to the corporeal. In this respect, although both senses surely remain operative in Goethe's use of the word—that is, the tremendous and the monstrous—Werther's abomination is not by any means a fully or even particularly well-imagined monster. Moreover, the word pregnantly terminates the letter, precluding any further elaboration: the universe ends in this vastness of a monster.

While Goethe's contemporary English translators have fairly consistently rendered Werther's chosen term for his universe as simply "monster," in the context of my argument it is particularly instructive to compare Goethe's original—"Ich sehe nichts als ein ewig verschlingendes, ewig wiederkäuendes Ungeheuer" (56)— with Thomas Carlyle's embellishment: "the universe is to me a fearful monster, for ever devouring its own offspring" (35). Here Carlyle presents us with an adumbration of the Lovecraftian representational strategy in more ways than one: not only does he provide some further personification of the indistinct, inchoate *Ungeheuer*—perhaps not quite literally "fleshing it out" with detail—his chosen image also anticipates the grotesquely maternal Shub-Niggurath, another amorphous entity only alluded to in Lovecraft's own works, but described in "The Whisperer in Darkness" as the *"Black Goat of the Woods with a Thousand Young!"* (*DH* 226).[12] Another case of Lovecraft's oft-lampooned linguistic acrobatics, perhaps, yet, even if we find his language frequently inadequate to his (anti-?)descriptive project, Werther's language seems inadequate as well, leaving his hostile universe as it were only on the cusp of monsterhood.

One might argue that Carlyle's supernumerary monstrification and indeed Lovecraft's tentacle-ization, because they seem to set

---

12. Although many subsequent depictions of Shub-Niggurath conform to the standard tentaculate model, HPL himself described her in a late letter as a "hellish cloud-like entity" (*SL* 5.303).

mankind against a monstrous being, dilute or cheapen the more impersonal cosmic horror of Goethe's original, in which, as a part of the nature Werther envisions, our bodies remain complicit in monstrosity. Here we are all eater and eaten, although we may feel the same disgust at the binary that Leopold Bloom feels in the "Lestrygonians" chapter of *Ulysses*, despite his own fondness for inner organs: "Eat or be eaten. Kill! Kill!" (139).[13] Even S. T. Joshi, that great advocate of Lovecraft's literary quality, has admitted that the impulse toward the tentacle monster "scares off" certain readers in an unfortunate way, and that therefore critical interest in Lovecraft has been limited to those "who can see beyond the tentacled monsters that adorn the cover of his books to the philosophical and literary substance of the work itself" (*Epicure* 15). Yet, as I hope to show, the Lovecraftian conception of the tentacle monster remains a fundamental part of that "substance," and Lovecraft assiduously circumvents the pulp conventions under which humans play heroes beset by inimical outer evils; Joshi himself tends to speak disparagingly of works like "The Dunwich Horror" and many of the later "Cthulhu Mythos" narratives that do conform to this popular model for their "naïve portrayal of a good-vs.-evil scenario" (*Icons* 105).

Indeed, in most of Lovecraft's fiction, not only are certain human cultists in direct collusion with tentacle monsters, but his narrators often learn of a far more sinister and far more fundamental connection between humanity and monstrosity. For instance, the narrator of Lovecraft's most fabulistic story, "The Outsider," discovers that *he* is the cosmic horror, "a leering, abhorrent travesty on the human shape" (*DH* 51),[14] and, in Lovecraft's short

---

13. We can find this image of a tentacle monster participating with its victims in a mutually destructive eater/eaten relationship echoed in a rather curious place: in the belly of the Almighty Sarlacc of the *Star Wars* universe. In the *Expanded Universe* short story by J. D. Montgomery, the great tentacled maw not only slowly digests its victims over a thousand years, but absorbs their personalities into its own, the eaten truly becoming the eater.

14. I find it no coincidence that Robert Waugh turns to "The Picture in the House"—a story that details a hapless narrator's encounter with a literal cannibal—to illustrate his conception of the Lovecraftian "image of complicity": "the narrator survives to beget and to feed on the reader" (8).

novel *At the Mountains of Madness*, a metadiegetic narrator even speaks of "Elder Things supposed to have created all earth-life as jest or mistake" (*MM* 22). Much more common than the speculation that grotesque beings created the human race, however, is the Lovecraftian narrator's discovery that he—or we—are descended from them, the most prominent examples being those two miscegenation fantasies "Facts concerning the Late Arthur Jermyn and His Family" and "The Shadow over Innsmouth." Yet more common still is a pervasive sense of the same sort of cosmic complicity that we find in Goethe: in Lovecraft, one does not so much run the Nietzschean risk of transforming into one of the monsters he fights, but that of recognizing he has been part of this greater, more terrible reality all along. Donald R. Burleson puts it best:

> As Nietzsche has said, gaze into the abyss and it will gaze back into you—you may discover, in fact, that you are the abyss, the one twitching nerve-end of the cosmos that writhes against itself. The experience of Lovecraft's fiction is an eternally frozen yet living moment of gazing into one's face in a mirror of devastating self-revelation. The Lovecraftian dichotomy deconstructs itself into, and reinscribes itself as, a perpetual aporia of mutual and self-reflection. ("On Lovecraft's Themes" 147)

In Lovecraft's embodiment of cosmic forces in his tentacle monsters, then, we see less a watering-down of Werther's horror than a different approach, a downswing (or upswing?) on the opposite side of the same unstable, gloom-ridden vision.

Although *Werther* manifestly contains a major kernel of "Lovecraftian" cosmic horror, Lovecraft remains little discussed in conjunction with Goethe. We can perhaps attribute such critical reticence in some quarters to a misunderstanding of Lovecraft's notorious repudiation of "romanticism," and, while Lovecraft does demonstrate a marked preference for, say, the grotesque over the sublime, Joshi provides a helpful corrective here: "The attack on what Lovecraft called 'romanticism' is one he never relinquished. The term must not be understood here in any historical sense—Lovecraft had great respect and fondness for such Romantic poets as Shelley, Keats, and Coleridge—but merely theoretically, as embodying an approach not only to literature but to life generally"

(*Life* 318). Indeed, along with several such insular Romantics, Lovecraft himself places Goethe in a tradition or proto-tradition of cosmic horror, reserving high praise for "his deathless master-piece *Faust*" in "Supernatural Horror in Literature" (26), after hav-ing declared in the previous paragraph that "the impulse and atmosphere are as old as man, but the typical weird tale of stan-dard literature is a child of the eighteenth century" (26). He fur-ther casts "the cosmic Goethe" as one of six divine poets in his lesser-known story "Poetry and the Gods" (*D* 352), a story which Joshi in fact describes as "one of the most peculiar items in Love-craft's fictional corpus," both because of its co-authorship with mystery woman Anna Helen Crofts and its relatively uplifting, consolatory theme—read, in Joshi's words, "its anomalous theme" (*Life* 237). Admittedly, unlike *Faust* and a volume of Goethe's po-etry, *Werther* does not appear in Joshi's catalogue of Lovecraft's personal library (68, items 359–61),[15] but if we continue to con-centrate our attention on the same August 18 letter—that most cosmic of Werther's epistles, and in its way the most "bodily" as well—we will see a veritable catalogue of Lovecraftian tropes and preoccupations, preoccupations which we may also track across his nineteenth-century predecessors.

I am primarily interested here in what we might describe as the most common fashion accessory of the tentacle monster: the trope of the lifted—or, more usually, rent—veil invariably ac-companies the recognition of cosmic monstrosity. Not only, then, does Werther allude in his letter to the casual destruction of a multitude of miniscule beings by a heedless giant, but he invokes the image of the curtain occluding the true horror of reality: "Something has been drawn away from my soul like a curtain and the panorama of eternal life has been transformed before my eyes into the abyss of an eternally open grave" (Hutter 65). Likewise,

---

15. We might see why Werther's saga of unrequited passion should prove on the whole less interesting than *Faust* to the notoriously "sexually sluggish" HPL (*Thing* 372n2). Indeed, when Michel Houellebecq asserts that "in his entire body of work, there is not a single allusion to two of the realities to which we gener-ally ascribe great importance: sex and money" (57), he overstates the point about money, but probably not so much concerning what HPL once termed "amatory phenomena" (*Lord* 82).

the narrator of "The Call of Cthulhu" famously begins by describing himself as another victim of revelation: "The most merciful thing in the world, I think, is the inability of the human mind to correlate its contents. [. . .] Some day the piecing together of dissociated knowledge will open up such terrifying vistas of reality, and of our frightful position therein, that we shall either go mad from the revelation or flee from the deadly light into the peace and safety of a new dark age" (*DH* 125). The narrator's slow penetration of the arcane mysteries confronting him effects only the gradual destruction of his sane universe—that plot trajectory of so many of Lovecraft's stories. Again, I am not arguing, based on these parallels, that we need reconfigure our understanding of Lovecraft's chief influences and place him squarely in the *Sturm und Drang* tradition, but this image of the lifted veil, the toxic revelation, is one of many in Werther's letter that boasts a literary lineage unto itself, and a lineage perhaps more available to Lovecraft and his own imitators.

In fact, the association of the lifted veil with a horror at once bodily and cosmic appears perhaps most strikingly in Poe and Hoffmann,[16] two writers whose respective relationships with Lovecraft could be and indeed have been explored in many other areas. In particular, I feel little need to belabor the Poe connection, for the formative and perpetual influence of Lovecraft's "God of Fiction" upon his work is not only well-documented but of such extent that

---

16. My study of "the veil of reality" is obviously not exhaustive, and I restrict myself to these two authors for their peculiar joint position between Goethe and HPL. Nevertheless, the appearance of the trope in George Eliot's aptly titled story "The Lifted Veil" merits a quick mention here for its rough contemporaneity, as well as for its glimmerings of the cosmic, as when the narrator feels himself caught "in the grasp of unknown forces" (33). Although Eliot applies the image of the veil to other concepts than all reality—including the barriers normally prohibiting clairvoyance and telepathy—her narrator eventually suffers under an eerily familiar burden of knowledge: "I was in the midst of such scenes, and in all of them one presence seemed to weigh on me in all these mighty shapes—the presence of something unknown and pitiless" (36). Helen Small speculates that Eliot's use of the term may derive from Shelley's "Lift not the painted veil which those who live / Call Life" or William Collins's "Ode to Fear," but also notes the long history of the representation of truth or death as veiled (88).

we frequently find the two authors conflated in popular culture (*SL* 1.20).[17] I would only note that, in "The Fall of the House of Usher"—among Lovecraft's stated favorite weird tales (*ASHL* 73)[18]—the narrator experiences a sensation very like Werther's even before being ushered into the madness of the house: "I looked upon the scene before me [. . .] with an utter depression of soul which I can compare to no earthly sensation than to the afterdream of a reveller upon opium—the bitter lapse into everyday life, the hideous dropping off of the veil" (90). Thus, while we may find familiar echoes of the tarn in "The Colour out of Space"—in the reservoir project itself or in "the yawning black maw of an abandoned well whose stagnant vapours played strange tricks with the hues of the sunlight" (*DH* 55)—the more overarching parallel in Lovecraft's philosophy of fiction revolves around that piercing of the insubstantial veil that protects humanity from the horror of reality.

Hoffmann, conversely, provides a strong counterpoint to Poe in several respects. For one, although Lovecraft mentions Hoffmann favorably in "The Rats in the Walls"—"Not Hoffmann or Huysmans could conceive a scene more wildly incredibly, more frenetically repellent, or more Gothically grotesque" (*DH* 42)—Joshi judges that "Lovecraft did not care greatly" for Hoffmann's stories (384n28). Moreover, his polite dismissal of Hoffmann in "Supernatural Horror in Literature"—"Generally [his stories] convey the grotesque rather than the terrible" (38)—is certainly much less flattering than the effusive chapter he dedicates to Poe's literal apotheosis as "deity and fountain-head of all modern diabolic fic-

---

17. For example, Roger Zelazny's pastiche of a Mythos novel *A Night in the Lonesome October* (1993) takes its title from Poe. And this phenomenon extends beyond the shared literary universe, even to the trading card game *Magic: The Gathering*, which pays direct homage to HPL with a tentacle monster called "Cosmic Horror," while "Phantom Monster," a similar creature card with companion artwork, bears a Poe quotation.

18. HPL also treats "Usher" at length in "Supernatural Horror in Literature" (45), and frequent echoes of the story can be heard throughout his writing career, beginning to end (roughly 1917–37). In "Facts concerning the Late Arthur Jermyn and His Family" (1921), the narrator tellingly declares, "The house of Jermyn no longer existed" (*D* 81), while "The Haunter of the Dark" (1935) plainly cites "Roderick Usher" at its conclusion (*DH* 115).

tion" (44). We can, however, detect a significant difference in
Hoffmann's approach to the problem of cosmic horror, best illustrated in his divergent application of the veil trope: in contrast to
Poe's and Lovecraft's shared vision of "the horrors that lurk ceaselessly behind life in time and in space" (*DH* 149), in *The Golden
Pot* [*Der goldne Topf*], Hoffmann uses the same metaphor of a veil
that conceals the truth of reality, but in order to offer us glimpses,
at least, of more benign, even congenial lurkings:

> Favourable reader, while you are in the faery region of glorious
> wonders, where both rapture and horror may be evoked; where
> the goddess of earnestness herself will waft her veil aside and show
> her countenance [. . .;] while you are in this region which the spirit
> lays open to us in dreams, make an effort to recognize the well-
> known forms which hover around you in fitful brightness even in
> ordinary life. You will then find that this glorious kingdom lies
> much closer at hand than you ever supposed. (Carlyle 18)

In Lovecraft, of course, what lays open to us in dreams—products
of that monstriferous sleep of reason—is much more often madness than wonder, and any bliss found in the Dreamlands melts
away beneath the perpetual shadow of cosmic indifference, never
offering any real solace from that inevitable apocalyptic syzygy,
the time "when the stars are right" for the Great Old Ones to arise
and annihilate human civilization.

Of course, a wider survey of Hoffmann's tales will uncover
plenty of horror both bodily and cosmic, and perhaps sometimes
in the intertwined manner that seems central to Lovecraft's sense
of cosmicism and the "true" weird tale. Even restricting ourselves
to *The Golden Pot*, we can find traces of cosmic horror that might
seem to belie Hoffmann's rather different construction of a veiled
ultimate reality. When, for instance, Veronica finds herself helpless before a witch's cauldron, Hoffmann's description of the event
much resembles Lovecraft's own dark sabbaths and their effect on
hapless witnesses: "She heard, indeed, the howling and raging
around her; all sorts of hateful voices bellowed and bleated, and
yelled and hummed; but she did not open her eyes, for she felt
that the sight of the abominations and horrors with which she was
encircled might drive her into incurable destroying madness"

(140). Scenes like this one further highlight the vertiginous moral gyrations the reader experiences throughout Hoffmann's narrative: is the Student Anselmus on his way to a realm of faery wonders, deluded into thinking so by demonic forces, or simply insane? Indeed, although the passage concerning the hidden fantasy realm romantically extols the "longing for an unknown Something" (120) and the glorious pursuit of "a loftier existence [for] man" (121), when the Student Anselmus's fancies first become demonstrably "real" in the home of the Archivarius Lindhorst, he experiences not joy but horror: "The strange sights which like a genuine necromancer [the Archivarius] had called forth [. . .] awakened a certain horror in the Student" (124).

In contrast to his extradiegetic narrator's cheerful adoration of the fantastic, Hoffmann's narrative at first gives us good reason to doubt the motives of the Archivarius Lindhorst, an elemental Salamander, and those of his daughter Serpentina, who seems to be some species of lamia. The narrator later reveals himself as both extradiegetic and homodiegetic when he meets the Archivarius, yet we still have equal cause to suspect *him* of the same sort of delusion that may or may not afflict the Student Anselmus: could they not both be victims of some elemental spell? For, ensnared by the snake-woman's beauty, Werther-like, the Student Anselmus strangely abandons his mortal love Veronica for his pursuit of the world beyond the veil, no matter the cost:

> "What else is it," said he, 'but that I love you with my whole heart and soul, and even to the death, glorious little golden snake; nay, that without you I cannot live, and must perish in hopeless woe, unless I find you again, unless I have you as the beloved of my heart. But I know it, you shall be mine; and then all that glorious dreams have promised me of another higher world shall be fulfilled." (121)

Curiously, however, after some harrowing trials—including his imprisonment in a small bottle—the Student Anselmus appears to succeed in his quest, and it is the resulting "happy ending" that in fact provides the most telling comparison with the Poe-Lovecraft model of horrific reality. We do, for example, see a similar moral vacillation between delusion and lofty fantasy in Lovecraft, most notably in his short story "Celephaïs," in which the protagonist's love of the faery dreamworld unto death earns him a decidedly ambiguous transcendence: he believes himself to have become a prince of a fantastic realm, while his body, we learn, is "mockingly" cast about by the tides in the physical world (*D* 89). Nevertheless, I would argue that, despite a similar moral uncertainty that mirrors similar gyrations between bodily and cosmic fear, *The Golden Pot* avoids becoming Hoffmann's "Celephaïs" because of the way in which its Paracelsian machinery promises to overcome Lovecraft's merciless materialism. In other words, although the sanguine coda to *The Golden Pot* does not conclusively establish the Atlantean elemental realm as superior to Veronica's own happiness in the mortal world of substance, the Paracelsian worldview it reflects does permit the coexistence of such incommensurable worlds, the interaction between which can generate conflict and horror, but which can also finally settle back into the harmony of respective chaoses. Hoffmann's decidedly Paracelsian veil, then, by its very nature conceals both terrors and wonders, stopping short of the ultimate horror at ultimate reality that arguably derives, in Lovecraft, at least, from his "mechanistic materialism" and resultant atheism (*Call* xiv), again necessarily ruling out the arrival of any salvific or even constructive knowledge obtained from beyond the veil. In the words of the cosmically beleaguered Nahum Gardner of "The Colour out of Space," in Lovecraft's universe "ye know summ'at's comin', but 'tain't n use . . ." (*DH* 71).

As should be readily apparent, the brutal, nihilistic apocalypse that will arrive with the awakening of Cthulhu and his kin enacts a kind of reverse Second Coming of Christ—one that is almost Yeatsian, in its way, a poet of whom Lovecraft indeed spoke in superlative terms (Joshi, *Life* 580; *ASHL* 61).[19] But before jumping

---

19. For a recent discussion of Yeats and HPL in the context of the political unconscious of modernism, see Willmott, *Modernist Goods*, esp. 80–96. For a more local treatment of the two writers, see also Burleson, "Swan Songs." The subject of HPL and Christian parody generally has, I think, received less critical attention, but, for the most extensive treatment, see Egan, "Dark Apocalyptic." Joshi repeats Egan's suggestion of a possible parody of Christ on the cross in "The Dunwich Horror" (*AHPL* 171n26), and David E. Schultz remarks on potential anti-Christian satire in *The Case of Charles Dexter Ward* (219n13) in his larger

from Hoffmann to the slouching beasts of the early twentieth century, we can also look beyond the standard proto-canon of the
nineteenth-century weird, for indeed Tennyson was not the only
major poet of his day to invoke the cosmic reach of the tentacle
monster. Browning, whom Lovecraft much admired despite a recorded distaste for the ostensibly "prosaic" character of his verse
(*SL* 4.109), has without doubt bequeathed to us the most salient
literary tentacle monster outside of Lovecraft or mythology:
namely, his redaction in *Caliban upon Setebos* of Shakespeare's
witch-god "Setebos / The many-handed as a cuttle-fish" (141–
42).[20] Caliban passes judgment on his dam's dark deity in a way
that further recalls the cosmic moral compass of the Great Old
Ones: "Thinketh, such shows nor right nor wrong in Him, / Nor
kind, nor cruel: He is strong and Lord" (98–99). Yet, while this by
turns spiteful and indifferent demi-demiurge terrifies Caliban with
his near-cosmic powers as well as his tentaculate physicality,[21]
Setebos must, of course, yield to a greater dark god, the Quiet, itself an impersonal impression of the void that more nearly ap-
proximates the net cosmicist effect of the entire Lovecraftian anti-

---

discussion of HPL's construction of an "antimythology" (200). Finally, see the less
critically rigorous but no less incisive tracking of the (anti-)Christian resonance of
HPL's fiction in Fred Van Lente and Steve Ellis's parodic evangelical tract "Why
We're Here."

20. To be sure, HPL had plenty of other precedents for his tentacle monsters, but
I have verified that *Caliban upon Setebos* does appear in the volume of Browning's poetry he owned, *Selections from the Poetical Works of Robert Browning*
(Chicago: Donohue, Henneberry, 189-), at pp. 324–37 (37, item 124). He praises
by name, however, only "the hideous poem 'Childe Roland'" (*ASHL* 22), which
HPL's devout follower Stephen King also obviously highly esteemed. Finally, although he attributes HPL's impulse toward the monologue more properly to
Poe, John Taylor interestingly remarks that "Lovecraft's strongest monologue
story is 'Pickman's Model,' *à la* Browning" (61). Now that Taylor has suggested
the possibility, one can't help but note the similarity between Fra Pandolf and
Fra Pickman: "That's my last shoggoth, painted on the wall . . ."?

21. Indeed, Browning's suggestively horrific incarnation of Setebos reappears as a
proper sci-fi tentacle monster in Dan Simmons's novels *Ilium* and *Olympos*. The
ubiquitous Shrike of his *Hyperion Cantos* also has more than a whiff of cosmic
horror about it, even possessing its own "Shrike Cult," although we might better
describe the entity as a multi-appendaged *thorn* monster.

pantheon, or of Werther's monophysitic Nature:

> But wherefore rough, why cold and ill at ease?
> Aha, that is a question! Ask, for that,
> What knows,—the something over Setebos
> That made Him, or He, may be, found and fought,
> Worsted, drove off and did to nothing, perchance.
> There may be something quiet o'er His head,
> Out of His reach, that feels nor joy nor grief,
> Since both derive from weakness in some way. (127–34)

Only here, set above but still implicated in bodily suffering, do we find ultimate reality: "This Quiet, all it hath a mind to, doth. / Esteemeth stars the outposts of its couch, / But never spends much thought nor care that way" (137–39). Although Caliban's recursive "natural theology" splits the cosmic horror into two entities, it is not always clear where one ends and the other begins. In fact, in a move that mirrors the same representational crisis I have been examining—a kind of "cosmos-body problem"—Caliban paradoxically turns his thoughts from this most disquieting entity back toward Setebos, the one more immediately responsible for both physical pain and the final fate of the world of flesh: "Shall some day knock it down again: so He" (199). Even the most oppressive sense of cosmic horror becomes localized in the body, and again and again in connection with these inscrutable cephalopods.

Of course, that horrific nineteenth-century rage of Caliban continued up through *fin de siècle* fiction, when the tentacle monster began to come into its own, making appearances in the fiction of Arthur Machen et al.—see, for one, "Novel of the Black Seal"—but also, indeed, throughout the works of H. G. Wells, himself the seer of a new kind of "cosmic" writing.[22] Long before the Cthulhu

---

22. I would venture to say that, of all the works I discuss here, Wells's corpus, as a whole, constitutes the most understudied influence on or analogue of HPL's own. HPL himself takes care to deny that Wells's short story "In the Abyss" "anticipates" his own tale of underwater cities, "The Temple" (*SL* 1.287), and, in his treatise on the weird, he mentions Wells only once, among a group of writers he places in "the romantic, semi-Gothic, quasi-moral tradition" (37). He goes on to explain the limitations of the approach of these authors in the area of cosmic horror: their other interests result in "a diluted product that can never achieve

cultists gibbered about the ultimate fate of humanity in the clutches of tentacled deities, the hero of *The Time Machine* (1895), at the far apochronicon of his temporal journey, discovers that the only living thing populating his twilight Earth is nothing other than a tentacle monster:

> A horror of this great darkness came on me. The cold, that smote to my marrow, and the pain I felt in breathing, overcame me. I shivered, and a deadly nausea seized me. [. . .] As I stood sick and confused I saw again the moving thing upon the shoal—there was no mistake now that it was a moving thing—against the red water of the sea. It was a round thing, the size of a football perhaps, or, it may be, bigger, and tentacles trailed down from it. (86)

To be sure, this grim vision of the tentacle monster(s?) that will inherit the earth anticipates Cthulhu and his reign of madness and destruction, and I would note the Time Traveller's emphasis on his decidedly corporeal reaction upon contemplating this "great darkness" at the end of time and its concomitant octopoid, a reaction that later in the passage carries him to the brink of fainting.

In spite of this obvious conjunction of tentacle monster and cosmic horror, however, it is a different Wells novel, *The War of the Worlds*, that will likely first come to mind in connection with any talk of tentacle monsters: indeed, the word "tentacle" appears in the text far more often than "tripod," the typical emblem of the Martians in the popular imagination. And, while those prodigious fighting-machines lash out with their own "steely tentacles" (78), the narrator prefers to focus our attention on the pilots, with their "Gorgon groups of tentacles" (34): "In a group round the mouth were sixteen slender, almost whiplike tentacles, arranged in two bunches of eight each. These bunches have since been named rather aptly, by that distinguished anatomist, Professor Howes, the *hands*" (175). The many hands of Setebos allow the Martians to manipulate their sophisticated machinery, but even these operations serve chiefly to facilitate their feeding, the glutting of the all-devouring

---

the concentrated essence" (37). Indeed, HPL may have justifiably said the same of any of the evanescent moments of cosmic horror I have identified, and his own work indisputably seeks to distill that "concentrated essence."

hunger that characterizes the tentacle monster. If Wells's monsters seem more refined—almost of the gentleman-vampire type, gorging themselves on the blood of humans but aseptically injecting it directly into their own bodies—they can never bypass the maw, and, in spite of the global, even interplanetary stakes of the events of the novel, its purest expressions of horror still focus on that mouth and on that halo of tentacle-hands.

Of course, that the destruction of human civilization in Wells's novel should be carried out by tentacle monsters rather than some other type of entity resonates only superficially with the Cthulhu Mythos; on the other hand, the decidedly "cosmicist" way in which Wells initially frames the extraterrestrial invasion begins to cross over firmly into what we now think of as Lovecraft Country, even if the action takes place across the pond from dark and dour Massachusetts:

> No one would have believed in the last years of the nineteenth century that this world was being watched keenly and closely by intelligences greater than man's and yet as mortal as his own; that as men busied themselves about their various concerns they were scrutinised and studied, perhaps almost as narrowly as a man with a microscope might scrutinise the transient creatures that swarm and multiply in a drop of water. (11)[23]

Not only do the Martians wreak physical horrors on mankind, draining the body of its vital essence, but their very existence al-

---

23. With at least four film adaptations to date and an uncountable number of derivatives, *The War of the Worlds*, much like HPL's own work, has escaped its creator to become almost hysterically prevalent in popular culture. For example, the first song from the progressive rock opera *Jeff Wayne's War of the Worlds* condenses and tightens this haunting opening, aided in presentation by Richard Burton's most fabulously histrionic voice: "No one would have believed, in the last years of the nineteenth century, that human affairs were being watched from the timeless worlds of space. No one could have dreamed we were being scrutinized, as someone with a microscope studies creatures that swarm and multiply in a drop of water. Few men even considered the possibility of life on other planets and yet, across the gulf of space, minds immeasurably superior to ours regarded this Earth with envious eyes, and slowly, and surely, they drew their plans against us."

ters his conception of his place in the universe, with their cosmic "minds that are to our minds as ours are to those of the beasts that perish, intellects vast and cool and unsympathetic" (12). Of course, by the end of the novel we understand the significance of the remark that these beings possess "intelligences greater than man's and yet as mortal as his own" (11). Although they threaten the human race with destruction, these monsters turn out to be inferior to the real ubiquitous beasties dwelling among us, in a sense revealing themselves as *false* Lovecraftian deities, only a different form of vain man, as indeed certain of Lovecraft's extraterrestrial races arguably do in works like *At the Mountains of Madness*: "the Old Ones were again supreme on the planet except for one shadowy fear about which they did not like to speak" (*MM* 66). Still victims of that same cosmic fear in spite of being hardier and more intelligent than humans, the Old Ones and the Martians may be higher in some cosmic hierarchy, but it is presumably a hierarchy that leads, eternally bafflingly, to the blind idiot god Azathoth, primal chaos—or, rather, back to where we started. Only chaos is always with us, and the end of even the most whimsical dream quest lies in "those inconceivable, unlighted chambers beyond Time wherein Azathoth gnaws shapeless and ravenous" (*The Dream-Quest of Unknown Kadath, MM* 404). Only chaos, in the cosmicist scheme, can claim to constitute ultimate reality.[24]

The *bacillus ex machina* in *The War of the Worlds* does much to contain the bodily and cosmic fear its apocalyptic host of tentacle monsters generates, and even the narrator's lingering doubts—the same veil, after all, has been torn away—yield to a final meditation on happiness restored, those thought dead returned to life and love. Likewise, in *The Time Machine* we catch a glimpse of infinite terror at the end of human time, but Wells does not dwell on it, returning us safely to the present and leaving his narrator, though bereft of his friend the Time Traveller, with a pair of white flowers from the future which testify that "gratitude and a mutual tenderness still lived on in the heart of man" (90), the novel's simi-

---

24. Paul Montelone comes to this same conclusion from a different angle, in his case praising "HPL's commendably honest acknowledgment of the pain and futility of human life: the world as Azathoth, and nothing besides" (3).

larly sentimental closing line. Rather than look to his Martians or
his Morlocks, then, I would in fact locate the most cosmic of
Wells's monstrosities in that Swiftian send-up of Verne, *The First
Men in the Moon*, a happy-go-lucky Lucianic translunar journey
that nevertheless contains several moments of unadulterated cosmic horror. In fact, Wells even populates the moon with tentacle
monsters that repel the scientist Mr. Cavor: "In [the moon's] re-
moter recesses, I am told, strange creatures lurk, some of them terrible and dangerous creatures that all the science of the moon has
been unable to exterminate. There is particularly the Rapha, an in-
extricable mass of clutching tentacles that one hacks to pieces only
to multiply; and the Tzee, a darting creature that is never seen, so
subtly and suddenly does it slay" (133). Cavor soon receives an opportunity to expound on the horror of these creatures:

> Among their catch was a many-tentaculate, evil-eyed black thing,
> ferociously active, whose appearance they greeted with shrieks
> and twitters, and which with quick, nervous movements they
> hacked to pieces by means of little hatchets. All its dissevered
> limbs continued to lash and writhe in a vicious manner. After-
> wards, when fever had hold of me, I dreamt again and again of
> that bitter, furious creature rising so vigorous and active out of
> the unknown sea. It was the most active and malignant thing of
> all the living creatures I have yet seen in this world inside the
> moon. (134)

The sea-borne monstrosity haunts Cavor's dreams in proper
Lovecraftian fashion, and, again, should we want to argue for a ge-
netic relationship between the cosmic horrors of Wells and Lovecraft, it may be significant that the only fictional work of Wells to
appear in Lovecraft's library is in fact *The First Men in the Moon*
(143, item 935). We may then perhaps view these moon monsters,
as China Miéville has referred to them, as more than simply *"prefiguring* those two idiot-savants of the tentacular, H. P. Lovecraft
and William Hope Hodgson" (xviii; emphasis mine).

Yet the horror of Cavor's many-legged creature pales before
the cosmic horror Bedford, the narrator, experiences elsewhere on
the moon; again, the visceral revulsion engendered by the tentacle
monster merely directs us towards the greater sensation of that

paradoxically bodily and cosmic fear. For, when Bedford learns that his sole voyaging companion has been taken below by the Selenites, he finds himself alone on the hostile lunar surface and experiences a sensation of terror much like Werther's in stemming from the totality of nature itself: "Over me, about me, closing in on me, embracing me ever nearer, was the Eternal, that which was before the beginning and that which triumphs over the end; that enormous void in which all light and life and being is but the thin and vanishing splendour of a falling star, the cold, the stillness, the silence—the infinite and final Night of space" (111). Although the Selenites themselves strike Bedford as horrifyingly grotesque in countenance—"It seemed as though it wasn't a face; as though it must needs be a mask, a horror, a deformity that would presently be disavowed or explained" (64)—he fears them far less than this oppressive sense of the Eternal, which results from a recognition of the limitations of both his body and his mind in the nameless, formless void. Yet, just as we see Werther accomplish at the conclusion of his August 18 letter, Bedford promptly begins to embody this abstraction: "The sense of solitude and desolation became the sense of an overwhelming Presence, that stopped towards me, that almost touched me" (111). The void acquires its own monstrous body, which then threatens the human body; moreover, few things better evoke the horrifically tactile than those shifting, clutching tentacular appendages.

We should not pass over Bedford's emphasis on the incompleteness of the cosmic monster's attempt to touch him, for many of Lovecraft's horrors operate in this same fashion, remaining always just beyond reach or perception; in other words, the veil cannot be permanently or completely removed, lest we lose our narrator to madness. We must be content, therefore, with second-hand revelations from the survivors of his tales, fleeting, fragmentary glimpses beyond the Mountains of Madness. Indeed, just as neither we nor the narrator ever learn what horror Danforth really saw in *At the Mountains of Madness*, the conclusion of Wells's novel suppresses any final revelation, offering us only the dampening silence of the Quiet. While Cavor had previously managed to transmit some messages back to the Earth about his time among the moon people—charmingly reminiscent of Gulliver's adventures in his various ambiguous utopias—the Selenites take action against him after they learn of humanity's warlike nature, fearing that he might give up the secret of Cavorite, which permits inter-planetary travel:

> It may be he made a hasty attempt to spell "useless" when his fate was close upon him. [. . .] Whatever it was we shall never, I know, receive another message from the moon. For my own part a vivid dream has come to my help, and I see, almost as plainly as though I had seen it in actual fact, a blue-lit shadowy dishevelled Cavor struggling in the grip of these insect Selenites, struggling ever more desperately and hopelessly as they press upon him, shouting, expostulating, perhaps even at last fighting, and being forced backwards step by step out of all speech or sign of his fellows, for evermore into the Unknown—into the dark, into that silence that has no end. (161)

It may seem curious that such a jaunty, jocose narrative should end in this melancholy manner, but I take it to emphasize that the brief moment of bodily fear Bedford experiences when the literal coldness of space threatens his personal survival transcends both the temporary and the bodily, pointing toward a genuine cosmic horror at the magnitude of the "imponderable menace" of the uni-verse ("The Dunwich Horror," *DH* 195). My use of the word "transcend" here does not, of course, imply that Wells's depiction of cosmic horror ever abandons bodily fear, and Bedford's final vi-carious experience of Cavor's sequestration in cosmic silence is anchored as firmly in his physical restraint by the limbs of those grotesque insects gripping his own as it is in the vastness of the void separating him from all human fellowship. Cavor—and Bed-ford back on Earth—find themselves captives of both the dark, silent Unknown and a palpably tactile Presence: the central repre-sentational paradox of cosmic horror.

This examination of Wells vis-à-vis Lovecraft has taken us far nearer to the latter's own generation—indeed, although nearly twenty-five years his senior, Wells outlived Lovecraft—and it has also taken us slightly higher up the ladder of literary respectability than might have a more standard accounting of Lovecraft's more directly observable influences in the nascent genre of weird fiction.

I have also already alluded to Lovecraft's appreciation of Yeats, but we may detect further reflections of a very Lovecraftian sort of cosmicism in some perhaps yet more surprising places, that is, not only in Algernon Blackwood, Lord Dunsany, or obscure issues of *Weird Tales*, but in the work of other "high literary" writers of his own time. Accordingly, I would like to conclude by way of a few comparisons with the embodied cosmic horror that appears in one of Conrad Aiken's most popular poems, "Tetélestai"; I am not suggesting that either author ever read the other, but rather advancing them only as two contemporary, like-minded "cosmos mariners," fellow "students of the skies."[25] In fact, Aiken wrote "Tetélestai" early in his career in 1917 (*Time's Stop* 25), the very year that Lovecraft was beginning to produce his own adult work—including the short story "Dagon," in Joshi's fair judgment the progenitor of "The Call of Cthulhu"[26]—making Aiken and Lovecraft's joint expression of transcendent fleshly fear not merely contemporary but veritably simultaneous.[27] Indeed, shortly after Aiken's invocation in the

---

25. The former designation derives from Aiken's celebrated epitaph: "Cosmos Mariner—Destination Unknown" (*Time's Stop* 4), and the latter from one of HPL's epithets for his somewhat tongue-in-cheek poetic stand-in *"Lucullus Languish, student of the skies,"* the hero of his 1916 poem "The Poe-et's Nightmare" (*AT* 18, l. 1). Although Languish's next epithet mock-heroizes him as a *"connoisseur of rarebits and mince pies"* (l. 2), "student of the skies" remains an apt description for HPL himself, as evidenced by his lifelong interest in astronomy (see Joshi, *Life* 50ff.).

26. In his headnote to "The Call of Cthulhu," Joshi argues that the later story "is manifestly an exhaustive rewriting of 'Dagon,' and could be said to begin a tendency found frequently in HPL's later tales whereby he reworks (usually to much better advantage) themes and conceptualizations utilized in earlier stories" (*Call* 393).

27. "Tetélestai" appeared in the December 1918 issue of the *Little Review*; for a partial history of its numerous anthologizations, see Bonnell, *A Bibliography* 144. The first professional publication of "Dagon," on the other hand, also represented HPL's first appearance in *Weird Tales*, a rather different venue from the influential little magazine that serialized *Ulysses* and featured regular contributions from T. S. Eliot. Since HPL was in fact inimical to some such instantiations of modernism, I should note that Joshi mentions Conrad Aiken in passing as one among a group of "level-headed modernists" who shared HPL's negative response to *The Waste Land* and "found the poem incomprehensible or at least ambiguous and incoherent" (*Life* 314). This comparison, while especially provocative in the con-

poem, the salutatory echoes of *Ecclesiasticus*—"How shall we praise the magnificence of the dead?" (I)—give way to a stunning metaphor for the same cosmic *indifference* so central to Lovecraft's own conception of cosmicism:

> Say rather, two great gods in a vault of starlight,
> Play ponderingly at chess, and at the game's end
> One of the pieces, shaken, falls to the floor
> And runs to the darkest corner; and that piece
> Forgotten there, left motionless, is I . . . (I)

Here Aiken has extended into a yet more fearful indifference that ancient image of the gods at play with the lives of mortal pawns, an image as popular in the Middle Ages—see Chaucer's *Book of the Duchess*, in which Fortune "captures" a bereft lover's queen— as in the twentieth century, where it reemerges in the 1981 Desmond Davis film *Clash of the Titans*. To the extent that divine abandonment and oblivion replace the sense of the gods' casual vindictiveness, Aiken's image also magnifies Gloucester's comparable but finally feebler flash of cosmic horror in *King Lear*: "As flies to wanton boys are we to the gods; / They kill us for their sport" (4.1.37–38).[28] Of course, Cthulhu and his ilk are less likely to kill for sport than for no mortally intelligible reason at all, and Aiken, like Lovecraft, seems unsatisfied with the already terrifying idea that the course of a human life changes at the whim of gods: no, these new twentieth-century gods must pay even *less* heed to humanity than boys do to insects. No Furies pursue Aiken's

---

text of my argument here, somewhat oversimplifies Aiken's relationship with Eliot, I think. For a perhaps unwarranted attempt to claim *Fungi from Yuggoth* as a work of modernist poetry, also see Oakes, "Modernism." Finally, although he leaves Aiken out of his exploration of HPL's stance *qua* modernism, Norman R. Gayford provides a much more compelling case for the claim that "Lovecraft was not isolated from the major literary arguments of his time" (273); Steven J. Mariconda echoes this view in his judicious remark that "Lovecraft was a product of the same social and cultural forces that the American Moderns were, and these common influences inform their respective artistic products" (20).

28. Often cited in conjunction with HPL, this line from *Lear* has exerted its own wide influence in science fiction and fantasy; see especially Robert Silverberg's "Flies" from the first *Dangerous Visions* (1967).

speaker; no Poseidon harries him; and it goes without saying that no Athena or Isis will step in to save him.

One will immediately observe that Aiken's starlit gods move—or fail to move—their game pieces without the aid of tentacles, yet subsequent passages in the poem begin to figure cosmic monsters that function, much like Lovecraft's and indeed much like Werther's, as the nexus of bodily fear and cosmic horror, perforce enacting the familiar shiftings between the poles of monstrification and abstraction: "Say that the fates of time and space obscured me, / Led me a thousand ways to pain, bemused me, / Wrapped me in ugliness; and like great spiders / Dispatched me at their leisure" (I). The speaker's initial description of the "fates of time and space" parallels a formulation of which Lovecraft was incredibly fond in the abstract—e.g., "the galling limitations of time, space, and natural law which for ever imprison us" (*CE* 2.176)—but Aiken effects a complex and deliberately paced transition from pure abstraction ("time and space") to a kind of inchoate quasi-personification ("wrapped me in ugliness") to a figuration of genuine spindly-limbed monsters with a straightforward simile, "great spiders" vastly different from the "giant" spiders that infest heroic fantasy,[29] and much more akin to Tolkien's cosmic devourer Ungoliant from *The Silmarillion*. Careful enjambment separates the spiders from their dispatching of the speaker—a leisurely annihilation again quite reminiscent of those heedless Great Old Ones—but in that preceding single line the fates have metamorphosed so quickly into great spiders that they perhaps finish wrapping the speaker in ugliness before we understand what it is they wrap him with, namely, physical deformity spewed forth from cosmic spinnerets and applied directly to the human frame. This arachnid image recurs in the third part of the poem, at which point the speaker imagines himself "caught in the web" of despair (III), but most noteworthy in the earlier passage is the stress laid on the speaker's affliction with such distinctly bodily torments even when confronted with distinctly cosmic monstrosities.

---

29. Even before the flowering of modern fantasy, HPL could remark on "the familiar overgrown-spider theme so frequently employed by weird fictionists" (*ASHL* 41). Stephen King, however, has notably brought Lovecraftian scale back to the "outer" arachnid in *It*.

"Tetélestai," like *Werther*, naturally covers more thematic ground than body horror and cosmic horror, but later sections of the poem remain rife with an anxiety about bodily decay and bodily powerlessness that we can further connect with the literary crisis-complex of representation that for convenience one might refer to as "Lovecraftian," but which I have endeavored to track long before the bard of Providence unleashed all his eldritch combinations of syllables upon the world.[30] For instance, at the same time that Aiken's speaker aspires to strike the heavens with his cries—"You stars and suns, Canopus, Deneb, Rigel, / Let me, as I lie down, here in this dust, / Hear, far off, your whispered salutation!" (II)—any attempt to order the universe fails when he retreats, inevitably, from the macrocosm: "I, the restless one; the circler of circles; / Herdsman and roper of stars, who could not capture / The secret of self" (III). We see that the old obsession with the bodily overtakes consciousness even in those moments when the speaker finally feels a master of his own universe, finds some handle on the heavens, attains an apparently Archimedean point in the cosmos. And it is not exclusively the weight of mortality, "the dust of death" (II), that so disturbs the speaker, but all bodily transformation, the entire impersonal process that carries man unwitting from cradle to grave: "I / Who laughed without knowing the cause of my laughter, who grew / Without wishing to grow, a servant to my own body" (III). Again, the real source of the terror remains indeterminate, focused alternately on the cosmic spiders that consume the body and the same enslaved body designed to consume, change, and die along with them, recalling Werther's regurgitating, self-devouring *Ungeheuer*. To be sure, over the course of the five movements in "Tetélestai," Aiken may find some degree of consolation in poetry itself, a humanistic commemoration of the dead, or in a meditative Unitarianism that fits the poetic self-image he would later develop as a "humanist

---

30. It seems that, as I am pursuing here myself, HPL himself readily sought to identify kindred evocations of cosmic horror even in brief portions of other works: "Moreover, much of the choicest weird work is unconscious; appearing in memorable fragments scattered through material whose massed effect may be of a very different cast" (*ASHL* 23).

and quester" ("Christ in Savannah" 111), but the poem's quite "Lovecraftian" representation of ultimate reality easily lends itself to an expression of ultimate fear.

We can now leave both Aiken and Lovecraft behind, grappling with their cosmic monsters in the early twentieth century, to see the tremendous surge of tentacle monsters in the past several decades, and not only in Mythos and "New Weird" fiction. In this incomplete teratology of mine, I have been less concerned with tracing the proper paternity of such Cthulhu-spawn to Werther or anyone else, but I have attempted to demonstrate that central to the ascendance of the cosmic tentacle monster lies an equivocation between the eternal desire to represent cosmic horror by means of a yawningly impersonal abstraction, or, alternatively and simultaneously, by means of a most visceral physical horror, some slimy loathsome many-appendaged thing. And, up until the moment of horrific revelation, the tentacle monster must wear the veil that conceals its true nature—and thus the nature of that more abstract reality—from our mundane, quotidian understanding of the universe, an understanding that Lovecraft finds "mercifully limited" in most people most of the time (SL 3.124). Of the works I have examined that offer glimpses of cosmic monstrosity, revealed from behind the universal veil and felt in the body, many of them do seem to swallow up the cosmic horror itself in their return to the other concerns that occupy them. And, although there are also those authors who, like Lovecraft, sustain the cosmic horror across an entire literary work, they do not necessarily defer to a Lovecraftian sense of finality: Aiken, for instance, charts new mythopoeic paths in his later work, struggling to forge a new conception of the universe after the veil has been torn away. Even so, to conclude with any such "solution" to this crisis of representation—which of course really speaks to a crisis of existence— would be to conclude on a note unrecognizable to the ears of either Werther or the typical Lovecraftian narrator; even a Hoffmann could not move them with any sublimely Paracelsian bid for freedom from the bodily fear he explores so relentlessly elsewhere in his work. For fantastic fiction of whatever stripe remains a mode obsessed with the bodily; even when the entire universe becomes the monstrous focus of attention rather than a humble human revenant or mere were-creature, the machinery of fantastic representation lumbers to imbue the eternally Protean with a form that mirrors our own physical suffering. In other words, the fundamental crisis of bodily versus disembodied (mis)representation in Lovecraft illustrates the natural consequence of the perverse pantheism to which Werther succumbs: when the universe itself becomes a malevolent god, that malevolence is reflected and magnified in his unstable creations, in us, the thinking lumps of tortured flesh, captives to mutability, bound fast by the restless formlessness of the tentacle monster.

Works Cited

Aiken, Conrad. *Collected Poems.* New York: Oxford University Press, 1953.

———. Review of *The World of William Clissold. Atlantic Monthly* 137 (November 1926): 20. Rpt. in. *H. G. Wells: The Critical Heritage*, ed. Patrick Parrinder. London: Routledge & Kegan Paul, 1972. 275–76.

Bonnell, F. W., and F. C. Bonnell. *Conrad Aiken: A Bibliography (1902–1978).* San Marino, CA: Huntington Library, 1982.

Browning, Robert. *Caliban upon Setebos; or, Natural Theology in the Island.* In *The Complete Poetical Works of Robert Browning.* 1895. Boston: Houghton Mifflin, 1973. 392–94.

Burleson, Donald R. "On Lovecraft's Themes: Touching the Glass." In *An Epicure in the Terrible: A Centennial Anthology of Essays in Honor of H. P. Lovecraft*, ed. David E. Schultz and S. T. Joshi. Rutherford, NJ: Fairleigh Dickinson University Press, 1991. 135–47.

———. "Strange High Houses: Lovecraft and Melville." *Crypt of Cthulhu* No. 80 (Eastertide 1992): 25–26, 29.

———. "Swan Songs: Lovecraft and Yeats." *Lovecraft Studies* No. 18 (1989): 14–17.

Cannon, Peter H. "Call Me Wizard Whateley: Echoes of Moby Dick in 'The Dunwich Horror.'" *Crypt of Cthulhu* No. 49 (Lammas 1987): 21–23.

Cerasini, Marc A. "Thematic Links in *Arthur Gordon Pym, At the Mountains of Madness* and *Moby Dick." Crypt of Cthulhu* No. 49 (Lammas 1987): 3–20.

"Cosmic Horror." *Magic: The Gathering* Card. *Gatherer.wizards.com.* Wizards of the Coast LLC, a subsidiary of Hasbro, Inc., 1995–2010. Web. Accessed 13 March 2010.

"Cthulhu for President: The Dawning of a New Era." *Cthulhu.org.* 2010. Web. Accessed 18 April 2010.

Egan, James. "Dark Apocalyptic: Lovecraft's Cthulhu Mythos as a Parody of Traditional Christianity." *Extrapolation* 23 (Spring 1983): 362–76.

Eliot, George. *The Lifted Veil and Brother Jacob.* Ed. Helen Small. New York: Oxford University Press, 1999.

Gayford, Norman R. "The Artist as Antaeus: Lovecraft and Modernism." In *An Epicure in the Terrible: A Centennial Anthology of Essays in Honor of H. P. Lovecraft,* ed. David E. Schultz and S. T. Joshi. Rutherford, NJ: Fairleigh Dickinson University Press, 1991. 273–97.

Goethe, Johann Wolfgang von. *Die Leiden des jungen Werthers.* Düsseldorf: Artemis & Winkler, 2004.

———. *The Sorrows of Young Werther.* Trans. Thomas Carlyle and R. D. Boylan. Mineola, NY: Dover, 2002.

———. *The Sorrows of Young Werther and Selected Writings.* Trans. Catherine Hutter. New York: Signet, 1962.

Hoffmann, E. T. A. *The Golden Pot.* In *Great German Short Stories,* ed. Evan Bates; trans. Thomas Carlyle. Mineola, NY: Dover, 2003. 105–68.

Houellebecq, Michel. *H. P. Lovecraft: Against the World, Against Life.* Trans. Dorna Khazeni. San Francisco: Believer Books, 2005.

Joshi, S. T. "The Cthulhu Mythos." In *Icons of Horror and the Supernatural,* ed. S. T. Joshi. Westport, CT: Greenwood Press, 2007. 98–128.

———. *H. P. Lovecraft: A Life.* West Warwick, RI: Necronomicon Press, 1996.

———. "Introduction." In *An Epicure in the Terrible: A Centennial Anthology of Essays in Honor of H. P. Lovecraft,* ed. David E. Schultz and S. T. Joshi. Rutherford, NJ: Fairleigh Dickinson University Press, 1991. 15–41.

———. *Lovecraft's Library: A Catalogue.* 2nd ed. New York: Hippocampus Press, 2002.

Joyce, James. *Ulysses: The Gabler Edition.* Ed. Hans Walter Gabler, with Wolfhard Steppe and Claus Melchior. New York: Vintage, 1993.

Knopf, Mack. "Things We Were Not Meant to Know: H. P. Lovecraft and Cosmic Horror." *Strangehorizons.com.* Strange Horizons, 18 June 2001. Web. Accessed 14 April 2010.

Lovecraft, H. P. *The Annotated Supernatural Horror in Literature.* Ed. S. T. Joshi. New York: Hippocampus Press, 2000. [Abbreviated in the text as *ASHL.*]

———. *The Call of Cthulhu and Other Weird Stories.* Ed. S. T. Joshi. New York: Penguin, 1999.

———. *Lord of a Visible World: An Autobiography in Letters.* Ed. S. T. Joshi and David E. Schultz. Athens: Ohio University Press, 2000.

Mariconda, Steven J. "H. P. Lovecraft: Reluctant American Modernist." *Lovecraft Studies* Nos. 42/43 (Autumn 2001): 20–32.

Maxwell, Richard. "Unnumbered Polypi." *Victorian Poetry* 47, No. 1 (2009): 7–23.

Miéville, China. "Introduction." In *The First Men on the Moon* by H. G. Wells. Ed. Patrick Parrinder. London: Penguin, 2005. xvii–xxviii.

Mitchell, Bruce. *An Invitation to Old English and Anglo-Saxon England.* Cambridge, MA: Blackwell, 1995.

Montelone, Paul. "The World as Azathoth—and Nothing Besides." *Lovecraft Studies* No. 37 (Fall 1997): 1–4.

Montgomery, J. D. [Daniel Keys Moran]. "A Barve Like That: The Tale of Boba Fett." In *Tales from Jabba's Palace*, ed. Kevin J. Anderson. New York: Bantam, 1996. 346–71.

Moorcock, Michael. *Wizardry and Wild Romance: A Study of Epic Fantasy.* London: Gollancz, 1987.

The Mountain Goats. "Lovecraft in Brooklyn." *Heretic Pride.* CD.4AD, 2008. CD.

Oakes, David A. "This Is the Way the World Ends: Modernism in 'The Hollow Men' and *Fungi from Yuggoth.*" *Lovecraft Studies* No. 40 (Fall 1998): 33–36, 38.

Osborn, Marijane. "Three Dragons." *ANQ* 20, No. 3 (2007): 63–65.

Paracelsus. *A Book on Nymphs, Sylphs, Pygmies, and Salamanders, and on the Other Spirits.* In *Four Treatises of Theophrastus von*

Hohenheim called Paracelsus. Ed. and trans. Henry E. Sigerist. Baltimore: Johns Hopkins University Press, 1941.

"Phantom Monster." *Magic: The Gathering* Card. *Gatherer.wizards.com.* Wizards of the Coast LLC, a subsidiary of Hasbro, Inc., 1995–2010. Web. Accessed 13 Mar. 2010.

Poe, Edgar Allan. *The Fall of the House of Usher and Other Writings.* London: Penguin, 2003.

Schultz, David E. "From Microcosm to Macrocosm: The Growth of Lovecraft's Cosmic Vision." In *An Epicure in the Terrible: A Centennial Anthology of Essays in Honor of H. P. Lovecraft*, ed. David E. Schultz and S. T. Joshi. Rutherford, NJ: Fairleigh Dickinson University Press, 1991. 199–219.

Shakespeare, William. *The Norton Shakespeare.* Ed. Stephen Greenblatt. New York: W. W. Norton, 1997.

Shreffler, Philip A. *The H. P. Lovecraft Companion.* Westport, CT: Greenwood Press, 1977.

Spivey, Ted R. "Christ in Savannah: Conrad Aiken's Religious Vision." *Essays in Arts and Sciences* 12, No. 1 (1983): 99–112.

———. *Time's Stop in Savannah: Conrad Aiken's Inner Journey.* Macon: Mercer University Press, 1997.

Tackett, Devon. "Hello Cthulhu." *Hello-cthulhu.com.* Tackett Devon, 24 December 2006. Web. Accessed 18 April 2010.

Taylor, John. "Poe, Lovecraft, and the Monologue." *Topic* 31 (1977): 52–62.

Tolkien, J. R. R. *The Two Towers: Being the Second Part of The Lord of the Rings.* 1954. Boston: Houghton Mifflin, 1994.

Van Lente, Fred, and Steve Ellis. "Why We're Here." *Fredvanlente. com.* Fred Van Lente and Steve Ellis, 2000. Web. Accessed 13 Mar. 2010.

Warrior, Valerie M. *Roman Religion.* Cambridge: Cambridge University Press, 2006.

Watkins, Calvert. *How to Kill a Dragon: Aspects of Indo-European Poetics.* New York: Oxford University Press, 1995.

Waugh, Robert H. "'The Picture in the House': Images of Complicity." *Lovecraft Studies* No. 32 (Spring 1995): 2–8.

Wayne, Jeff. "The Eve of the War." In *Jeff Wayne's Musical Version of The War of the Worlds.* 1978. Columbia Records, 2005. CD.

Wells, H. G. *The Definitive Time Machine: A Critical Edition of H. G. Wells's Scientific Romance.* 1895. Ed. Harry M. Geduld. Bloomington: Indiana University Press, 1987.

———. *The First Men in the Moon.* 1901. Mineola, NY: Dover, 2001.

———. *The War of the Worlds.* 1898. New York: Epstein & Carroll, 1960.

Willmott, Glenn. *Modernist Goods: Primitivism, the Market and the Gift.* Toronto: University of Toronto Press, 2008.

Briefly Noted

Three Lovecraft scholars have recently made ventures into Lovecraftian fiction. Peter Cannon's *Forever Azathoth: Pastiches and Parodies* (Subterranean Press, 2011) is a generous sampling of his Lovecraftian tales, including the amusing "Scream for Jeeves" trilogy of stories. This volume is issued in only a limited hardcover edition, and an augmented edition—adding the substantial novelette "The Madness out of Space"—is forthcoming from Hippocampus Press. Kenneth W. Faig, Jr., has issued a "micro-edition" of his volume *Lovecraft's Pillow and Other Strange Stories* (Moshassuck Press, 2011), containing 15 of his varied narratives, many on Lovecraftian themes. A selection of these tales—along with Faig's earlier volume, *Tales of the Lovecraft Collectors* (1995)—will be published by Hippocampus Press in 2012. Finally, S. T. Joshi has written a 75,000-word novel, *The Assaults of Chaos*, with Lovecraft as the protagonist. Publication by a small press will probably occur in due course of time.

Lovecraft and I

Caitlín R. Kiernan

[The following is a speech delivered at the H. P. Lovecraft Film Festival in Portland, Oregon, on October 2, 2010.—ED.]

Oh, where to start.

First off, I think that when you're a Guest of Honor it means you're *being* honored. But, truthfully, I feel very much the other way around about this turn of events, having been invited to appear as a Guest of Honor at the Lovecraft Film Festival. *I'm* honored to have been *asked*, and honored that the Festival has gone to considerable trouble and expense to get me here. I certainly couldn't have managed it otherwise. It doesn't help that I'm a bit of a recluse, and not much given to travel. Just getting me out of the house can be a chore. Getting me to cross the county and back, well, that's something I've not done in more than a decade. But when I was asked to be here, I couldn't very well say no. Lovecraft's work has been too great an influence on my own writing to have possibly said no, and, as I've stated, it was an honor.

Then, when I was asked to speak at the opening ceremonies, I said yes. After all, it was *another* honor, being asked, and so again, I couldn't exactly say no. Still, I had no clue whatsoever as to what I was going to say up here at the podium. I'm truly not good at this sort of thing. I'm never sure where to begin or where to end. I ramble. I lose my train of thought. But I pondered and pondered *and* pondered, and finally, at the last minute—which was Wednesday afternoon—I figured it out.

I'll begin here, with the day I first encountered H. P. Lovecraft. Oddly, I found him in Trussville, Alabama, on a yellow school bus. I was seventeen years old. It was a rainy morning in the spring of 1981, and Lovecraft was lying all alone on an empty seat, in the form of a library book from the Birmingham Public Library that someone had accidentally left behind when they got off. It was, in fact, the original 1965 Arkham House edition of *Dagon and Other Macabre Tales*. The black-and-white cover, by Lee Brown Coye (1907–1981), depicts a decrepit, bug-eyed man clad all in rags, a monstrous figure that reminded me at once of Captain Ahab Ceely. The bug-eyed man is wielding a harpoon, which, as one might expect from a decrepit sort of Captain Ahab Ceely, has impaled an albino sperm whale. Turns out, Coye had something of an obsession with *Moby Dick*, and whales are a recurring motif in his artwork. But the man on the book's cover was a giant, by comparison to the whale, which, I'd soon learn, echoes a passage from "Dagon." Lovecraft writes:

> It was the pictorial carving, however, that did most to hold me spellbound. Plainly visible across the intervening water on account of their enormous size, were an array of bas-reliefs whose subjects would have excited the envy of a Doré. I think that these things were supposed to depict men—at least, a certain sort of men; though the creatures were shewn disporting like fishes in the waters of some marine grotto, or paying homage at some monolithic shrine which appeared to be under the waves as well. Of their faces and forms I dare not speak in detail; for the mere remembrance makes me grow faint. Grotesque beyond the imagination of a Poe or a Bulwer, they were damnably human in general outline despite webbed hands and feet, shockingly wide and flabby lips, glassy, bulging eyes, and other features less pleasant to recall. Curiously enough, they seemed to have been chiselled badly out of proportion with their scenic background; for one of the creatures was shewn in the act of killing a whale represented as but little larger than himself. I remarked, as I say, their grotesqueness and strange size; but in a moment decided that they were merely the imaginary gods of some primitive fishing or seafaring tribe; some tribe whose last descendant had perished eras before the first ancestor of the Piltdown or Neanderthal Man was born. Awestruck at this unexpected glimpse into a past beyond the conception of the most daring anthropologist, I stood musing whilst the moon cast queer reflections on the silent channel before me.

Of course, as we soon learn, the figures in the bas-relief are *not* imaginary, and the proportions are likely *not* that far off.

But anyway, for me that's how the love affair with Lovecraft began—a stark black-and-white cover, with the name *Dagon* emblazoned in crimson. As I teenager, I admit that I had the somewhat reprehensible habit of judging a book by its cover. I was even worse about this as a child. Fortunately, I fell in love with Coye's cover at once. And it was just lying there on the seat of the school bus, with no one in sight to lay claim to it. I checked to see if anyone was watching. Nobody was. I felt a distinct thrill in picking it up and hurrying away with it clutched in my arms. I suppose I should have given it to the bus driver, or taken it to the lost and found . . . or something. But I was too intrigued. I had to know what was inside. So I spent several days and nights devouring *Dagon and Other Macabre Tales*. I sat up late at night when I ought to have been asleep. I hid it inside my algebra textbook during class. These things sound horridly cliché, I know, but they're true. And as I read, I fell for the author of these stories, just as I'd fallen for Lee Brown Coye's cover art.

After reading the collection, I'd realize how effectively that cover art evoked the mood of the stories, their atmosphere, the overall *frisson*. And any admirer of HPL's knows that, to him, the success or failure of any weird or macabre tale hinges on whether or not the author has managed to evoke *mood*, first and foremost. No amount of rotting New England seaports or arcane texts or slithering tentacles can ever take the place of expertly crafted mood. You get the mood right, or you give it up. So, in that sense, Coye's cover is spot on. It drew me in, and I discovered not only the title story, but such dark gems as "The Hound," "The Strange High House in the Mist," "The Lurking Fear," "The Doom That Came to Sarnath," and, perhaps, most importantly, the essay "Supernatural Horror in Literature." I read *Dagon and Other Macabre Tales* cover to cover, and some of the stories I read more than once. Then I reluctantly dropped the book into the return bin at the Trussville branch of the library. I have often regretted not keeping it. It's not like I was the one who carelessly left it lying on the school bus. It's not like I was the one who'd be in trouble for losing it. But I didn't keep it. I returned it back into the world.

So, that was my initiation, my introduction to Lovecraft. A left-behind library book with an odd, grotesque, eye-catching cover created by a man who, by coincidence, died that same year.

Now, at the time, I had no idea that these were far from Lovecraft's best stories, and it would be several years yet before I'd figure that out, before I'd discover the wonders of *At the Mountains of Madness*, and "The Colour out of Space," and "The Shadow over Innsmouth." I was a voracious reader, but it wasn't easy finding Lovecraft in Alabama in 1981, and I was very busy with high school, and then college, and many other authors, besides. My life became consumed with my studies in paleontology, geology, and biology, and I didn't find my way back to Lovecraft until 1988 or so. In part, it was reading T. E. D. Klein's sublime novel *The Ceremonies* and then his collection *Dark Gods* that reminded me of that rainy day on the school bus and what I found there. While at the University of Colorado in Boulder, I found the other Arkham House volumes in the college library, and I devoured them immediately.

I think it's no coincidence that my fondness for Lovecraft was cinched about this time. I was working as a paleontologist, and continuing my education in that subject. For me, conceiving of vast gulfs of time and space had become part of my everyday life, though I was aware it was something most people seemed never to pause to consider. Here we are, an infinitesimal speck in a largely unknowable and entirely indifferent universe. Here we are, only a momentary incarnation of matter and energy. Eternity and infinity stretch away all around us. We see it in the stars, and in quantum mechanics, in rocks that were already ancient before the evolution of multicellular life, and we see it in the profusion of plants and animals that inhabited this world before us, preserved now as fossils. We see it in the coming of our own species, and all the ages of human history. For me, this awareness of what geologists call "deep time" was both mundane and marvelous. Still, I wasn't that accustomed to finding it in literature. But here it was in Lovecraft, and here it was in spades.

Few other speculative fiction writers, and certainly very few prior to Lovecraft, seem to have so thoroughly comprehended the profundity of deep time and its consequences for humanity. Lovecraft not only comprehended it, he spent his life writing stories that, among other things, sought to convey the truth of our place in the cosmos. Sure, the monsters were nice, and the disintegrating ancestral castles, and the mutant fish people—but for me, it was his appreciation for time and his ability to convey a cosmic perspective in fiction. He knew, instinctively, the power of these revelations. Time and space is scary shit. If it weren't, Galileo wouldn't have been forced to recant, and we wouldn't still have creationists yammering about biblical myths more than a century and a half after Darwin published his great book. Lovecraft didn't just write creepy stories. In his own way, he subverted religious dogma and said, "Look, we're so tiny, and we'll be gone before you know it. And nothing and no one cares. And this is terrifying, but it's also grand."

I should wrap this. I've already mentioned the trouble I have finding endings. But here we are, twenty-nine years and a couple of odd lifetimes after that day on the school bus. I now live in Providence, Rhode Island, Lovecraft's city, the city he declared himself to exemplify. I certainly never planned for things to work out that way, but fate's an odd and wondrous and disquieting thing. I regularly walk the same redbrick sidewalks he walked, past houses where he lived, and I visit libraries and museums he visited. On a regular basis, I pass the observatory where a young Lovecraft watched the stars. And I sometimes leave tokens of appreciation on his modest headstone at Swan Point Cemetery.

My own fiction has been receiving comparisons to his since my second novel, *Threshold*, was published in 2001. I've never quite known what to make of these comparisons, except that I find them flattering. Indeed, I find, when I read them, that I am honored. And humbled.

Thank you.

Lovecraft and the Sublime: A Reinterpretation

Alex Houstoun

At this point, a great deal has been written about H. P. Lovecraft and his literary themes in regard to both Edmund Burke and Immanuel Kant's understanding of the sublime, the most prominent of these pieces being "Lovecraft and the Burkean Sublime" by Dale J. Nelson (*Lovecraft Studies* 24) and "H. P. Lovecraft and the Semiotic Kantian Sublime" by Bradley A. Will (*Extrapolation,* Spring 2002). The components that apparently link Lovecraft to these concepts of the sublime are his tendency to describe objects and creatures in terms of their lack of form, seemingly infinite size, contradictions to the rules of reality, and/or general might compared to that of his human characters. Furthermore, Lovecraft's narrators and characters frequently fail to classify what they experience in comprehensible terms: they are left speechless or babbling senselessly in a state of awe and terror. When a character does attempt a description of what he witnesses, it is often contradictory or utterly beyond human understanding, for example this passage from "The Call of Cthulhu": "The Thing cannot be described—there is no language for such abysms of shrieking and immemorial lunacy. . . . A mountain walked or stumbled" (*DH* 153). However, to say that Lovecraft was aiming to convey a sense of the sublime within his works is to completely misunderstand his philosophical goals as a writer.

In his own words, Lovecraft was a writer of "cosmic horror" and, while there are similarities to the Burkean and Kantian concepts of the sublime, the effect intended is quite different. Cosmic horror has the goal of revealing to the character his, and humanity's, ultimate insignificance within the cosmos through a sensation of complete and overwhelming terror. The unknown creatures and objects in Lovecraft's stories, while described in a similar style to the sublime, are meant to reveal mankind's pathetic state and destroy the concept of humanity's self-importance and power within the world—referring both to the earth and the cosmos at large. Whereas, in the Kantian sublime, there is the idea that one can ultimately derive pleasure from moments of terror as he comes to understand and appreciate the transcendent power in sublime objects, there is no such escape for Lovecraft's characters. Rather, there is a total collapse of the self. Lovecraft's characters are left in a state of utter despair as they try to grapple with the complete destruction of what was once their concept of reality. It is this absolute lack of recovery or any sort of greater, positive, knowledge that creates the true horror in Lovecraft's stories. In looking at a selection of some of Lovecraft's best-known work, it is clear that there are elements that appear to be similar to the Kantian and Burkean ideas of the sublime, but, ultimately, Love-craft's cosmic horror goes in a significantly different direction.

To understand how it is that cosmic horror is frequently con-fused with the sublime, it is first necessary to define both Kant and Burke's understanding of the term, Lovecraft's concept of cosmic horror, how there are basic similarities between the two, and how they ultimately differ. For Burke, the sublime can be found in anything that is "in any sort terrible, or is conversant about terrible objects" because terror is "productive of the strong-est emotion which the mind is capable of" (35). Burke additionally states that one experiences the sublime most powerfully in mo-ments of "astonishment," when "all [the soul's] motions are sus-pended, with some degree of horror" (49). Furthermore, Burke goes on to list a variety of characteristics that can endow an object with a sense of awe and, therefore, make it sublime for the human subject: obscurity, power, vastness, and, building off of vastness, the sense of infinity.[1]

---

1. "To make anything very terrible, obscurity seems in general to be necessary . . . all is dark, uncertain, confused, terrible and sublime to the last degree" (Burke 50–51); "I know of nothing sublime, which is not some modification of power" (Burke 55); "Greatness of dimension is a powerful cause of the sublime" (Burke

Kant's concept of the sublime bears an initial resemblance to Burke's in that he states that the sublime "must always be great" and "must be simple," but Kant additionally elaborates on what it is about the sublime that causes the subject such delight in witnessing it (340). The sublime, when it first appears to the subject, completely overwhelms his senses, he experiences a failure to understand what is in front of him, and it is this failure that causes the initial reaction of total awe. However, Kant argues that the subject's "reason" begins to work after this first instance of awe and that "reason" then attempts to compensate for and understand what the subject's senses were incapable of grasping. Reason allows the subject to draw an "abstract conclusion," as Will elaborates, using God as an example; "we cannot empirically prove the existence of God, but we can *reason* . . . that God exists . . . we behave *as if* God exists" (Will 8; author's emphasis). The sublime object elicits a similar sort of reaction. The subject feels a mix of respect and humility toward this object that is beyond comprehension. Because of the parallels between the sublime object and the subject's rationale of God, the subject takes a sort of pleasure in the terror and awe he experiences; there occurs in his reasoning a "sublimity of the mind" that is generated when the subject becomes aware of the relationship between the sublime object and God, and the subject becomes, in the words of Vivian Ralickas, conscious of his own "moral vocation" (365).[2]

Lovecraft offers the clearest insight into his idea of cosmic horror within his introduction to the essay "Supernatural Horror in Literature". In this essay he states that the primary goal of the supernatural horror writer, himself included, is to create "[a] certain atmosphere of breathless and unexplainable dread of outer, unknown forces . . . particular suspension or defeat of those fixed laws of Nature which are our only safeguard against the assaults

---

61); "Infinity has a tendency to fill the mind with that sort of delightful horror, which is the most genuine effect and truest test of the sublime" (Burke 62).

2. I owe a great deal to Ralickas's article, "'Cosmic Horror' and the Question of the Sublime in Lovecraft," as it was the first piece I read that articulated my own misgivings and apprehensions about classifying HPL's fiction within either Burke or Kant's respective definitions of the Sublime.

of chaos" (*D* 368), and this can only be achieved through a "degree of imagination and a capacity for detachment from every-day life" (*D* 365). Lovecraft also states that "we remember pain and the menace of death more vividly than pleasure" (*D* 367), and it is because of this that individuals are so struck by the unknown and bizarre as "the oldest and strongest kind of fear is fear of the unknown" (*D* 365).

Given these quotations, it is apparent that cosmic horror has a similar sort of basis with the sublime; just like Kant and Burke's definition of the sublime, Lovecraft, through cosmic horror, is attempting to create a scenario in which the subject is faced with a totally new marvel that overwhelms the senses and body and freezes his faculty of understanding. But it is important to note that Lovecraft already dramatically differs from the sublime. His focus on the concept of memory and the remembrance of "pain and death" is a radical modification of Kant and Burke's sublime. Both Kant and Burke wrote about the sublime as a momentary effect—once the subject's sense of awe fades, the sublime experience ends. Cosmic horror, on the other hand, remains with the subject past the initial moment of awe and terror; it is an effect that does not end, as the memory is just as powerful as the moment that first generated the horror.

Lovecraft also differs from both Kant and Burke in regard to what he chooses to focus on in these moments of awe. In their writings on the sublime, both Kant and Burke are fixated on the relationship that the sublime object, or scenario, has with the human subject. Within Kant's sublime, the subject, through his reason, derives a pleasure from the object because he sees a transcendent power that he can recognize as being an extension and amplification of part of his own self. Lovecraft totally rejects this notion that the human subject should be the focus within cosmic horror, and he very plainly writes: "The true 'hero' of a marvel tale is not any human being, but simply a *set of phenomena*" (*MW* 118; author's emphasis). Lovecraft's human characters are meant as nothing more than a means for the reader to experience the phenomena of his stories, and it is the character's inability to properly understand and describe the phenomena that conveys its true sense of might. As Michel Houellebecq bluntly states, "[the characters'] sole function, in fact, [is to] *perceive*" (68).

Additionally, Burke writes about how the sublime allows the subject to feel a sense of appreciation for "the Godhead" because within the sublime the subject recognizes the ultimate power of his respective deity: "we shrink into the minuteness of our own nature . . . If we rejoice, we rejoice with trembling" (58). On the other hand, Lovecraft completely rejects any sort of belief in a "Godhead" or any other deity figure: "The idea of a deity is a logical and inevitable result of ignorance, since the savage can conceive of no action save by volition and personality like his own" (*MW* 165). Returning to the previously made point, Lovecraft refuses to shift his focus from anything but the phenomena being described. There is no "Godhead" responsible for the objects within cosmic horror; in fact, the very notion of a "deity" being present or responsible for any aspect of the world or cosmos is the "result of ignorance." In this rejection of a deity or "Godhead," Lovecraft draws all attention directly to cosmic horror as shown through the phenomenon's pure unbridled power.

Having established these basic definitions, it is now possible to address the issues, and errors, that come up in arguing that Lovecraft is writing about the sublime in his fiction. In his essay on Lovecraft and the Burkean sublime, Nelson contends that both authors are attracted to "objects and situations which—'at certain distances'³—arouse awe and terror" (2) and that this makes a reasonable basis for saying that Lovecraft is writing about the sublime. Yes, both authors are drawn to objects and situations that inspire terror and awe, but Nelson fails to account for the need for an objective distance in order for a subject to achieve Burke's sublime. If Nelson were to look at a scenario in Gothic literature in which the sublime is apparent and compare it to Lovecraft's own writing, he would be able to see how magnificent his error is.

An example of the sublime, as a result of conditions Nelson describes, can be clearly seen within the second volume of Mary Shelley's *Frankenstein* when Victor Frankenstein is in Mont Blanc with his family. In this section of the novel, Victor goes out into

---

3. Edmund Burke, *Philosophical Enquiry*, ed. J. T. Boulton (University of Notre Dame, 1968), 40. This footnote was originally included in Nelson's essay.

nature and is awed by the landscape in a manner that clearly reflects Burke's concept of the sublime:

> These sublime and magnificent scenes afforded me the greatest consolation that I was capable of receiving. They elevated me from all littleness of feeling; and although they did not remove my grief, they subdued and tranquilized it . . . [The summit of Montanvert] filled me with a sublime ecstasy that gave wings to the soul, and allowed it to soar from the obscure world to light and joy. The sight of the awful and majestic in nature had indeed always the effect of solemnizing my mind, and causing me to forget the passing cares of life. (63–64)

Central to Victor's account of his experiences in this landscape is his remark that "a sublime ecstasy gave wings to the soul" and allowed him to figuratively soar away from "the obscure world" to a state of "light and joy." What Victor is describing in this moment is the elevation of his human spirit to a condition that seems to be interwoven and conscious of the workings of the Divine—Burke's "Godhead." The grief Victor has been suffering since the murder of his brother is temporarily "subdued and tranquilized" as he experiences these brief moments of the sublime in which he is raised from "all littleness of feeling"—the state of mankind—and is free to contemplate, and wonder at, the role of Divinity in the creation of nature.

However, it is also important to realize—and this pertains to the "certain distances" mentioned by Nelson—that it is Victor's ability to leave these landscapes when he chooses that equally allows him these sublime experiences. Victor knows that, while the landscape around him may be "awful and majestic," with the approach of the evening he will rejoin his family in their apartments. Victor's isolation from humanity and the "littleness of feeling" are checked by an awareness of his surroundings—Mont Blanc—and, however overwhelmed the scenes may make him, Victor is capable of returning to humanity when he desires. Victor's knowledge of his surroundings becomes the objective distance necessary to the subject in order to experience the sublime; no matter how "awful" the nature around him may be, Victor always knows, in the back of his mind, exactly where he is, and this knowledge allows him to enjoy and experience the sublime in his exploration.

On the other hand, Lovecraft intentionally removes any sort of safe distance between his subjects and objects so as to maximize the sensation of terror and deny reason, or thought, a chance to intervene. The short story "Dagon" provides such an example of this undermining of the necessary objective distance when the narrator awakens and finds himself on an alien expanse of land: "When at last I awakened, it was to discover myself half sucked into a slimy expanse of hellish black mire which extended about me in monotonous undulations as far as I could see" D 15). Critical to this scenario is the narrator's comment that he was literally "half sucked into" this new world about him. The fact that he is physically submerged in this "hellish black mire" completely denies him the necessary distance that Burke argues is critical for one to experience the sublime; the narrator is awed by the environment, but his focus is more immediately directed at the environment's active consumption of his self. Whereas Victor is capable of taking pleasure in Mont Blanc because he knows where he is and how to return to his family (humanity), the narrator of "Dagon" is terrified because he has no knowledge of his environment and is shocked to find that his body is becoming part of the "hellish black mire" that now surrounds him. Given the psychological state of the narrator, it should be clear that this scenario reinforces Lovecraft's belief that the phenomena should be the primary focus within a fantastical tale. The human subject, the primary focus in both Burke's and Kant's sublime, is literally being swallowed up by the object that is meant to be a source of awe and to inspire the sublime—this phenomenon is overwhelming and erasing all evidence of humanity.

"Dagon" is not the only instance where Lovecraft has removed the necessary objective distance for a sublime experience; this lack of a safe barrier between the subject and object is a critical component in his cosmic horror and can be seen just as sharply in "The Call of Cthulhu." Upon landing on, and investigating, R'lyeh, Johansen and his crew are not filled with awe for what they see; rather, "something very like fright had come over all the explorers" (DH 151), and this "something" develops more into the feeling of terror as the men continue their exploration of R'lyeh. Just like the narrator of "Dagon," Johansen soon finds himself completely surrounded by an alien environment; there is no way for any of the sailors to ground, or relate, what they are seeing to normal human experience because they have been totally cut off from the world they know. This issue is further compounded in Thurston's remark that "the geometry of the place was all wrong. One could not be sure that the sea and the ground were horizontal" (*DH* 151). R'lyeh is a realm that defies human understanding; Johansen literally cannot come to terms with the land that he is standing on.

Thurston's comment about the geometry of R'lyeh being unnatural brings to light how Lovecraft's cosmic horror contradicts Kant and Burke's interpretations of the sublime. For Kant, sublimity hinges on the subject's ability to recognize the "sublimity of his own mind" (Ralickas 384). However, without any sort of objective distance, or removal from the object, Johansen is left with nothing that his mind recognizes as natural: "In this phantasy of prismatic distortion [the door] moved anomalously in a diagonal way, so that all the rules of matter and perspective seemed upset" (*DH* 152). What is occurring here is not a sublimity of the mind, but a complete rupturing of all that Johansen thought he had known. The very "rules of matter and perspective" seem to be bending and breaking all around him, and with them goes Johansen's reason, which was dependent on what he had considered to be the laws of nature and reality. Without his senses and reason to partially understand and rationalize R'lyeh, Johansen is trapped in a continued state of total terror and denied any form of a sublime experience.

Returning to "Dagon," it is also clear that the narrator is unable to utilize his reason and is denied both a Kantian and Burkean sublime. On top of lacking the objective distance necessary to experience awe, the narrator is overwhelmed by the sheer magnitude of his surroundings:

> Though one might well imagine that my first sensation would be of wonder at so prodigious and unexpected a transformation of scenery, I was in reality more horrified than astonished. . . . Perhaps I should not hope to convey in mere words the unutterable hideousness that can dwell in absolute silence and barren immen-

sity. There was nothing within hearing, and nothing in sight save a vast reach of black slime; yet the very completeness of the stillness and the homogeneity of the landscape oppressed me with a nauseating fear. (*D* 15)

This passage directly contradicts Burke's sublime as he writes that "succession and *uniformity*" are parts of what constitutes "the infinite," and the infinite is "the most genuine and truest test of the sublime" because there are "scarce any things which can become the objects of our senses, that are really and in their own nature infinite" (62; author's emphasis). Burke goes on to state that there are also scenarios in which "the eye" is unable to "perceive [the] bounds of [objects]" and this creates an "artificial infinity" (62, 63). The issue is that Burke's artificial infinite requires the human subject's willingness to suspend disbelief and ignore any checks to his imagination that reveal that what he is witnessing is not actually infinite. These checks act as a barrier, another form of the necessary objective distance, to keep the subject safe. For Lovecraft's characters, there are no barriers. The narrator has no means of checking his imagination or even knowing if there is an end to his surroundings; he is completely overwhelmed and left in a state of unending terror. His senses are utterly strained and the narrator is filled with a nauseous fear by the "absolute silence," "stillness and the homogeneity" to such a degree that his reason abandons him in his attempts to comprehend his surroundings and, instead, focuses on setting out to find "the vanished sea and possible rescue."

Another component of Lovecraft's cosmic horror that is falsely identified with the sublime is the recurrence of magnificent heights and even greater depths throughout his landscapes and realms. Nelson claims that Lovecraft's description of "those primordial lost realms" is, in fact, exactly the same as Burke's sublime quality, *vastness:* "Greatness of dimension is a powerful cause of the sublime . . . we are more struck looking down a precipice, than looking up at an object of equal height" (Burke 61). However, there is a critical difference between the two in that Burke's sublime merely requires "looking down" into these depths, whereas Lovecraft's characters not only look down, they enter the depths, and, most importantly, there is something waiting for them at the bottom that denies any potential sublime experience because of the knowledge it brings to the characters.

The strongest case against this misinformed attribution of the sublime is "The Rats in the Walls," whose "black carrion pits" and subterranean world, according to Nelson, are prime "instances of [the] sublime" (5). In the tale, the narrator, known only as Delapoer, and later as de la Poer, returns to his ancestral home in England, Exham Priory, and, upon the completion of its reconstruction, begins to hear the sounds of rats scurrying behind his walls down and down into the depths of the house. Anxious to uncover the origins of this mysterious sound, de la Poer and a group of six other men go into the sub-cellar of the home and then descend, through a hidden passage, even further until they arrive in a "twilit grotto of enormous height" (*DH* 41). This grotto is most certainly described in language similar to the sublime; it is noted that the grotto "stretch[ed] away farther than any eye could see; a subterraneous world of limitless mystery" (*DH* 41–42), and, when the men first come upon it, they are most certainly filled with something very similar to the awe that precedes the sublime: "A few steps more, and our breaths were literally snatched from us by what we saw. . . . Of seven cultivated men, only Sir William Brinton retained his composure" (*DH* 41).

The grotto discovered by de la Poer and his companions should bear a rather uncanny resemblance to those who, like Lovecraft, are well versed in the works of Edgar Allan Poe. The subterranean realm beneath Exham Priory is strikingly similar to the vault described by Poe's narrator in "The Fall of the House of Usher." The vault within Poe's tale is first introduced to the narrator in the form of a painting done by Roderick Usher, and the language in which the narrator describes his reaction to the scene is noteworthy:

A small picture presented the interior of an immensely long and rectangular vault. . . . Certain accessory points of the design served to convey the idea that this excavation lay at an exceeding depth below the surface of the earth. No outlet was observed in any portion of its vast extent, and no torch, or other artificial source of light was discernible; yet a flood of intense rays rolled throughout, and bathed the whole in a ghastly and inappropriate splendor. (325)

Just like de la Poer, the narrator of "Usher" is witnessing a great depth, but this narrator's reaction is much more akin to that of an individual witnessing the Burkean sublime. The narrator remarks that Usher's rendering of the vault, and the depth it resides in, create an "inappropriate splendor" that seemingly causes him delight as the viewer. This remark, that the splendor of the vault is "inappropriate," seems to coincide with Burke and Kant's belief that the sublime object should fill the subject with a delightful terror. The narrator is in some manner repulsed by the scene and dubs it "ghastly and inappropriate," but he is also deriving a pleasure from it because, despite being "ghastly," the scene is still a "splendor." Additionally, there is the matter of the "intense rays" that seem to fill the vault. As the narrator remarks, there seems to be no natural point from which the rays originate, and so their inexplicable existence within the vault can be seen as evidence of divine creation. These rays fill the cavern with a splendor that arouses a pleasurable terror in the narrator, and their lack of an origin reminds the narrator of the role of an almighty creator—the "Godhead." While he is not as explicit as Victor, it appears that the narrator, in looking at Usher's representation of the vault, seems to experience the sublime.

While Poe's narrator is able to derive a pleasure from looking at Usher's painting of the vault, he experiences no such joy when he enters the real vault beneath the house of Usher. Gone is any sort of splendor—there is nothing marvelous in the depth in which the vault is located. The narrator remarks that "the vault in which we placed it . . . was small, damp, and entirely without means of admission for light" (329). What was pleasurable, and sublime, from a distance—when the narrator was looking down into the vault—has become ugly, unpleasant, and tied with death as the narrator and Usher deposit the body of Madeline within the vault. Without the objective distance necessary for both the Kantian and Burkean sublime, the narrator is left feeling nothing but a grim sense of disgust as he helps Usher with his sister's body.

Just as Poe's narrator is denied any sense of splendor and the sublime when he enters the vault, so too is de la Poer, and he goes to great lengths to convey that the twilit grotto does not inspire any form of pleasure for any of the explorers. The very nature of the

grotto, the fact that it seems endless and suggestive of untold horrors and awful truths about the de la Poer family, initially taxes de
la Poer's imagination to such an extreme that he only has one way
of describing the place: "It was the antechamber of hell . . . We shall
never know what sightless Stygian worlds yawn beyond the little
distance we went . . . this grisly Tartarus" (*DH* 44). Additionally, the
vastness of the phenomena seems to directly rupture the very nature of the Kantian sublime because, rather than any of the explorers achieving a sublimity of the mind, their trip into the vast depths
of Exham Priory leads to disturbing revelations and a complete up-
setting of what they had perceived to be the nature of humanity; as
de la Poer remarks, "I wonder that any man among us lived and
kept his sanity through that hideous day of discovery" (*DH* 42).

It is the "discovery," or truth, uncovered in the depths of Exham of Priory that most severely prevents a proper sublime reading of "The Rats in the Walls" and emphasizes the awful nature of
cosmic horror. Within Lovecraft's fiction there is consistently a
strong tie between physical depths and time, in that time seems to
become akin to a literal depth and characters are capable of tran-
scending time by descending deeper into the earth. As de la Poer
and his team move deeper underground, there are continual references to how each step further into the earth is similar to a step
further back in time. The grotto itself is comprised of a multitude
of various relics from different time periods, from "English *graffiti*
. . . as recent as 1610" to Roman ruins and monuments that seem
to suggest an even earlier time (*DH* 43; author's italics). This progression back in time ends with de la Poer realizing the awful
truth of his family; the reason the de la Poers have been hated and
feared through all history is because their home—but most importantly the realm beneath it—served as the site for horrors and
practices that go beyond barbarism and the savagery of primitive
man. It is revealed that the ancient de la Poers took part in the
torture and mutilation of both animals and human beings; they
were cannibalistic; and, worst of all, they kept humans caged in
such disgusting conditions that they devolved into some sort of
gigantic, fleshy, ratlike entities. In the horrifying conclusion of the
story, de la Poer also undergoes a form of devolution and devours
his close friend Capt. Norrys.

De la Poer's temporary madness carries with it a significant weight in relation to the history of his family and humanity. Throughout the story, de la Poer emphasizes the fact that his only tie to the ancient inhabitants of Exham Priory is his name—and at the start of the story he denies even this with his Americanized spelling, "Delapoer." This insisted removal is meant to cut off de la Poer from the awful rumors that surround his household, but additionally to signify his standing as a cultured and educated gentleman. However, his actions within the grotto completely negate this separation this as he acts exactly as the primitive and barbaric inhabitants of that subterranean realm. With his regression comes the implication that man has not advanced at all from his original primal state, and that all it takes to return to this mania is the right trigger. As de la Poer's speech gives way before he attacks Norrys, so do all aspects of humanity and civilization. The sublime is meant to raise man above nature—to reaffirm his rightful place as master of the natural world—and yet in de la Poer the exact opposite unfolds. He gives in to the vilest aspects of his family's history and embraces the madness that seems to arise from within. There is no moment of sublime tranquility or a sense that de la Poer and his team have benefited from what Nelson and Will claim is a sublime experience; rather, as Ralickas puts it, "de la Poer and his team confront the intrinsic bestiality of human nature and succumb to the devastating force of cosmic horror" (383).

Perhaps the greatest misinterpretation of the sublime in place of cosmic horror occurs in the matter of Lovecraft's continual referral to an object or phenomenon's obscure nature. No example of this stands out more clearly than "The Colour out of Space," in which the narrator is told of a meteorite that landed on Nahum Gardner's farm and the strange gaseous beings—released from the meteorite—that go about slowly destroying all the land and life on the Gardner property. Prior to the destruction of the Gardner farm, a group of Arkham scientists take back a sample of the meteorite to run tests, and, through these tests, they come upon something that utterly baffles them: "[the sample] had acted quite unbelievably in that *well-ordered* laboratory . . . upon heating before the spectroscope it displayed shining bands *unlike any known colours of the normal* spectrum . . . bizarre optical properties, and other things which puzzled men of science are wont to when faced by *the unknown*" (*DH* 58; emphasis added).

Will, in his article on the Kantian sublime, argues that this event is a clear example of the sublime because the sublime "hinges on one key point—the success or failure of the faculty of understanding to grasp the object in question" (10). In this scenario, it is clear that the object fails to conform to the "well-ordered" and "normal" laws of nature that the scientists are used to, thus creating a failure in their comprehension. The fact that the scientists are so utterly astonished and baffled by the object reveals "an awareness of the lack of rational grounds of our idea of limitlessness" and signifies that "[they have] experienced the sublime" because "the faculty of reason [generates] an abstract idea of the ungraspable object" (Will 12, 11). The scientists are left with no deeper insight to the nature of the object that they test. All they are capable of concluding is that the meteorite does not conform to their understanding of natural law, but they are equally able to reason that such an object is capable of existing as evident by the fact that they are interacting with the object.

It seems that Will is quite correct in his analysis that the Arkham scientists experience the sublime within this story, but to say that because these characters experience the sublime the whole story is about the sublime is entirely erroneous and ignores all that occurs at the Gardner farm. The entire narrative is focused on Nahum Gardner and the fate of his farm and family as a result of the "colour out of space," and it is their experience with the phenomenon that Lovecraft is concerned with exploring. The Arkham scientists are secondary characters and benefit from the necessary objective distance needed in order to have a sublime experience. The scientists appear at the farm, take a sample, run their tests, and are awed by the results, but the sample inexplicably vanishes before anything else can occur; that is the end of their time with the object along with the Gardner farm. With the disappearance of their personal sample they no longer are exposed to the phenomenon and its incomprehensible nature. Their experience has a clear start and end point.

On the other hand, the Gardners lack the objective distance that is critical for a sublime experience and that benefits both the narrator and Arkham scientists. The meteorite arrives on the Nahum's property and does not leave until the entire family has died. As a result, and prior to their death, the Gardner family's continual exposure to the phenomenon—an object that absolutely confounds their understanding—begins to take a severe toll upon their minds: "Winter came early, and was very cold. Ammi saw Nahum less often than usual, and observed that he had begun to look worried. The rest of his family, too, seemed to have grown taciturn" (*DH* 61). Nahum admits to Ammi that he is "disturbed" because something is odd about the footprints of animals on his property, but he cannot completely explain it: "something [was] not quite right about their nature . . . they were not as characteristic of the anatomy and habits . . . as they ought to be" (*DH* 61). What is disturbing Nahum is that the very nature of his land, and the animals upon it, is becoming unknown to him. Everything that he once seemed to understand is beginning to change, but not in a way that he can clearly recognize—he is left with nothing more than a growing sense of dread but nothing to base this feeling off of. Will says that in order for the subject to have a sublime experience, "the faculty of reason must generate an abstract idea of the ungraspable object" (11), and it is clear that Nahum and his family are experiencing a total failure of their reason as well as their understanding. They are completely incapable of generating an "abstract idea" that could rationalize what is taking place on their farm, and instead they are stuck with a growing sense of terror.

As time progresses, things continue to grow more and more bizarre on the Gardner property: "no sane wholesome colours . . . everywhere those hectic and prismatic variants of some diseased, underlying primary tone without a place among the known tins of earth. . . . In May the insects came, and Nahum's place became a nightmare. . . . The boughs surely moved, and there was no wind" (*DH* 63–64). This degradation of the land—its seemingly inexplicable transformation and outright contradiction to known nature—is reflected by the mental decay of the Gardners. One by one, they all succumb to madness, not by any direct object or event but because of the obscure nature of their surroundings and the seemingly unknown force behind it:

the poor woman screamed about things in the air which she could not describe. In her raving there was not a single specific noun . . . Thaddeus went mad in September after a visit to the well . . . lapsing into an inane titter or a whisper about 'the moving colours down there'. . . . "Nothin' . . . nothin' . . . the colour . . . it burns . . . cold an' wet, but it burns . . . it lived in the well . . . I seen it . . . a kind o' smoke . . . suckin' the life out of everything . . . it beats down your mind." (*DH* 64–71)

In each of these instances, it is clear that the cause of insanity in the Gardner family members is the inability of their "faculty of reason" to create the necessary "abstract idea" needed in order to deal with obscurity of the phenomenon plaguing their land. Without this "abstract idea," the subject's mind is unable to generate an "indirect knowledge" (Will 10) of the phenomenon; it is, therefore, denied any sense of enjoyment and left, instead, with the feeling of an unyielding terror.

This is most clearly illustrated in the Gardner family's failure to explain what it is that is driving them insane; they each suffer a total collapse of language and expression, because the phenomenon they are dealing with is completely outside of human understanding and reason. Mrs. Gardner is reduced to screaming about indescribable "things in the air," and Thaddeus is only able to classify the entities as "moving colours." Neither of these descriptions actually work to dissolve the mystery of what they are trying to express, but it is Nahum who most clearly emphasizes this point in the direct contradictions of his words. What he is trying to explain apparently contradicts its very nature, or the human concept of nature, and this impossibility of being both "nothin'" and something—of being cold yet burning—emphasizes what can become of the obscure if it is left unchecked by reason. The fact that these phenomena defy human reason and understanding turns them into a violent force that destroys the Gardner family both mentally and physically. This is clearly not in any way the sublime. This is cosmic horror, and it has obliterated the subjects—the unfortunate Gardner family—exposed to it.

In establishing how Lovecraft's fiction fails to be classified as the sublime, there has been a recurring theme of the characters

being unable to understand the phenomena that they are confronted with. The men of de la Poer's exploration team lose their
composure and, according to de la Poer, their sanity because of
the grotto and what they learn about the de la Poer family's history; the narrator of "Dagon" ultimately commits suicide because
he witnessed "it"; after his experience on R'lyeh, Johansen is found
babbling madly and, later, seems to embrace his coming death or
murder; each member of the Gardner family goes insane because
of the "things" and "colours" that are slowly devouring their land.
However, while these characters are denied any form of direct
knowledge about the specific phenomena they witness, they do
gain a different type of insight. As Lovecraft wrote in his essay
"Nietzscheism and Realism," "in the cosmos the existence or non-
existence of the earth and its miserable inhabitants is a thing of
the most *complete indifference*" (*MW* 175; emphasis added), and it
is this truth—the revelation that humanity is not as significant as
once believed—that Lovecraft's characters are forced to recognize.
Their madness and terror are a combination of being confronted
by a phenomenon that they are completely unable to grasp and
the knowledge that the existence of such a thing signifies the error
in their understanding of reality. Whereas the sublime is interested
in exalting man's dominance over nature, cosmic horror forces a
"collapse of signification" that leaves the character in one of three
potential states: insane by the burden of such a knowledge, dead
or preparing to embrace death, or completely rejecting his previous role within humanity (Ralickas 365).

    "Dagon" offers possibly the most compact and precise example
of Lovecraft's intended affect with cosmic horror. After the narrator sets off in the hope of locating the ocean, he comes upon "an
abyss which had yawned at the bottom of the sea since the world
was young" that reminds him of Satan's descent in *Paradise Lost* (*D*
17). The narrator then moves down into the pit only to discover,
standing at the center, a "Cyclopean monolith" that is covered in
forms that are "grotesque beyond the imagination" (*D* 17, 18). The
narrator is at first disgusted with these carvings— "damnably human . . . despite webbed hands and feet, shockingly wide and
flabby lips, glassy bulging eyes, and other features less pleasant to
describe"—but rationalizes that they must be the representations

of some "primitive fishing or seafaring tribe" (*D* 18). However, this theory falls apart when one of these creatures suddenly appears and, as the narrator states, "I think I went mad then" (*D*18).

The reason for the narrator's madness is slightly more complex than just the sight of the creature. It must first be noted again that, when the narrator initially found himself upon this land, he was alarmed that he had become "half-sucked" into "the nasty mud"—the alien environment that he had encountered was literally swallowing him up. This caused a crisis within the narrator as he seemed to realize that he was losing all aspects of both the world he knew and himself, and so he went off in search of rescue and the desired return to human civilization. In entering into this abyss, the narrator completely submerges himself and severs all ties with humanity—his trip becomes akin to both Satan's initial journey into hell and a movement back in time to when "the world was young." It is this issue of time that becomes central to the narrator's madness. In seeing the creature, living evidence of what he assumed to be primitive lore, the narrator suddenly becomes aware of humanity's own insignificance in terms of time and strength in the world. The creature is a signifier of an entire form of existence that greatly predated mankind and will seemingly continue to exist regardless of mankind's self-believed control of the world.

What is worse is, while this single "vast, Polyphemus-like" (*D* 18) monster is unaware of the narrator and humanity's existence, that could all change: "I dream of a day when they may rise above the billows to drag down in their reeking talons the remnants of puny, war-exhausted mankind" (*D* 19). The narrator fears that this creature, and the rest of its kind, could cause the end of mankind, but he is equally aware that these "Polyphemus-like" creatures are entirely indifferent to humanity because of how insignificant mankind ultimately is in terms of the greater cosmos. The course of human existence will come and go and will have no effect on the monstrosity witnessed by the narrator; his life is absolutely meaningless in the face of such an entity—the reality he has known is shattered.

This is then echoed in the narrator's final lines before he takes his life: "The end is near. I hear a noise at the door, as of some immense slippery hand lumbering against it. It shall not find me. God, *that hand!* The window! The window" (*D* 19; author's emphasis). It should be noted at once that it is absurd to believe that the creature has actually arrived at the narrator's door. To accept that this entity could somehow track the narrator, arrive in San Francisco, and locate the narrator's abode without being detected, despite the fact that it is the size of a whale, absolutely discredits Lovecraft's ability as a writer. What seems actually to be the case is that the memory of the creature is so powerful that the thought of its hand is enough to speed the narrator's suicide. This action should recall Lovecraft's words, "we remember pain and the menace of death more vividly than pleasure" (*D* 367). While the creature did not deal the narrator any physical pain, its existence has become an assault upon the narrator's mind and sense of self. The creature symbolizes death, not just of the narrator, but of humanity as a whole. It is a creature that existed and ruled the land long before mankind, and it has the power to obliterate humanity should it choose to do so.

With this effect the creature becomes a combination of both horror and terror. In his treatise *The Gothic Flame*, Devendra P. Varma writes: "The difference between Terror and Horror is the difference between awful apprehension and sickening realization: between the smell of death and stumbling against a corpse." The creature brings with it the "sickening realization" that humanity is a matter of "complete indifference" in the grander scope of the cosmos, and yet it also carries the "awful apprehension" that, at any time, these entities could rise from the depths of the ocean. This is cosmic horror—the dual impact of the unbearable truth of existence and the fact that the only thing that has allowed humanity to exist for so long is sheer luck. There is no deity or "Godhead" watching over humanity, there is no reason that mankind should believe itself to be the masters of the world, there is nothing preventing a different, utterly alien species from completely obliterating all traces of man, and, worst of all, there is nothing even to guarantee that human civilization will even be remembered, or matter, to anyone but those who helped build and take part in it. The cosmos is indifferent to the actions and fate of man—for, ultimately, he is nothing. The narrator chooses to kill himself because there seems to be little other choice left to him. His life is meaningless when looked at from a cosmic perspective, and without drugs left to delude his mind, every living moment is filled with the memory of that creature and the dread that it and the rest of its race will rise from the floor of the oceans and smite humanity.

In his closing remarks, Will writes, "Lovecraft's use of the Kantian sublime is the crucial feature that sets his work apart from others" (20). As should be made apparent by this essay, Lovecraft's work entirely fails to be read as sublime and, arguably, openly contradicts the requirements necessary for a sublime experience. His characters always lack the necessary objective distance needed to experience both the Kantian and Burkean sublime, and Lovecraft amplifies sublime characteristics such as size, obscurity, and depth to such a degree that they completely engulf his characters, cutting them off from any form of humanity and relentlessly beating them until they submit to these phenomena. What the characters actually experience is cosmic horror— the overwhelming realization that humanity's position within the world, and the cosmos, is not at all as secure and permanent as they had previously believed. The elements that Will, Nelson, and others have mistaken for the sublime are really the attributes and testaments to the incomprehensible power and awe of these comic entities.

"It was just a colour—but not any colour of our earth or heavens" (*DH* 79), the narrator of "The Colour out of Space" says toward the end of his narrative. While this "colour" is seemingly incomprehensible to all those who encountered it, it brought with it an awful sort of realization: there are entities far beyond the human scope of reason and understanding, and the fact that such things have not done to the earth the same thing that was done to the Gardner's farm has nothing to do with the perceived power and significance of humanity. It is pure luck that humanity has not been eradicated at this point, but even this does not matter because, in the terms of these unknown phenomena—otherworldly colours, alien monsters of the deep, and horrors the size of mountains—and in comparison to the cosmos, humanity's full existence, whenever it does come to an end, will still amount to only a miniscule and insignificant moment.

Works Cited

Burke, Edmund. *On Taste; On the Sublime and Beautiful; Reflections on the French Revolution; A Letter to a Noble Lord*. Ed. Charles W. Eliot. New York: P. F. Collier & Son, 1937.

Houellebecq, Michel *H. P. Lovecraft: Against the World, Against Life*. Translated by Dorna Khazeni. San Francisco: Believer Books, 2005.

Kant, Immanuel. "The Beautiful and Sublime." In *The Portable Enlightenment Reader*, ed. Isaac Kramnick. New York: Penguin, 1995.

Nelson, Dale J. "Lovecraft and the Burkean Sublime." *Lovecraft Studies* No. 24 (Spring 1991): 2–5.

Poe, Edgar Allan. *Poetry and Tales*. Ed. Patrick F. Quinn. New York: Library of America, 1984.

Ralickas, Vivian. "'Cosmic Horror' and the Question of the Sublime in Lovecraft." *Journal of the Fantastic in the Arts* 18 (2007): 364–98.

Shelley, Mary. *Frankenstein*. Ed. J. Paul Hunter. New York: W. W. Norton, 1996.

Varma, Devendra P. *The Gothic Flame*. New York: Russell & Russell, 1966.

Will, Bradley A. "H. P. Lovecraft and the Semiotic Kantian Sublime." *Extrapolation* 43 (Spring 2002): 7–21.

―――――――――

Briefly Noted

Foreign interest in Lovecraft remains strong, as testified by the publication of Lovecraft's *Teoria dell'Orrore* (Milan: Edizioni Bietti, 2011), edited by Gianfranco de Turris and translated and annotated by Massimo Berruti and Claudio De Nardi. This substantial volume contains many of Lovecraft's essays on supernatural literature, from the *In Defence of Dagon* essays to "Lord Dunsany and His Work" to "Supernatural Horror in Literature." Another volume of note is *The Best of H. P. Lovecraft* (2010), published by Crows Nest, an imprint of Allen & Unwin in Crows Nest, NSW, Australia. This is the first volume of Lovecraft's work that originated from an Australian publisher; the 624-page book contains ten of Lovecraft's best tales and costs $29.99 in Australian dollars.

Lovecraft: A Gentleman without Five Senses

Roland Hölzing

Everybody has five senses. At least medicine tells us so in respect to sound human beings. Whoever has less is called ill. Almost everybody prefers one sense to the others. However, the way these five answer to the will of the person differs very much: eyes may be shut, appearances may be altered (within limits) according to one's wishes, data of touch can only be sampled from close objects and under further restrictions, smell and taste need close distance and are transmitted chemically. Hearing and sight work over greater distances and, finally, sound, sight, and smell sometimes molest us without warning.

About Lovecraft we know that he not only wrote and received written text (which, as is often overlooked, is an optical impression), but effectively read aloud his own stories as well as delivered speeches. "Lovecraft could very easily have become an actor, because he read the manuscript with real effect" (Eddy 10). The effects of his rendition—in sound as well as in acting—brought him applause even as an infant of two years reciting "Mother Goose" (Joshi, *Dreamer and Visionary* 12), and he kept on enjoying the effect throughout his life, as far as we know. He did a dramatic declamation of horror stories visiting a graveyard together with a beautiful woman one night in 1933. This left the lady somewhat irritated (*Dreamer and Visionary* 337). Further, his whole self-stylization as a "gentleman" was kind of permanent play-acting:

He liked to consider himself an aged recluse, writing his aunts as "My darling daughter" and "My dear grandchild" and signing his letters "Grandpa". He affected the language, attitudes, and even spelling . . . of an eighteenth-century English Tory. . . . When his friend Morton taxed him with being a poseur, he blandly replied: "But isn't it an artistic pose?" (de Camp 4)

We know of no further inclination in respect to acting, though. If there was, he didn't live it but followed his inclination toward a quiet life. His financial situation as well would permit neither a histrionic nor a gentlemanly life in public. His voice was somewhat shrill, "piping," and could adopt different tones. Apart from this its quality seems to have been unspectacular.

The way Lovecraft presented himself to the world was strictly conservative: shirt with tie, trousers, and jacket. This almost unchanging style had several advantages: he presented a controlled and reliable picture to the outside without too much thought, and it was rather inexpensive. Especially so, since he avoided fashion as best as he could. Finally, this dress code helped to cover most of his body. In "The Dunwich Horror" Lovecraft invented one Wilbur Whateley, who looks like a distorted self-portrait. I wonder whether the sentences characterizing Wilbur's body might reflect Lovecraft's hostile attitude toward his own: "aside from the external appearance of face and hands, the really human element of Wilbur Whateley must have been very small" (*DH* 176)

Obviously, to Lovecraft the optical sense and its data were much more important than many scholars have realized. Writing about "mythical" multicolored sunsets, silhouettes, or panoramas of cities, beings with fishlike attributes or withered trees—all these are optical impressions, only sometimes stretched beyond reality and transformed into something fantastic or bizarre. The traditional saying "in his mind's eye" hints at just this mechanism—from gathering visual input to making up a fantasy-image.

This dominant interest in pictures is documented from Lovecraft's childhood days. As a six-year-old, visiting a friend, he found an illustrated edition of Coleridge's *Rime of the Ancient Mariner*. But the words didn't matter to him. The illustrator's name mesmerized him: "for didn't I know the dark, supernal magic of the Doré pictures in our Dante & Milton at home? I opened the book—& behold a hellish picture" (Joshi, *Dreamer and Visionary* 18). It is the pictures, not the words, the boy was after, and he was absolutely fond of Gustave Doré. An inability to read would not have been surprising at this age, but this was not Lovecraft's problem. At the age of four he had started by digesting Grimm's *Fairy Tales* and the *Arabian Nights* with some secondary effect: "how many young dream-Arabs have the *Arabian Nights* bred! I ought to know, since at the age of 5 I was one of them! . . . It was then that I invented for myself the name of Abdul Alhazred" (*SL* 4.8). Surely, when he found the illustrated Coleridge, he really was more interested in pictures than in words.

But not all the visual scenes Lovecraft invented in his stories are pleasing. Instead, we find two quite different types:

- If the scene takes place in daylight or bright dawn/dusk, the emotions described are mainly loving and longing. These scenes are quite seldom and short.
- If the scene is artificially lit, in deep dusk, close to or completely dark, the main impression is fear. Such scenes are easily found and sometimes go on over several pages.

So we find two most important senses: dominant by far is sight, and the second, much weaker one is hearing/sound. Touch, smell, and taste for most people are much less important than the other two—as long as these can be used. If people (at least of Western civilization) are restricted to these three senses, the preferred input of information is missing and people tend to feel uneasy, even frightened. If—as with this author—his most important sensory input fails or becomes unreliable, the only literature that can be produced will be a literature of fear.

Lovecraft describes inorganic matter (e.g., stone) in a way that suggests organic corruption or similar processes. Generally, these are accompanied by nauseating smells. In his stories, taste and smell, darkness and loathing are quite often connected: notice one, and soon the others will be found. On the other hand, hardly anything in his literary works tastes good. Nice smells tend to be labeled "sweet" but won't be differentiated any further. I suppose the reason for this is that agreeable impressions generally are faked, not felt: "sweet odours linger about strange gardens" ("The White Ship" [*D* 36]); "bright and fragrant the flowers" (*D* 39); "sweetness of flowers" ("The Quest of Iranon" [*D* 112]).

The tactile sense most often is stimulated by night-gaunts who will tickle one sadistically: "He screamed again and again, but whenever he did so, the black paws tickled him with greater subtlety" (*The Dream-Quest of Unknown Kadath* [*MM* 335]. Orientation in space sometimes is missing, too: "Human utterance can best convey the general character of our experiences by calling them *plungings* or *soarings*" ("Hypnos" [*D* 166]). The only positive memories of touch are from contact with cats (Eddy 6), but these hardly are exploited literally. Only his Randolph Carter in *Dream-Quest* initiates a contact with cats: "And because he loved nothing on earth more than a small black kitten, he stooped and petted the sleek cats of Ulthar" (*MM* 314).

Finally, one sense its missing—taste. Taste is missing to an alarming degree. People in Lovecraft's stories hardly ever drink or eat. Wine is "potent," i.e. effective (*MM* 385). Obviously there is no taste, but it makes one gossipy and numb (*MM* 312, 317). Only ghouls or cats enjoy feeding ("licking their chops with unusual gusto" [*MM* 314]), but Lovecraft doesn't try to explore their delights.

Out of Lovecraft's own life we are told of ice-cream sprees (he "continued triumphantly through the whole twenty-eight flavors, consuming more that two quarts of ice cream" [de Camp 72]), and his coffee at least contained four spoonfuls of sugar (Eddy 7, 53). But his alter ego Randolph Carter is not permitted such delights. Coming back to his childhood home in "The Silver Key," he "ate his supper in silence" (*MM* 417).

If ever one finds a positive, beautiful scene the impression is almost solely optical. Generally it deals with landscape, often with buildings. Sometimes there are silhouettes of whole cities, as in the beginning of *Dream-uest*: "All golden and lovely it blazed in the sunset, with walls, temples, colonnades, and arched bridges of veined marble, silver-basined fountains of prismatic spray in broad squares" (*MM* 306). Sometimes single houses are described precisely. Apart from literary works, this happens in descriptions of Charleston and Quebec. To the author, these two almost rivaled Providence. Judging by his enthusiastic words, Lovecraft forgot his greatest love for a time while visiting these two cities: "Never have I beheld a place [Charleston] which appeals more thoroughly to me. The climate is marvellous . . . it was possible to sit outdoors all day and enjoy it" (*CE* 4.67); "the suggestion of dreamlike exoticism [in Quebec] is intensify'd by the strange, slender spires which rise on every hand . . . for a moment it is hard to connect this breathless vitsa with unmagical reality, or to realize that one is not being wafted bodily into the midst of some vast picture vivid with adventurous expectancy" (*CE* 4.179). In between the words we find some sketches by hand. Some are maps, others deal with details of the houses. In particular, the large porches on Charleston's eighteenth-century houses are shown as well as described in detail (*CE* 4.86f.).

In Lovecraft's literary works such extended descriptions of positive, brightly lit spaces hardly ever appear. Seldom do we read about brighter areas, serving as a contrast to the general darkness of the scenery. Some of these rare examples are to be found in *Dream-Quest*. Apart from its beginning (cited above; it goes on for more than half a page in print, hinting melancholically at Carter's longing for something lost), we find something beautiful and almost from this earth later on: Carter meets his old friend Kuranes, who can't return from the dreamlands to the waking world, since his body died there. As a substitute he dreams up some small Cornwall-within-dreamland and reigns there as king: "had formed a mighty longing for the English cliffs and downlands of his boyhood . . . on the coast nearby he had built a little Cornish fishing village" (*MM* 354). A few pages earlier, Lovecraft paints a paradiselike landscape, only to show us within a few lines one very special inhabitant: "So Carter set out alone over the golden fields that stretched mysteriously beside a willow-fringed river. . . . Once in a while he paused to watch a carnivorous fish catch a fishing bird, which it lured to the water by shewing its tempting scales" (*MM* 348f.).

Obviously, Lovecraft made up whole stories like a painting, and in his mind's eye the reader can examine the scene and find more and more details that support the idea he started to nurse a lot earlier. "Lovecraft's stories are like paintings in that they are static . . . in the beginning he sketches out what's going to happen in the story and then he proceeds to fill in things in more detail" (David E. Schultz, cited in Joshi, *A Subtler Magick* 257). There are no surprises, only confirmations. But this method allows the stories to be read several times over, contrary to simple "whodunit" stories. No surprise is waiting at the end. In a deconstructionist sense, we read the text for the first time every time, because our memories of the last reading change our ideas while re-reading.[1] With whodunits, this would cause boredom; with Lovecraft's texts, we discover new details, connect things differently, and so on.

It seems to me that perhaps optical fantasies were an important thing to keep Lovecraft in life and alive: the "Vor-Lust" that awaits the reapparition of

> fragments expressed in unknown or half-known architectural or landscape vistas, especially in connexion with a sunset. . . . [T]he impression [is] that the scene in question represents something I have seen & visited before under circumstances of superhuman liberation & adventurous expectancy . . . [These images extend] back in my experience to my very first memories at the age of 1¾ . . . (SL 3.197)

As a summary I find that of all the five senses Lovecraft mainly used sight—in respect to his inspirations as well as in writing and perhaps, to some extent, even in the layout of his stories. But this most important ability is what is least reliable for his characters, sometimes even totally missing. The author tells us about how his characters manage with their fundamental deficit. Hearing may help, but more often it only strengthens the fear, the sense of smell only (with very rare exceptions) adds to or triggers fear in the subject. Touch seldom and negatively occurs and taste is totally absent. This perfectly mirrors a man who always dressed correctly and who presented only a controlled and very restricted image of his body. This person made contact via mail and voice (corresponding to eye and ear). Bodily smells are painstakingly avoided and personal contact (not to speak of intimacies) are hardly ever welcomed. Taste in the sense of sweet, sour, etc., only exists in relation to edibles and is therefore restricted to the purse's capacities. While the characters in his stories tend to get

---

1. "A thing repeated from an anterior instance is a thing changed, by virtue of the fact that its new appearance is a repetition." Donald R. Burleson, *Lovecraft: Disturbing the Universe* 20f.

molested by these "sensual" irritations, the author himself—for a time, anyway—believed himself to be free from these things: a classical case of repression. "As an adult he actually thought of himself as a man virtually without emotions—a disembodied intelligence" (de Camp 42).

This optically oriented man who always tried to look like a gentleman without actually being able to afford it (Joshi, *Dreamer and Visionary* 66) always built his stories around fear. If sight is diminished, frightening sounds, smells, and contacts threaten to enter one's consciousness. Starting from this basic assumption, the aliens' offer in "The Whisperer in Darkness" almost perfectly seems to suit Lovecraft's wishes: separation of the (almost immortal) brain from the body, cosmic voyages, command of sight, hearing, and speech (*DH* 257) under omission of touch, smell, and taste. Together with a stainless body of Yuggoth-metal that doesn't need to be looked after! But the one thing missing is terrible: total dependency on other beings who have to plug in the sensory cables. This dependency—or, put differently, this loss of control—is dreadful for Lovecraft's character Wilmarth, and from this cosmic fear the author probably was running all through his life. But—in literature at least—he never got over it.

Works Cited

Burleson, Donald R. *Lovecraft: Disturbing the Universe*. Lexington: University Press of Kentucky, 1990.

de Camp, L. Sprague. *Lovecraft: A Biography*. Garden City, NY: Doubleday, 1975.

Eddy, Muriel. *The Gentleman from Angell Street*. [Providence, RI: Privately printed,] 1961.

Joshi, S. T. *A Dreamer and a Visionary: H. P. Lovecraft in His Time*. Liverpool: Liverpool University Press, 2001.

———. *A Subtler Magick: The Writings and Philosophy of H. P. Lovecraft*. San Bernardino, CA: Borgo Press, 1996.

Endless Bacchanal: Rome, Livy, and Lovecraft's Cthulhu Cult

Dennis Quinn

To me the Roman Empire will always seem the central incident
of human history.

—H. P. Lovecraft, Letter to R. H. Barlow,
13 June 1936 (*SL* 5. 266)

The Oldest and Strongest Emotion

A dangerous cult has come to town! People of the town begin to
disappear not to be found again. Strange sounds in the night
frighten the citizens. Women and children are induced into the
nocturnal orgies and other unspeakable debaucheries. The cult
teaches that its members are above the civil laws. Initiates are delivered as victims to the priests, who lead them away to a dark
place with shouts and the beating of cymbals and drums. The
bodies of the sacrificed are taken away to dark caves to be devoured by black creatures in the night. Authorities are called in to
help root out the dangerous cult. What they find is that the evil
teachings have infected more people then they had imagined. The
evil has to stop! The cult must be rooted out, its members punished to prevent it from taking over the town. The very existence
of civilization is at stake!

This scenario sounds almost cliché. It has appeared in dozens of
pulp horror stories and B-horror movies, and certainly sounds familiar to any reader of the works of H. P. Lovecraft, particularly in part
II, "The Tale of Inspector Legrasse," in his masterpiece, "The Call of
Cthulhu" (1926). But this story is much older. It is, in fact, a summary of an account written two thousand years ago by one of

Rome's greatest historians, Titus Livius, better known today by students and scholars as Livy (59 B.C.E.–17 C.E.). His account of the infamous Bacchanalia, which appears in Book 39 of his mammoth *History of Rome*, tells of an orgiastic, human-sacrificing cult of the Greek god Dionysus, which Roman authorities worked diligently to uncover and brutally stamp in 186 B.C. The event set the tone for how Romans dealt with cults believed to be immoral, aberrant, impious, and foreign. Indeed, how Romans dealt with the cult of Bacchus in the second century B.C.E. became the model for how persecuting Roman authorities dealt with Christianity, and subsequently how Christians dealt with pagan mystery cults from Emperor Theodosius I (379–395 C.E.) throughout late antiquity.

Roman history is a subject Lovecraft knew quite well, as can be seen in the numerous books on Rome in his library, and his many mentions of ancient Roman topics in his work. Specifically, Livy's view that this deranged cult that honors a god was dangerous to the stability, moral tenets, and very existence of the Roman world was fertile ground for Lovecraft's imagination. The event was the seed of his creation of the cult of Cthulhu. The Roman account in a second-century B.C.E. bronze tablet inscription entitled the *Senatus Consultum de Bacchanalibus* (the official Roman decree prohibiting the cult of Bacchus in Rome), Roman histories of the nineteenth century, and, more important, the account of the suppression of the Bacchanalia in Livy 39 had a profound influence on Lovecraft's crafting of "The Tale of Inspector Legrasse" section in "The Call of Cthulhu." Indeed, there are many instances in which he makes specific references to Greco-Roman history, and he often evokes classical myths. Roman civilization in particular served as utopia of sorts for Lovecraft—a time when he saw realization of the truest expression of conservative values and republican virtues.

Lovecraft longed for ancient Rome. He even dreamed about being Roman. In a letter he wrote to Donald Wandrei in 1927 (later published as "The Very Old Folk"), while "The Call of Cthulhu" was under consideration for publication, we see Lovecraft rubbing elbows with Roman magistrates who play important parts in Livy's account of the suppression of the Bacchanalia. Lovecraft had this dream just a few months after completing "The Call of Cthulhu." Seeing the cult that Inspector Legrasse encounters in light of this letter, and in light of the prevailing influence of Livy on Lovecraft's creation of the cult, we can see in sharp relief the fact that the Cthulhu cult as presented in this story is a retelling of Livy's Bacchanalia account seen through Lovecraft's burgeoning myth-cycle, which was subsequently named the Cthulhu Mythos.

Lovecraft and Rome

Scholars over the past several decades have often acknowledged the inclusion of classical themes in Lovecraft's fiction. His interest in and great familiarity with classical mythology can be clearly seen in the setting, structure, and important plot elements in stories such as "The Tree" (1920), "Hypnos" (1922), "The Rats in the Walls" (1923), and "The Very Old Folk" (1927). In one of his first major short stories, "The Tomb" (1917), the main character, Jervas Dudley, becomes inspired to enter the tomb after reading the *Lives* by Plutarch (*D* 6), the first-century C.E. Greek-turned-Roman citizen philosopher and biographer, whose works lined the shelves of Lovecraft's uncle's library. But even in the some perhaps less obvious stories, the classical influence lies just below the surface, difficult to detect, but bubbling up enough to discern. For example, classical influence, particularly the Greek classic Homer's *Odyssey* and the Roman Virgil's *Aeneid*, even the Roman historian Lucian, is apparent in Lovecraft's epic novella, *The Dream-Quest of Unknown Kadath* (Joshi 1986, 31–32). S. T. Joshi has shown that "Greek and Roman mythology and religion seems to have played a role in shaping" the work (*H. P. Lovecraft: A Life* 33). Even the demythologized *At the Mountains of Madness* contains, as Peter Cannon noted, "a subtle strain of traditional mythology [which] helps anchor the invented mythos of the novel" (103).

"The Call of Cthulhu" is another case in point. Many critics have pointed to various influences on this story, such as Guy de Maupassant's "The Horla," Arthur Machen's "Novel of the Black Seal," A. Merritt's "The Moon Pool," and the Theosophical writings of Helena Petrovna Blavatsky (Joshi and Schultz 28–29). These are clear in structure, plot elements, and references in the tale. But "The Call of Cthulhu" has also been noted for its classical references. For example, Peter Cannon (66) points to the classical motifs in part 3 of the story, "The Madness from the Sea," in which Lovecraft calls the city of R'lyeh a "monstrous Acropolis" (*DH* 166), the god Cthulhu is compared to "Polytheme cursing the fleeing ship of Odysseus," who is "bolder than the storied Cyclops" (*DH* 153) in pursuit of the unfortunate sailors of the *Alert*. Drawing from Homer's *Odyssey*, Lovecraft creates a new vision entrenched in his own pseudomythology by combining classic old tales with new flair. Additionally, Stephen R. Wilk stresses the classical motifs in "The Call of Cthulhu" by drawing parallels between the description of the Cthulhu bas-relief and the Gorgon described in Hesiod's *Shield of Heracles* in that the creature possessed a "scaly body" and rudimentary wings. Wilk writes:

> It seems to me that the analogy can be pushed further in that beholding the Gorgon, in particular the Gorgon Medusa, had negative effects indeed—namely, turning one to stone. The mere gaze at the great Cthulhu killed and drove insane nearly all the crew of the *Vigilant*. And, not to push the analogy too far, the very image of Medusa and other Gorgons in Greek paintings, with the snakes encircling the head, looks, to the unfocussed eye, something like the many tentacles of an octopus. (215)

Wilk stressed that "A number of horror writer H. P Lovecraft's odd beings have their roots in Greek mythology" (215).[1] Further, Jason C. Eckhardt noted "There is little argument about the presence of Greek and Roman mythology in the writings of H. P. Lovecraft" (25). Thus, as these scholars and others have noted, "The Call of Cthulhu" in many ways harkened back to Lovecraft's fascination with the Greco-Roman world. However, as these scholars have noted, the influence was primarily via classical myth. But this is only part of the story. Roman history in general and in particular the Roman historian Livy must also be considered part of the ingredients in the classical stew from which Lovecraft concocted his tale of subversive cultists and an evil god that threat-

---

1. George T. Wetzel has noted that "The Call of Cthulhu" has some allusions to classical myth by adding "extravagantly to the descriptions, making his creatures seem much more loathsome than their original antecedents" (Wetzel 1959, 278).

ened to destroy the world.

In December 1933, less than four years before his death, H. P. Lovecraft summed up his lifelong love of Roman civilization in a letter to his friend Clark Ashton Smith:

> Rome is a subject which has fascinated me uncannily since I first heard much of it around the age of six. From the moment I picked up any idea of its nature, history, and characteristics, and held in my own hands the actual Roman coins (about two dozen—now in my possession) of my grandfather's collection, I have had the most persistent sensation (out of which occultists would make a case of metempsychosis, and of a pseudo-scientist one of hereditary memory) of some ineluctable connection with the ancient *Respublica*. (*SL* 4.332)

His reference to metempsychosis is telling, not because Lovecraft believed that he was literally reincarnated from or indwelled by someone an ancient Roman (he was a well-known materialist and atheist); but to use such strong language to describe his connection to ancient civilization only punctuates the fact that Lovecraft was unabashedly obsessed with Rome. In the same letter he insisted that it "is utterly impossible, too, for me to regard Rome in a *detached* way. As soon as I get behind the age of the Saxons on England, say 450 A.D., my sense of personal connection with my own blood-ancestors of the north utterly vanishes—giving place to a natural and unshakable feeling of *being a Roman*" (*SL* 4.332). If one follows this remarkable statement, one can see how his immersion in the Roman world may have colored his creation of fiction writing.

As S. T. Joshi's catalogue of Lovecraft's library shows, Lovecraft owned several editions of classical Latin in his library, such as Caesar, Cicero, Horace, and Livy. Lovecraft often bragged about his comfort in reading the language of the Romans.

> In school I took Latin as a duck to water, but found all other languages alien and repellant. French seemed to me a pitiful decadence-product; German a hateful tongue from across the Rhine-Danube frontier. Greek I liked and respected—but I found it difficult, and tended to translate it mentally into Latin. Nor have I

ever quite ceased to have Roman dreams of the most puzzling vividness of detail. (*SL* 4.334)

He often attempted to show off his knowledge Latin by inserting quotations of the ancient language into a number of his stories. At the climactic ending of "The Rats in the Walls," Lovecraft has the narrator exclaim the Latin, "Magna Mater! Magna Mater!" before he descends into prehistoric gibberish (*DH* 45). It is the Latin version of his fictional book, the *Necronomicon*, which comes down to the unfortunate characters in his stories, the original Arabic having been lost. However, his citations of Latin usually come primarily from encyclopedias, for example, the Latin quote in "The Horror at Red Hook," which Lovecraft took from the ninth edition of the *Encyclopaedia Britannica* or from authors' quotations that Lovecraft lifts from the text, such as the Latin epigraph at the beginning of "The Tomb."

It should be noted that the epigraph attached to his short story "The Festival" (*Efficiunt Daemones, ut quae non sunt, sic tamen quasi sint, conspicienda hominibus exhibeant*), which is attributed to Lactantius in the standard editions of Lovecraft, is not actually from Lactantius at all. As S. T. Joshi has pointed out (Lovecraft, *Call of Cthulhu* 385n1), Lovecraft got the quotation from his own copy of Cotton Mather's *Magnalia Christi Americana* (1702), which cites it as Lactantius' *Divine Institutes* 2.15. We can also see this same quote in the work of Cotton's father, Increase Mather. It is an epigraph in his demonological work *Cases of Conscience concerning Evil Spirits Personating Men* (1693). After a search in Lactantius' works, however, even in the edition of *Divine Institutes* the Mathers may have actually owned, I was unable to locate the quotation. Furthermore, this fourth-century Christian author was a teacher of rhetoric. He wrote with classical Latin flair, surpassing even Augustine in Latin eloquence, and is sometimes referred to as the "Christian Cicero." The quotation attributed to Lactantius in "The Festival" does not seem Lactantian. Indeed, it may be a much later Latin, perhaps medieval, though its source is completely unknown to me. So where did Increase Mather get this quotation? The Mathers, like many of his contemporary seventeenth- and early eighteenth-century divines, often quoted classical and patristic Latin from inaccurate collected works or *florilegia* rather than directly from the original text, and thus sometimes misquoting their sources (Wright 34). Most of these have yet to be properly indexed, and modern editions are sorely lacking. It seems that this supposed quotation from Lactantius might have been one such misquotation from the Mathers' *florilegia*. It is also possible that Increase Mather misquoted from memory a passage from Lactantius.[2] Thus, it is may be more correct to say that it is a quotation from Increase Mather misquoting Lactantius rather than from the fourth-century Church Father himself. So Lovecraft got his Latin quotations (and misquotations) from various secondary locations, which is understandable since he had little access to scholarly research libraries.

Explicit references to Roman civilization are also common in Lovecraft's stories. For example, in "The Rats in the Walls," finished in 1923, the main character discovers that his ancestral home rests upon an ancient Roman temple in honor of Attis, replete with Latin graffiti in the basement. In one passage, the main character is puzzled by the Latin writing on an "unknown altar designs," showing that his confusion is heightened by the discrepancy between Roman writing on un-Roman altars (*DH* 40). Thus, the narrator's knowledge of Roman religious practices leads to the discovery that something more sinister than simple classical paganism had been going on. De la Poer notes the Latin inscriptions in the sub-cellar: "'P. GETAE. PROP . . . TEMP . . . DONA . . .' and 'L. PRAEC . . . VS . . . PONTIFI . . . ATYS . . .'" When describing the graffiti, he explains, "The reference to Atys made me shiver, for I had read Catullus and knew something of the hideous rites of the Eastern god, whose worship was so mixed with that of Cybele" (*DH* 37).

In another tale completed two years later, the terrible Roman cult of this goddess is mentioned again in "The Horror at Red Hook." As Lovecraft describes it in his characteristically purple prose:

> Satan here held his Babylonish court, and in the blood of stainless childhood the leprous limbs of phosphorescent Lilith were laved. Incubi and succubae howled praise to Hecate, and headless moon-

---

2. The closest I can find to a discussion on the power of demons to deceive humans is Lactantius' Divine Institutes 2.16. However, it should be stressed that neither the quotation itself nor anything close to it can be found here.

calves bleated to the Magna Mater. Goats leaped to the sound of thin accursed flutes, and Ægypans chased endlessly after misshapen fauns over rocks twisted like swollen toads. Moloch and Ashtaroth were not absent; for in this quintessence of all damnation the bounds of consciousness were let down, and man's fancy lay open to vistas of every realm of horror and every forbidden dimension that evil had power to mould. (*D* 260)

For Lovecraft, New York was a veritable melting pot of multiple traditions woven together to create an evil confused mass of worshippers that could only be up to no good. Here, the worst of ancient religions is mixed with what Lovecraft believed to be inferior races, degrading even more into a horrific conglomeration of ancient foreign cults and New York's immigrant population to exemplify his learning in ancient abhorrent religions alongside his modern xenophobic worldview.

Lovecraft was often inspired to write stories set in Rome or with Roman characters, but he was not always able to keep pace with his aspirations. This is clear in a story idea outlined in a letter to Lillian D. Clark in 1925. In it, Lovecraft envisions a story in which Romans settled America long before Columbus, leaving behind archaeological evidence in modern Rhode Island:

> I'd like to write a tale of a digging of a Westminster St. Subway—or a Providence—Pawtuket subway—& the incidental discovery of broken Corinthian columns bespeaking the forum of some unknown Roman town at the head of Narragansett Bay. A trireme under Cn. Pomponius Falco during the war against the Mediterranean pirates in Cicero's time is hurled by a storm thro' the Pillars of Hercules & into the vast Atlanticus. At length it reaches a pleasant bay inhabited by copper-skinned barbarians, & after a treaty is drawn up, a town is built on the side of the pleasant hill named MUSOSICUM—as the settlers interpret the name Mooshasuck, which they hear from the barbarians. (Letter to L. D. Clark, cited in de Camp 244)

Lovecraft never wrote this story; however, it reveals that he was attempting to find ways to connect his beloved Rome with his New England home. Certainly, his many letters reveal a primary motivation in his thought which is echoed in his literature.

This letter was written just a year before he wrote "The Call of Cthulhu."

The Bacchanalia in Lovecraft's Library

Having seen the extent to which classical Roman fascinated Lovecraft, we now turn to his knowledge of Livy, the author of the classic account of the suppression of the Bacchanalia. It is clear that he was familiar with the Roman historian and his account of the foreign cult. This is evident from the books Lovecraft possessed in his personal library and how hints of the Bacchanalia of 186 B.C.E. can be discerned in a latter he wrote to a friend shortly after he wrote "The Call of Cthulhu." Although no complete catalogue of his library exists, since many of his books were scattered shortly after his death, according to S. T. Joshi's reconstruction (2002) of the remaining books of his library, it is certain that he possessed more than a dozen volumes on Roman history, almost a half a dozen historical fictions set in Rome, and numerous ancient Roman authors in translation and Latin.

The great historian Livy's account of the development of Roman civilization is at the heart of all histories of Republican Rome; and this is certainly the case for the books in Lovecraft's library. For instance, one of Lovecraft's books, *The Story of Rome, from Its Earliest Times to the End of the Republic* (1885; *LL* 355), by Cambridge professor Arthur Gilman, emphasizes the foreign nature of the cult and its capacity to damage Roman civilization: "Then the abominable worship of Bacchus came in, and thousands were corrupted and made vicious throughout Italy before the authorities were able to put a stop to the midnight orgies and crimes that daylight exposed" (124). Similarly, in another one of his books, Leonhard Schmitz's *A Manual of Ancient History* (1886; *LL* 762), it is noted that "it had been found necessary to prohibit the celebration of the Bacchic festivals (Bacchanalia), which had been introduced from Southern Italy and formed a focus for every vice and licentiousness" (340). This idea of "foreign" cult was reflected in the nineteenth-century British imperialist worldview. The highborn British establishment, from which many of the historians in Lovecraft's library arose, held a total contempt for foreigners. It is no secret that the British imperialist worldview, with which many of these historians agreed, held that foreigners mostly brought a degrading effect on high civilization. Indeed, Livy was suspicious of "the subjective superstition of foreign religions, which he repeatedly condemns for the mental illness or the bodily corruption which they cause" (Walsh 61). Echo of this is clear in these nineteenth-century historians.

Similarly, views of women in nineteenth-century historiography reflected common Victorian ideals. For example, according to another historian's work in Lovecraft's library, Henry George Liddell's *A History of Rome from the Earliest Times to the Establishment of the Empire* (1858–99; *LL* 532), it is argued that the cult of Bacchus was extremely dangerous because it targeted Roman women:

> A sure sign of corruption is to be found in the dissolute manners that were discovered among the women. In 186 B.C., the Consul Posthumius was accidentally informed that there were not only in Rome, but in many Italian towns, secret societies, in which young men and women were dedicated to Bacchus; and that, under the cloak of religious ceremony, every kind of license and debauchery was practiced. (449)

This view of the Bacchanalia was common in nineteenth- and early twentieth-century Roman historiography: it was foreign and feminized. And it is this image of the Bacchanalia that was transmitted to Lovecraft, as he understood the bifurcation of religious activity into legitimate rites and illegitimate cults.

Another history of Rome in Lovecraft's library was William Smith's *A Smaller History of Rome* (1889; *LL* 824). In it, Smith takes a slightly different view of the cult of Bacchus. It was introduced to Republican Rome because, in the second century B.C.E., "A love of luxury and the general depravity gradually spread through Italy" (154). The cult of Bacchus was for Smith a symptom of the decline of the Roman Republic rather than the one of the causes, as the other works in Lovecraft's possession maintained. The cult of Bacchus was

> A striking instance of the growing licentiousness of the times was brought to light in 186 B.C. It was discovered that the worship of Bacchus had been introduced from Southern Italy into and other

towns, and that secret societies were formed, which, under the cloak of worship, indulged in the most abominable vices. A stringent inquiry was made into these practices; and a decree of the senate was passed, forbidding the worship of Bacchus in Rome and throughout Italy. (154)

This is a somewhat more refined view of the cult; nevertheless, the cult was viewed as a corruption and degradation from pure Roman religion. Although the Roman magistrates were able to crush the cult before it could spread more widely, it was only a part of Rome's problems. Nevertheless, Smith still emphasizes the disruptive nature of the cult, "under the cloak of worship," which consisted, not of proper religious piety, but rather "the most abominable vices."

Lovecraft was an atheist who considered even Christianity to be a danger to all thinking people. As James Egan has commented, the whole of the so-called Cthulhu Mythos can be understood as "systematic, deliberate parodies of several aspects of Christian religious thought. . . . His penchant for satire and ridicule make Christianity a likely target in his fiction as surely it was in his correspondence" (362). But some Enlightenment critics of Christianity have seen a direct relationship between the bizarre rituals of the cult of Bacchus and later cults.

One of the most important representatives of this Enlightenment view was Edward Gibbon, the author of the most popular and influential book on the fall of Rome ever written. According to Gibbon's *Decline and Fall of the Roman Empire* (1776–88), a copy of which Lovecraft possessed in his library (*LL* 351), it was foreign cults like that of Bacchus, which he called "abhorrent mysteries," that paved the way for the rise of Christianity. Gibbon writes, "The Polytheists were disposed to adopt every article of faith, which seemed to offer any resemblance, however distant or imperfect, with the popular mythology; and the legends of Bacchus, of Hercules, and of Aesculapius, had, in some measure, prepared their imagination for the appearance of the Son of God under a human form" (2.211).

Lovecraft would certainly have agreed with Gibbon's assessment; so too with Gibbon's notion, which goes back to the Roman and then later Christianized view, that secret cults that went on at night should be considered the height of credulity and must be treated with contempt and suspicion. In fact, it is this fear that is at the heart of Lovecraft's construction of the Cthulhu cult. The Cthulhu cultists were primarily foreigners, but instead of comprising mainly of women, the "lesser sex" for male Roman patricians, but it consisted of people of darker skin, which Lovecraft considered to be inferior. It is possible Lovecraft could have gotten the broad outlines of the Cthulhu Cult from some of his several books on Roman history he possessed in his library; but Livy casts a long shadow in all subsequent histories of Rome. Thus, we turn now to a close reading of Lovecraft's cult scene in "The Call of Cthulhu" alongside Livy's account of the suppression of the Bacchanalia.

Indeed, Lovecraft was quite familiar with the Bacchanalia. Although not as common as his use of "eldritch" or "gibbous," Lovecraft uses the term "bacchanalian" or its variants quite often in his works. For example, in the tale "The Hound" (1922), this word is used to describe the ominous bats circling the graveyard: "Madness rides the star-wind . . . claws and teeth sharpened on centuries of corpses . . . dripping death astride a bacchanale of bats from nigh-black ruins of buried temples of Belial" (*D* 178). Also, in the story "The Temple" (1920) the ritual carvings appear to include participants of a deranged ritual: "In the centre yawns a great open door, reached by an impressive flight of steps, and surrounded by exquisite carvings like the figures of Bacchanals in relief" (*D* 9). And in "The Tomb" (1917), "One morning at breakfast I came close to disaster by declaiming in palpably liquourish accents an effusion of eighteenth-century Bacchanalian mirth" (*D* 6). So Lovecraft was certainly throwing "bacchanalia" around in his writing; as the word was also being thrown back at him. In 1924, just a few years before Lovecraft wrote "The Call of Cthulhu," his friend Samuel Loveman wrote a poem called "Bacchanale," which he dedicated to the Old Gent. Lovecraft said of the poem that it "has a certain fascination which I cannot define" (*Mysteries of Time and Spirit* 42). It is unclear why Loveman used that title for a dedication to Lovecraft, but the poem itself seems inspired by Euripides' play *The Bacchae*, with its references to Agave, Pentheus, and the Maenads (Loveman 74). Nevertheless, the choice of this title for Loveman's poem honoring

Lovecraft seems quite prophetic. The fascination Lovecraft held for
the poem may have been due to his underlying interest in the original account of the suppression of the Bacchanalia in Livy—the account that would lie at the heart of his crafting of the Cthulhu cult
scene in one of his best and best-known works.

Livy and Legrasse

While trying to reconstruct the books and stories that influenced
Lovecraft, it is important to say at the outset that much of that influence was subtle, latent, and perhaps even invisible to Lovecraft
himself. What is clear, however, is that his vast reading and erudi-
tion in a great number of topics from various sources underlie
much of his literary genius. What is to follow is a comparison between Livy and Lovecraft's constructions of aberrant cult activity. I
think it will become clear that the similarities between the two are
far deeper than coincidence, and could not have been simply
gleaned from the general knowledge he gained from historical sur-
veys of Republican Rome, as seen in books from his library. The
larger structure of the narrative of "The Tale of Inspector Legrasse"
as well as some points of detail can come only from the account of
the suppression of the Bacchanalia by Livy himself.[3]

Lovecraft knew Livy well. He possessed two copies of Livy's
History of Rome in his personal library: I. W. Bieber's *Selections
from the First Five Books* (1872), which does not contain the ac-
count of the Bacchanalia, and a complete copy of Livy's *History of
Rome* translated George Baker (1830) in two volumes (*LL* 538–
39), which does. Furthermore, in his essay "The Literature of
Rome," published in *Collected Essays* (2004), Lovecraft calls Livy
"The sole great prose writer of the Augustan aera." He also gives

---

3. As some scholars have noted, "It is very difficult to discern the actual facts in
the romanticized account in Livy." Martin P. Nilsson, "The Bacchic Mysteries of
the Roman Age," Harvard Theological Review 46 (1953): 175–202 (193). Other
scholars, such as P. G. Walsh, "Making a Drama out of a Crisis: Livy on the Bacchanalia," Greece and Rome 2nd Ser. 43 (1996): 188–203, have seen the account
in Livy to have some important seeds of fact. This will not concern us, since it is
the account in Livy that is the most important to forming a basis for HPL's story,
not the historicity of the event.

Livy credit as an historian who writes with the liveliness of fiction, even if he is a bit superstitious. Lovecraft writes, "The style of Livy is of utmost elegance, though as an historian he is marred by too great credulity in legends and unreliable authorities. His narrative flows along with the ease and liveliness of fiction, and makes reading of the most pleasing sort" (*CE* 2.28). It is not clear whether he is referring to the Latin original, which he does not seem to have owned, or one of the translations he had on his shelves. I suspect the latter, since the Baker translation is a relatively lively one, for its nineteenth-century origin.[4] All quotations of Livy are from the Baker translation.

"The Tale of Inspector Legrasse" describes the cult practices of the worshippers of Cthulhu in the Louisiana swamp country, and it is in this section that much of the information about the nature of the danger the cult poses for the world. This section has many parallels with Livy's account of the Bacchanalia. In both, the methods described to gain the information include eyewitness reports and testimony from adherents of the religion. The section begins with the inspector of Louisiana police showing up at the 1908 American Archaeological Society's annual conference in St. Louis with a strange statue he has acquired during a raid on a bizarre cult in the swamps south of New Orleans.

> The statuette, idol, fetish, or whatever it was, had been captured some months before in the wooded swamps south of New Orleans during a raid on a supposed voodoo meeting; and so singular and hideous were the rites connected with it, that the police could not but realise that they had stumbled on a dark cult totally unknown to them, and infinitely more diabolic than even the blackest of the African voodoo circles. Of its origin, apart from the erratic and unbelievable tales extorted from the captured members, absolutely nothing was to be discovered; hence the anxiety of the police for any antiquarian lore which might help

---

4. The ninth edition of the *Encyclopaedia Britannica* that HPL possessed, and which many scholars have noted he used slavishly in his stories—"The Horror at Red Hook," for instance—does not have an entry on the "Bacchanalia" and only alludes to the incident in its "Livy" essay. But the Roman Bacchanalia, as seen in Livy, is clearly an influence on HPL's "The Call of Cthulhu."

them to place the frightful symbol, and through it track down the
cult to its fountain-head. (*DH* 133)

At first, the cult is surrounded by great mystery, but it is clear
that it is very dangerous. The origin is not immediately known,
but the fact that it is a foreign cult, perhaps from Africa, is para-
mount. This quotation from the beginning of the section sets the
tone and summarizes what will come later. The use of color and
racial imagery permeate the account, like much of the racial categorization in many of Lovecraft's stories. In Livy, it is class, ethnic-
ity, and gender that are most pervasive, since these are the
categories that concerns him the most.

The story of Legrasse begins with a report by "squatters" from
the swamps and lagoon country from the south of New Orleans,
characterized as "mostly primitive but good-natured descendants
of Lafitte's men," who "were in the grip of stark terror from an
unknown thing which had stolen upon them in the night." The
threat is social, cultural, and cosmic. The reference to night rituals
seems common enough in literary accounts of "evil cults" during
Lovecraft's era. However, the next few sentences, when compared
to Livy, sound familiar:

> It was voodoo, apparently, but voodoo of a more terrible sort than
> they had ever known; and some of their women and children had
> disappeared since the malevolent tom-tom had begun its incessant
> beating far within the black haunted woods where no dweller ven-
> tured. There were insane shouts and harrowing screams, soul-
> chilling chants and dancing devil-flames; and, the frightened mes-
> senger added, the people could stand it no more. (*DH* 136)

For Livy, women and children are especially vulnerable in the
cult: "a great part of them are women, and this was the source of
the evil; the rest are males, but nearly resembling women, actors
and pathicks, in the vilest lewdness; night revellers, hurried on, by
wine, noise of instruments, and clamours, to a degree of mad en-
thusiasm" (39.15). Gender and class are two central constructs in
Roman social power, so the fact that women and men are on the
receiving end of sex acts by other men further punctuates the vile
nature of this cult for Roman aristocrats. Further, Livy's account

of the cult of Bacchus was of screams, drums, and flames in the night, which lead to the consul's conclusion that something needed to be none about the cult for the safety of the citizens of Rome: "Many of their audacious deeds were brought about by treachery, but most of them by force, and this force was concealed by loud shouting, and the noise of drums and cymbals, so that none of the cries uttered by the persons suffering violation or murder could be heard abroad" (39.8).

Instead of holding hearings in which witnesses come to them, as did the Roman consuls and senate, Lovecraft's tale has the police doing what they do best: go out to investigate the cult themselves, led by Inspector Legrasse. What they find is an exploration into prejudices of Lovecraft, similar to the classism, sexism, and homophobia of Livy, but in Lovecraft's case the practitioners of the cult are all seen through his usual lens of xenophobia and racism, revealing that constructing "cults" is a function of projecting one's prejudices on to whatever group is considered to be the Other. Note Livy's report on the nature of the nocturnal celebrants:

> [The] night encouraging licentious freedom, there was nothing wicked, nothing flagitious, that had not been practised among them. There were more frequent pollutions of men, with each other, than with women. If any showed an uncommon degree of reluctance, in submitting to dishonour, or of disinclination to the commission of vice, they were held as victims, and sacrificed. (39.13)

What was for Livy the danger of Greek effeminacy, homosexual acts, female leadership, and gender and class mixing was for Lovecraft a degenerate group of foreigners and racial inferiors who threaten to infect the larger mainstream culture. The critic Gavin Callaghan maintains that "The Call of Cthulhu" is the "supreme expression of Lovecraft's racist-paranoiac vision" (11). This is most certainly correct. While Legrasse and his men "plunged on unguided into black arcades of horror that none of them had ever trod before" (*DH* 137), Lovecraft was not only describing the darkness of the night, but also the skin of the residents of the region and that of the revelers. Lovecraft often describes them as people of mixed race. "The region now entered by the police was

one of traditionally evil repute, substantially unknown and un-
traversed by white men" (*DH* 137). Later in this section, he characterizes revelers as a "hybrid spawn" (*DH* 138), "men of a very
low, mixed-blooded, and mentally aberrant type. Most were sea-
men, and a sprinkling of Negroes and mulattoes, largely West Indians or Brava Portuguese from the Cape Verde Islands, gave a
colouring of voodooism to the heterogeneous cult" (*DH* 139).
Thus, though Livy and Lovecraft have their own racial, cultural,
social, and gender biases, they use them to the same effect: aberrant religions come from "lesser" people who threaten to bring
high civilization into decline or death. Thus, Lovecraft simply
translates the Roman aristocratic Other to the early twentieth-
century white New England aristocratic Other. Both feared the
corrupting influences of foreigners.

As the account of the Cthulhu cult continues, the parallels between Livy and Lovecraft become more obvious. Livy describes a
Greek mystery cult that intrudes on Roman social norms and dis-
rupts the religion of their ancestors. Livy's account of the Bacchanalia states that the cult arose from a foreigner, a "Greek of mean
condition," who is a "low operator in sacrifices," who came to
Rome as "a teacher in secret mysteries" (39.8). The emphasis on
class and secrecy permeates the account, as does the idea that the
cult is a growing menace to the social and moral order of the state.
The cult grows steadily like an infection, "like that of a pestilence"
(39.9), first to a few, but then "communicated to great numbers,
both men and women" (39.8). The following is Livy's summary of
the main crimes (civil, religious and moral) perpetuated by the
worshippers of Bacchus:

> To their religious performances were added the pleasures of wine
> and feasting, to allure the greater number of proselytes. When
> wine, lascivious discourse, night, and the mingling of sexes had
> extinguished every sentiment of modesty, then debaucheries of
> every kind began to be practised, as every person found at hand
> that sort of enjoyment to which he was disposed by the passion
> most prevalent in his nature. Nor were they confined to one spe-
> cies of vice, the promiscuous intercourse of free-born men and of
> women; but from this store-house of villainy proceeded false wit-

nesses, counterfeit seals, false evidences, and pretended discoveries. In the same place, too, were perpetrated secret murders; so that, in some cases, even the bodies could not even be found for burial. (39.8)

Lovecraft's Cthulhu cult is a mystery religion of sorts, much like the cult of the god Bacchus, and both Livy's and Lovecraft's deviant cults conduct human sacrifice. In Livy, the celebrants of Bacchus perpetrated secret murders so that, in some cases, even the bodies of the victims could not be found for burial. In Lovecraft, bodies were also disappearing in the ritual murders (*DH* 136). The reason for the disappearance of citizens is the same for both: the sacrificed are being taken away by the "gods" and devoured. For Livy, "men were carried off by the gods, when, after being fettered, they were dragged into secret caves" (39.8). Lovecraft also mentions a terrible but powerful figure who took the human sacrifice: "All denied a part in the ritual murders, and averred that the killing had been done by Black Winged Ones which had come to them from their immemorial meeting-place in the haunted wood" (*DH* 140). This is perhaps one of the most telling parallels: Both Livy and Lovecraft tell of dark and mysterious figures taking human victims off to be devoured.

Lovecraft seldom makes any allusions to sex in his writings. He rarely even has a woman in his stories at all. However, the account of Inspector Legrasse contains a very unusual reference, though veiled, to the practice of ritual sex during the cult of Cthulhu—another direct connection between the two works. Lovecraft describes what Legrasse and his men witnessed. "Animal fury and orgiastic license here whipped themselves to daemoniac heights by howls and squawking ecstasies that tore and reverberated through those nighted woods like pestilential tempests from the gulfs of hell" (*DH* 137). Livy's account is makes explicit references to sex acts between men and women and between men and men. Lovecraft is not so blunt. In his description of the revelers, he then makes the second of his few not too subtle hints that sexuality was part of the cult of Cthulhu: "It was inside this circle that the ring of worshippers jumped and roared, the general direction of the mass motion being from left to right in endless Bacchanal between the ring of bodies and the ring of fire" (*DH* 138). He had already mentioned that the revelers were "void of clothing." Livy's revelers are naked and drunk. Although allusion to wine is absent from Lovecraft's cult, the sexual aspect of Livy's account clearly shines through. There is also a possible wink and a nod to Livy when he characterizes the Cthulhu cult as an "endless Bacchanal."

Details about both Livy's and Lovecraft's cults are revealed by interrogating alleged cultists. In Livy, several captured initiates testified before consuls and senators; in Lovecraft, detectives gain information through inquisition also. Moreover, the apprehended cultists for both accounts are reluctant to release any information for fear their gods may punish them. For the main source of information of the Bacchanalia in Livy's account, the fear of divine retribution was what kept the main informant Hispala reluctant to divulge cult secrets: "she stood in great dread of the gods, whose secret mysteries she was to divulge; and also of men, who, should she be seized as an informer, would certainly put her to death" (39.12). Hispalia also feared for her life if she did not provide the information to the Roman official Postumius. However, he ensured her safety if she provided information (39.13). For Lovecraft, fear of punishment is also clear. When Castro was compelled through enhanced interrogation techniques to reveal more "Meanwhile no more must be told. There was a secret which even torture could not extract" (*DH* 139).

Another telling parallel between Livy and Lovecraft is the philosophy espoused by the cultists, which is the notion that their members are above the law. The Bacchanalian cultists of Rome were accused of violating the purest of Roman values, preaching "personal defilements, or murders, or were stained with the guilt of false evidence, counterfeit seals, forged wills." Moreover, they felt themselves immune to the laws of the state. "To think nothing unlawful was the grand maxim of their religion" (Livy 39.13). Similarly, Lovecraft's cult is promised by their god Cthulhu to live their lives in moral turpitude and in disregard to the laws of the land:

> The time would be easy to know, for then mankind would have become as the Great Old Ones; free and wild and beyond good and evil, with laws and morals thrown aside and all men shouting

and killing and revelling in joy. Then the liberated Old Ones would teach them new ways to shout and kill and revel and enjoy themselves, and all the earth would flame with a holocaust of ecstasy and freedom. (*DH* 141)

For both accounts, there is a sense that the cult is spreading and it is a great threat to the society. Residual fears remain for both. Both Livy and Lovecraft leave a sense of heightened fear that the authorities must remain vigilant in order to ensure the cult does not continue. In Rome, Livy expresses the sense of fear that permeated society well after the event had been so severely repressed. Livy portrays the Roman consul emphasizing the magnitude of the threat: "never was there in the state an evil of so great magnitude, or one that extended to so many persons, and comprehended so many acts of wickedness." The initiates into the Bacchanalia perpetuate all sorts of fraud and violence on private citizens of Rome, but soon the Roman state will be at risk of being taken over by the cultists.

> The impious assembly, at present, confines itself to outrages on private citizens; because it has not yet acquired force sufficient to crush the commonwealth: but the evil increases and spreads daily; it is already too great to find employment among the private ranks of life, and aims its views at the body of the state. Unless you take timely precautions, Romans, their nightly assembly may become as large as this, held in open day, and legally summoned by a consul. At this present moment, they dread your collected body; but, in a short time, when you shall have separated, and retired to your several dwellings, they will again come together. They will hold a consultation on the means of their own safety, and, at the same time, of your destruction. Thus united, they will cause terror to every one. You, therefore, ought to pray, that all your kindred may have behaved with wisdom and prudence; and if lust, if madness, has dragged any of them into that abyss, to consider such a person as the relation of those with whom he conspired for the perpetration of every wickedness, and not as one of your own. (Livy 39.16)

Overrun by effeminate and irrational people inspired by a foreign dangerous god, the only course for Roman citizens is to stamp out the cult of Bacchus as quickly and severely as possible. For the consuls, this cult was not a religion in the traditional Roman sense, but a social and political threat. Romans feared the cult might usurp social control and moral order from their great civilization, destroying traditional Roman values. It was a false piety for Livy: "When the authority of the gods is held out, as a pretext, to cover vice, we become fearful, lest, in punishing the crimes of men, we may violate some divine right connected therewith" (39.16). This dread is echoed in Lovecraft, tinged with his characteristic cosmic fear:

> This was that cult, and the prisoners said it had always existed and always would exist, hidden in distant wastes and dark places all over the world until the time when the great priest Cthulhu, from his dark house in the mighty city of R'lyeh under the waters, should rise and bring the earth again beneath his sway. Some day he would call, when the stars were ready, and the secret cult would always be waiting to liberate him. (*DH* 139)

In the end, both stories show that the most dangerous leaders of the cult are either put to death or imprisoned. For Livy, some of the cultists were executed, others imprisoned. The Senate then posted a reward for information leading to the arrest of the leaders of the cult, and several prominent citizens were arrested and confessed their guilt (39.17). Then, trials were conducted in the towns. Simple initiates who did not themselves perpetuate any grievous acts were thrown in Roman prisons. Many were executed:

> But those who had forcibly committed personal defilements, or murders, or were stained with the guilt of false evidence, counterfeit seals, forged wills, or other frauds, all these they punished with death. A greater number were executed than thrown into prison; indeed, the multitude of men and women who suffered in both ways, was very considerable. (39.18)

Their altars and statues were demolished, the cult was effectively outlawed in its present form, and the original informants were all rewarded with money and higher social status (Livy 39.19). Similarly, Lovecraft's cultists were dealt with swiftly and harshly: "Only two of the prisoners were found sane enough to be hanged, and the rest were committed to various institutions" (*DH*

139–40). Not only were the people involved in both accounts eliminated from society, but both accounts stress the destruction of cultic sites. For Livy, statues and cult sites of the Bacchanalia are systematically destroyed. For Lovecraft, "The image on the monolith, of course, was carefully removed and carried back by Legrasse" (*DH* 140). Both accounts conclude with a sense that, though the cult has been eradicated for now, steps need to be taken no be sure that they do not come back. A real sense of fear permeates both accounts, since they both portray times when their civilizations were in danger of being transformed—ruined by degenerate cultists who bring a horrific teaching into their midst.

Roman Dream

The view of subversive secret cults in Livy must have made an impression on Lovecraft, who had such a fondness for the standard practices of the refined, conservative, upper-class Roman. In fact, we can see this similar view of foreign secretive cults in his "Roman dream," which was from letters he wrote to Donald Wandrei and others shortly after completing "The Call of Cthulhu." In fact, the best way to understand the way Lovecraft fashioned the cult scene in "The Tale of Inspector Legrasse" from "The Call of Cthulhu" is by a close reading of the letter he wrote to Wandrei in November 3, 1927, which would later be edited and published as the short story "The Very Old Folk," alongside this comparison between Lovecraft and Livy.

When Lovecraft submitted the manuscript of "The Call of Cthulhu" to Farnsworth Wright, editor of *Weird Tales*, in October 1926, it was rejected. This was devastating to Lovecraft. By this time, he had sparked up a friendship with Wandrei, who was well connected with Wright. Lovecraft shared "The Call of Cthulhu" with Wandrei, who loved it, and subsequently hand delivered the manuscript to Wright for reconsideration. Wright accepted "The Call of Cthulhu" in July 1927 (*SL* 2.149), and a few months later Lovecraft wrote a letter to Wandrei wherein he recounts, or constructs, a vivid dream he had where he was a Roman governor of the town of Pompelo, Spain, who is called to hear testimony from soldiers who become concerned about a group of "very old folk" who are conducting bizarre rituals, including sacrifice, using drums, conducted by people of what the Roman magistrates consider to be low intelligence, and a number of other elements reminiscent of what he wrote in "The Call of Cthulhu."

Lovecraft writes, "It appeared that I was a provincial quæstor named L. Cælius Rufus, and that I had been summoned by the proconsul, P. Scribonius Libo, who had come from Tarraco some days before." Lovecraft's dream was also set in Spain, in "the tiny provincial town of Pompelo, at the foot of the Pyrenees in Hispania Citerior" (*Mysteries of Time and Spirit* 177). Livy mentions a Lucius Scribonius Libo in a list of commissioners that a "city prætor, constituted . . . for conducting colonists thither [Spain]" (39.23). There is a possibility that P. Scribonius Libo is modeled on a character in the novel *The Bloody Poet* (1927) by Dezsö Kosztolányi (*LL* 507) who is named Rufus Scribonius Proculor. The character Scribonius Curio also appears in the novel, by William Sterns Davis called *A Friend of Caesar* (1900; *LL* 225). Also, Balbutius and Cina, who both appear as fellow Romans in Lovecraft's dream, are named as characters in Kosztolányi's book. There is little doubt that Lovecraft's imagination was filled with scenes, structures, and characters from the many books he read.

The dream is set sometime in the Late Republic. It is not clear when, but it is clearly after the Bacchanalia suppression in 186 B.C.E., since the *Senatus Consultum de Bacchanalibus* is cited as justification to persecute the cult. Lovecraft even acknowledges that, after he awoke, his role in the dream reminded him of that of the proconsul Aulus Postumius, who prosecuted the revelers of the Roman Bacchanalia. Lovecraft remembers, "A. Postumius being consul, had executed so many Roman citizens for the practice of the Bacchanalia matter kept ever in memory by the *Senatus Consultum de Bacchanalibus*, graven upon bronze and set open to every eye" (*Mysteries of Time and Spirit* 180). Furthermore, the letter to Wandrei discussed above spells Postumius without the *h*, as it is spelled in his copy of Livy. The other history texts he owned, the Liddell book for instance, spells the name Post*h*umius. Therefore, Lovecraft follows the spelling in the Baker translation of Livy rather than in the other book he owned that referenced him. This clearly letter shows Lovecraft's familiarity with Livy's Bacchanalian affair, as well as with the *Senatus Consultum de Bacchanalibus* inscription. Furthermore, the fact that Lovecraft had this dream and shared it with Wandrei shortly after Farnsworth Wright accepted "The Call of Cthulhu" for *Weird Tales* after Wandrei's prodding may be of greater significance than even Lovecraft realized. Both the "Roman dream" and "The Call of Cthulhu" have elements of Livy's account of the Bacchanalia resting just below the surface. Could it be that Lovecraft realized his debt to Livy in his creation of the Cthulhu cult and expressed it through this account of his dream?

This we may never know. Nevertheless, it is clear that there are many parallels between Lovecraft's story about the Cthulhu cultists in "The Call of Cthulhu" and Livy's account of the cult and Roman government's treatment of the worshippers of Bacchus. Though not literally taken from Livy, as Lovecraft did for his account of the satanic rituals in "The Horror at Red Hook," which was lifted from the *Encyclopaedia Britannica*, the whole structure of Lovecraft's narrative is similar in that the account was obtained through interrogation of participants. The significance of this dependence upon Livy's and subsequent Roman historians account of the Bacchanalia on "The Call of Cthulhu," one of Lovecraft's most important works in the formation of the so-called "Cthulhu Mythos," rests in two main areas: 1) how subsequent Cthulhu ritual scenes are constructed in later literature; and 2) how religions, based on the Cthulhu Mythos, use the creation as a ritual model. In both, we can see a direct link back generally to Roman fears about foreign cults, and in particular Livy's account of the cult of Bacchus, which has, at its core, at least a kernel of truth about actual practices on the ancient religion.

Gruesome Passages

It is interesting that Lovecraft makes no mention of Livy's account of the Bacchanalia in his "Supernatural Horror in Literature" (1927; revised 1933–35). Lovecraft acknowledged Roman literature as the source for other modern weird tales. For example, he points to the influence of "the werewolf incident in Petronius, the gruesome passages in Apuleius, the brief but celebrated letter of Pliny the

Younger to Sura, and the odd compilation *On Wonderful Events* by the Emperor Hadrian's Greek freedman, Phlegon" (*Supernatural* 25). The documentary nature of "The Call of Cthulhu" and its attempt to be a true account seems to be the key to understanding this lacuna. Since Lovecraft wanted this story to sound like an historical account, it seems only logical that he would have drawn from one of the most respected Roman historians. He fully acknowledged the importance of ancient literature as an influence of one of his favorite authors, Lord Dunsany, whom he imitated in many early tales and who continued to cast a long shadow on his overall corpus. And for Dunsany, Lovecraft maintains that "His system of original personal and place names [were] drawn from classical" and other sources, and is "a marvel of versatile inventiveness and poetic discrimination" (*Supernatural* 67–68). The same can be said for Lovecraft. The more we peer into his letters, fiction, and even his dreams we may discover that his "ineluctable connection with the ancient *Respublica*" had become greater than Lovecraft himself ever realized.

Appendix

Select Lovecraft Books on Rome, from S. T. Joshi, *Lovecraft's Library: A Catalogue* (New York: Hippocampus Press, 2002). References are to item number.

1. Historical Works

Andrews, Ethan Allen. *A Copious and Critical Latin-English Lexicon.* New York: Harper & Brothers, 1854 (*LL* 28)

Apuleius, Lucius. *The Golden Asse of Lucius Apuleius.* Trans. William Adlington. London: Chapman & Dodd, 1898 (1566). (*LL* 37)

Baird, James S. S. *The Classical Manual: An Epitome of Ancient Geography, Greek and Roman Mythology, Antiquities, and Chronology.* New York: Sheldon & Co., 1871. (*LL* 59)

Caesar, C. Julius. *Commentaries on the Civil War.* Trans. Unknown. New York: Hinds & Noble, n.d. (*LL* 146)

———. *Caesar's Commentaries.* Interlinear translation by James Hamilton et al. Philadelphia: D. McKay, 19—. (*LL* 147)

———. *Commentaries of Caesar on the Gallic Wars*. Interlinear translation by unknown. New York: Hinds & Co., 1893 (?). (*LL* 148)

Church, Alfred J. *Stories from Livy*. New York: Dodd, Mead, 1883. (*LL* 173)

Cicero, M. Tullius. *Select Orations*. Interlinear trans. By Thomas Clark. Philadelphia: D. McKay, 1870 (1861). (*LL* 174)

Corte, Matteo della. *Pompeii: The New Excavations (Houses and Inhabitants)*. Valle de Pompeii: Tip. De F. Sicignano, 1927. (*LL* 197)

Creighton, Mandell. *History of Rome*. New York: American Book Co., 19——. (*LL* 210)

Gibbon, Edward. *The History of the Decline and Fall of the Roman Empire*. With Notes by the Rev. H. H. Milman. New York: A. L. Burt, 1845. 5 vols. (*LL* 351)

———. *A Student's Gibbon: The History of the Decline and Fall of the Roman Empire*. Abridged, Incorporating the Researches of Recent Commentators, by William Smith. New York: Harper & Brothers, 1864. (*LL* 352)

Gilman, Author. *The Story of Rome, from Its Earliest times to the End of the Republic*. New York: G. P. Putnam's Sons, 1885. (*LL* 355)

Liddell, Henry George. *A History of Rome from the Earliest Times to the Establishment of the Empire*. New York: Harper Brothers, 1858–99. (*LL* 532)

Livy. *Selections from the First Five Books, Together with the Twenty-first and the Twenty-second Books Entire*. With an Interlinear translation . . . By I. W. Bieber. Philadelphia: D. McKay, 1872. (*LL* 538)

———. *The History of Rome*. Translated from the Original, with Notes and Illustrations, by George Baker. London: Johns & Co., 1830. 2 vols. (*LL* 539)

Lohr, Friedrich. *A Day in the Life of Rome: Being a Revision of Lohr's Aus den Alten Rom, with Numerous Illustrations by Edgar S. Shumway*. New York: Chautauqua Press, 1885. (*LL* 542)

Myers, Philip Van Ness. *Ancient History*. <1904> Uncertain edition. (*LL* 635)

Osborn, Edward Bolland. *The Heritage of Greece and Rome*. New York: George H. Doran, 1924 or 1925. (*LL* 656)

Pellisson, Maurice. *Roman Life in Pliny's Time*. Translated from the French by Maud Wilkinson. With an Introduction by Frank

Justus Miller. Meadville, PA: Flood & Vincent, 1897. (*LL* 681)

Schmitz, Leonhard. *A Manual of Ancient History, from the Remotest Times to the Overthrow of the Western Empire, A.D. 476*. New York: Sheldon & Co., 1868.(*LL* 762)

Sewell, Elizabeth M. *The Child's First History of Rome*. New York: D. Appleton & Co., 1883. (*LL* 783)

Smith, Sir William. *A Smaller History of Rome, from its Earliest Times to the Establishment of Empire*. With a Continuation to A.D. 476 by Eugene Lawrence. New York: Harper & Brothers, 1889. (*LL* 824)

Steele, Joel Dorman. *Brief History of Rome: With Select Readings from Standard Authors*. New York: American Book Co., 1885. (*LL* 841)

Suetonius. *Lives of the Caesars*. Unknown edition, probably English translation. (*LL* 855)

2. *Historical Fiction*

Davis, William Sterns. *A Friend of Caesar: A Tale of the Fall of the Roman Republic, 50–47 B.C.* New York: Macmillan, 1900. (*LL* 225)

Kosztolányi, Dezsö. *The Bloody Poet: A Novel about Nero*. By Desider Kostolanyi. With a Prefatory Letter by Thomas Mann. Translated out of the German by Clifton P. Fadiman. New York: Macy-Masius, 1929. (*LL* 507)

Macaulay, Thomas Babington. *Lays of Ancient Rome; with Ivry and The Armada*. Illustrated by J. R. Weguelin. New York: Bay View Publishing Co., n.d. (*LL* 560)

White, Edward Lucas. *Andivius Hedulio: Adventures of a Roman Nobleman in the Days of the Empire*. New York: E. P. Dutton, 1923. (*LL* 924)

Works Cited

Callaghan, Gavin. "The Occult Lovecraft," *Fate* 60, No. 8 (2007): 10–21.

Cannon, Peter. *H. P. Lovecraft*. Boston: Twayne, 1989.

de Camp, L. Sprague. *Lovecraft: A Biography*. Garden City, NY: Doubleday, 1975.

Eckhardt, Jason C. "Cthulhu's Scald: Lovecraft and the Nordic Tradition." *Lovecraft Studies* No. 8 (Spring 1984): 25–29.

Egan, James. "Dark Apocalyptic: Lovecraft's Cthulhu Mythos as a Parody of Traditional Christianity." *Extrapolation* 23 (Spring 1983): 362–76.

Joshi, S. T. "Attis and Cybele: A Translation of Catullus 63." *Crypt of Cthulhu* No. 72 (Roodmas 1990): 6–8.

———. *H. P. Lovecraft: The Decline of the West*. 1990. Berkeley Heights, NJ: Wildside Press, 2000.

———. "H. P. Lovecraft and *The Dream-Quest of Unknown Kadath*." *Crypt of Cthulhu* No. 37 (Candlemas 1986): 25–34.

———. *H. P. Lovecraft: A Life*. West Warwick, RI: Necronomicon Press, 1996.

Joshi, S. T., and David E. Schultz. *An H. P. Lovecraft Encyclopedia*. 2001. New York: Hippocampus Press; 2004.

Lactantius. *Divinae Institutiones et Epitome Divinarum Institutionum*. In *Lactantius Firmianus: Opera Omnia*. Ed. S. Brandt and Georg Laubmann. Vienna: Corpus Scriptorum Ecclesiasticorum Latinorum 19, 1890.

Lovecraft, H. P. *The Annotated Supernatural Horror in Literature*. Ed. S. T. Joshi. New York: Hippocampus Press, 2000.

———. *The Call of Cthulhu and Other Weird Stories*. Ed. S. T. Joshi. New York: Penguin, 1999.

———. *Mysteries of Time and Spirit: The Letters of H. P. Lovecraft and Donald Wandrei*. Ed. S. T. Joshi and David E. Schultz. San Francisco: Night Shade, 2002.

Loveman, Samuel. *The Hermaphrodite and Other Poems*. Caldwell, OH: Caxton Printers, 1936.

Mather, Cotton. *Magnalia Christi Americana*. 1702. Hartford: Silas Andrus & Son, 1955.

Mather, Increase. *Cases of Conscience concerning Evil Spirits Personating Men*. Boston: Benjamin Harris, 1693.

Walsh, P. G. *Livy: His Historical Aims and Methods*. Cambridge: Cambridge University Press, 1967.

Wetzel, George T. "Notes on the Cthulhu Mythos." In *The Shuttered Room and Other Pieces* by H. P. Lovecraft and Divers Hands. Ed. August Derleth. Sauk City, WI: Arkham House, 1959. 278–86.

Wilk, Stephen R. *Medusa: Solving the Mystery of the Gorgon*. Oxford: Oxford University Press, 2000.

Wright, Thomas Goddard. *Literary Culture in Early New England, 1620–1730*. New Haven, CT: Yale University Press, 1920.

"Cool Air," the Apartment Above Us, and Other Stories

Robert H. Waugh

"Cool Air" is not a story that has the metaphoric virtues of Love-craft's early works such as "The Outsider" or "The Picture in the House." It is a sober story, and so since it is a later work it avoids their excesses, the hyperbolic style that we find in them and such other works as "Herbert West—Reanimator" or "The Hound." But it has none of the expansive quality we find in "The Call of Cthulhu," "The Dunwich Horror," or "The Shadow over Innsmouth." It falls between the stools; it is neither this nor that, it is purely what it is, and so it has few exponents.[1] I have not been one of them, so it is only now, after avoiding it for these many years, that I have decided to have a close look at it. This essay is something of an apology to an accomplished, cool story; in any case, we see immediately that, though it may be a minor virtue of the story, the story is now more relevant than it once was as we read thinking of cryogenics and the possible fate of a deliquesced Walt Disney. But this is as much to say that the story is one of Lovecraft's first experiments in moving the weird tale into the broad genre of science fiction; there is a touch of the old style, worthy of "The Hound," in such broad assertions that "fiendish things were in the air" (*DH* 206), but later that summer he was to write "The Call of Cthulhu" in which his transformation of the genre was complete.

---

1. S. T. Joshi, however, believes it to be "Lovecraft's most successful evocation of the horror to be found in [...] America's only true megalopolis" (391), though to describe it as the best of Lovecraft's New York stories is perhaps to damn with faint praise.

In looking at the story I have various goals in mind. I wish to look at the story itself, in and of itself, but I also wish to look at it as an example of a story with a particular kind of setting such as we find in "The Picture in the House," "The Music of Erich Zann," and "Dreams in the Witch House" and that we find also in Thomas Pynchon's story "Entropy." Simply put, these stories present a contrast in a house between a lower story where daily life proceeds merely as daily life does and an upper story where life proceeds in a very different fashion that we may call archetypal or ideal, depending upon our preference for language. Two different atmospheres, different in vertical orientation and different in narrative concerns, are at work in these stories.

I

> [. . .] the parching Air
> Burns frore, and cold performs th'effect of Fire.
> (Milton, *Paradise Lost* 2.594–95)

These stories complicate the pattern of Lovecraft's own experience, who enjoyed the library of his beloved grandfather but especially that part of the library banished to the attic where the young boy found the classics of the eighteenth century which were to have such a profound influence upon his own style (*SL* 3.407–8). This is the same pattern we see in such stories as *The Princess and the Goblin* or *Lilith* by George MacDonald. In each of them the protagonist discovers that the upper stories of the homes where they take place have contact with or are filled by divine powers. In the first work the Princess finds that her grandmother lives in the top of the tower, but this is a grandmother that more than the typical fairy godmother resembles the goddess Isis, in whose robes "stellae dispersae coruscebant, earumque media semestris luna flammeos spirabat ignes" [the scattered stars shone and in their midst the half-moon breathed out flames of fire] (Apuleius 11.4), fused with the figure of the Shekinah, the Wisdom that was with God in the creation, often understood as a type of the Holy Spirit (Prov. 8:22–31); this grandmother has cosmic affinities that mean good by her granddaughter. Her bedroom is open to the moon and stars and her bath is full of healing (111–17). The garret in *Lilith* is more complex. Early in the book the terrified narrator compares it to a brain that is much larger than the house upon which it rests (16); and through a mirror it gives access to a landscape in which the main narrative of the novel is played out in an even more pointed fashion than *The Princess and the Goblin*, returning to origins in the figures of Adam and Eve and Lilith. In both cases the narrow smallness of daily life is contrasted to a life that is more spacious and significant, binding together the present and the past; the upper story offers a spiritual adventure in which such figures as the archetypal old wise woman find a place. This pattern is of course transformed in "Cool Air."

With these comments as a background let us consider a preliminary analysis of the story "Cool Air." It begins very quietly with an unnamed narrator addressing an unknown friend: "You ask me to explain [. . .] why I shiver more than others upon entering a cold room" (*DH* 199). In his account the exterior setting engages us first. As the last of Lovecraft's stories set in New York this story has a certain distance that the others do not and thereby achieves a greater realism. It is not simply that he has taken as its setting the brownstone on West 14th Street where his friend George Kirk lived and thus achieves a certain typicality (Joshi 390–91). Most striking I think is that the time within the story is objective; the climax in which Dr. Muñoz's ammonia cooler fails him takes place in October, not in the height of summer as we might expect. The time has no symbolic significance at all; it is such a time as one would find in the city, profane and indifferent. At least so it seems, though October in the midst of fall points ahead to the deep cold of winter.

Another aspect of this realism is Lovecraft's handling of his racist understanding of the city. The abhorrence expressed in "The Horror of Red Hook" is here nuanced. Though the landlady Mrs. Herrero is introduced as "a slatternly, almost bearded Spanish woman" she figures in the story as a sympathetic character who expresses concern for her tenants; and though the other lodgers are introduced as "mostly Spaniards a little above the coarsest and crudest grade" (*DH* 200), they are not at all threatening and the description has no bite to it, despite the grudging phrase "a little above." As for Dr. Muñoz, though the narrator confesses, "I shivered as I crossed the threshold into a large apartment" (*DH* 201), he treats the man with the utmost respect and sympathy, "a man of birth, cultivation, and discrimination" (*DH* 201), a man "of striking intelligence and superior blood and breeding" (*DH* 202). The racist epithets do not carry a great pejorative charge here. The worst character, whose race the narrator never identifies, is the "seedy-looking loafer" (*DH* 206) whom the narrator hires to provide the doctor with the ice in his emergency; but the man understandably flees "screaming and mad-eyed" when he sees the results of Dr. Muñoz's disintegration (*DH* 206). As a part of this subdued style the narrator offhandedly comments that the "hot water is not too often cold," a remark that shall be important later (*DH* 200). No one in the story is a monster unless it be the doctor himself, caught up in his project to live forever and mired at last in his disintegration.

More charged in the story is the contrast between the interior of the house, especially the interior that the doctor has created for himself, and the outside world. Outside is "the clangour of a metropolis" (*DH* 199). The apartment house itself is quiet, despite "the din of street cars" which "proved a serious annoyance" (*DH* 200). At the conclusion the narrator insists upon "the clatter of cars and motor trucks ascending clamorously from crowded Fourteenth Street" (*DH* 207), a hot scene that contrasts tellingly to the cold death in the doctor's room. The narrator intends to "hibernate" in the apartment house (*DH* 200). The verb is well chosen, since hibernation is not simply a sleep during the winter but a turning down of the activity of the organs to achieve a lower metabolism, an action that Dr. Muñoz has pursued in an extreme fashion. Both men exist in opposition to the world outside, a world of loud, vainglorious motion, that nevertheless the narrator must appeal to; and thus the opposition between the inside and the outside is not clear-cut.

Three more details about the doctor need to be observed. He wears "a pince-nez shield" (*DH* 202) that shields his eyes from the outside world; visually like the narrator aurally the doctor cannot bear the glare of the outside world. The phrase, however, might suggest an aggressive shield that he uses in his war against mortality, for he is "the bitterest of sworn enemies to death" (*DH* 202), one who must in the climax of the story "hurl defiance at the death-daemon" (*DH* 205). He is not, however, as far as we can observe, on the offensive, for in the last pages of the story—nay, for the last eighteen years—he conducts a hopeless siege in a body that has already been breached. One step in his disintegration occurs when "a spasm caused him to clap his hands to his eyes and rush into the bathroom" (*DH* 205); the narrator never sees his eyes again, for the shield has been useless. Furthermore, the better the narrator has come to know him the clearer it is that the doctor has no heart or at least no heart beat; he jests that he will "someday teach [the narrator] to live [. . .] without any heart at all" (*DH* 203). Yet he does have a heart insofar as he sympathizes with the narrator and with other people who have been injured, like the plumber. But he cannot help himself; though he believes he must be as emotionless as possible, as cold as possible, to stop the advance of his death, he rages at his fate (*DH* 204–5); and his rage infects the narrator with a rage also (*DH* 206). The doctor cannot die a Stoic death. The most remarkable aspect of the complex we are describing is the baths he takes. "All day," Mrs Herrero reports, "he take funnee-smelling baths, and he cannot get excite or warm" (*DH* 200). It reaches the point that the baths are "incessant" (*DH* 204). Given his demand for a cold apartment, we suspect that these baths are cold indeed. The implication seems to be, given his use of spices, incense, and "pungent chemicals" (*DH* 204), that the baths form part of his hygiene to preserve his body, but we cannot escape the suggestion that he is possessed of a terrifying rage for purity. This detail may indicate a racist environment in the story which at our first reading we missed. Would the doctor have found an excuse for attending the ancient auto da fés in Spain? But there is more to his purity which we shall explore shortly.

It may be important to note that the doctor does not stand alone in his efforts, for a certain Dr. Torres had shared his experiments, nursed him through his significant illness some eighteen years earlier, and died because of his efforts (*DH* 203); the truth of the matter is that Dr. Muñoz had himself died at that time. Is Dr. Torres, then, simply an alter ego of the doctor, a man's story in which the doctor's story is truly revealed? His name means "tower" and points at the verticality that is so basic to this story and the others we shall examine. The name Muñoz, a name borne by many Spaniards,[2] means "son of Muño (a hill) or of Nuño (ninth)" ("MUÑOZ—Name Meaning & Origin"). There is some uncertainty here; and I should note that in investigating various Spanish dictionaries I found nothing to support this assertion of the web site. I am no scholar in Spanish philology (and Lovecraft was not either), so I cannot decide the matter; but the name may be related to the Latin *mons*, which means "mountain" and is related to such words as *eminere* (to rise out), *prominere* (to stand out), and *minax* (threatening) and is cognate to the Breton word *menez* (mountain) (Pokorny 1.726). It seems then likely that both Torres and Muñoz are words that point at the verticality so important to the story, the aspiration to be above the merely human.

Finally, in these preliminary remarks, I want to emphasize a detail at the end of the story in which the narrator describes the "awful, blind hand" with which the doctor in his fatal deliquescence attempts to write the reason for his death. The radical mixed metaphor of the phrase "blind hand" (*DH* 207) may be reminiscent of Milton's phrase "blind mouths" in his attack upon the ignorant, shallow greed of the Anglican clergy ("Lycidas" 119). The hand in Lovecraft's phrase refers to the script in the doctor's note, a script that fails to communicate because of the condition of man's physical hand, which may be taken as a synecdoche for his body, for that hand has become a claw not capable of easily dealing with the business of manipulating the pencil (*DH* 207), and his blind body was blind, senseless, from its birth. The word *blind* refers literally to the doctor's loss of sight as he dies, but it also refers to the condition of the script, which is smeared, scrawled, and nauseous. Twice the narrator says that it is a piece of paper "hideously smeared" or "stickily smeared" (*DH* 207). There is some irony in the word "smear," since it originally referred to an anointing with oil in order to bless (*OED* "Smear");

2. Luis Muñoz Rivera was an important Puerta Rican politician, "largely responsible for the Jones Act (signed March 4, 1917), granting U.S. citizenship to Puerto Ricans" ("Luis Muñoz Rivera"). I think it possible that this man was the source of the name, though the name was popular at the time.

now the oil is simply the mess that remains of the body in its death, devoid of all sacrality. The word "scrawl" is related to "crawl," in both cases related to the inability to move the pencil across the page and to the degradation of the man. Two very similar phrases in the last two paragraphs, "nauseous words" and "noisome scrawl," once more refer to the physical state of the body, its smell, but each also refers to the moral state of the man who attempted to evade death.

A tacit contrast to this decrepitude of the hand lies in the cool air that early in the story "creeps" (*DH* 199), later "rushes" (*DH* 201), and then "blasts" (*DH* 201). What begins as a simple explanation for being "afraid of a draught of cool air" (*DH* 199) concludes in an apocalyptic scene reminiscent of the judgment in "Lycidas" rendered by St. Peter upon a faithless clergy. But what is being judged, and in what way is the doctor faithless or corrupt? The answer is I think simple; he has been a sworn enemy of death, an enemy of the natural processes through which we live and die. This scene is of course replayed in the conclusion to "The Thing on the Doorstep" in which another body in deliquescence, because it is another mentality that believes in the power of the will to evade death, attempts to write and in a fury presents the narrator "a large, closely written paper impaled on the end of a long pencil" (*DH* 301) accompanied by "a gust of insufferably foetid wind" that "almost flung [the narrator] prostrate" (*DH* 301). Some of the message comes through, some is torn away, and some willfully destroyed; but the truth of the matter is that these blind hands know not of what they write.

Let us now situate this story within others that deal with the same configuration of the two levels. The earliest is "The Picture in the House," in which the narrator arrives in a chill rain at a house he had not intended to enter; it cannot be any warmer inside except for the second floor where the fresh blood drips onto the floor and the ceiling of the room below. From one point of view the structure seems to conform to MacDonald's, for here the difference between the lower and the higher stories appears to be a model of that developed by Plato in *The Republic*, in which the lower world, this everyday world, is a mere reflection or participation within the higher world, which is the true reality. Below we have the picture in the book of an African charnelhouse five centuries removed from the characters; above, at this instant, a real charnelhouse is dripping its actual blood in the attempt of the old man to live forever. This ideality lies in a secret knowledge. In "Cool Air" the higher story also obtrudes into the lower by dripping into it; in that case, however, it is the ammonia that drips down, not quite as potent a material as blood. On the other hand, the picture does have an immediate, subtle effect upon the two characters who find themselves unaccountably moved by it. Though Plato thought art merely a mimetic mode that clumsily imitates the actual reality, this story affirms the energy that reaches out from the picture, primitive as it is. Methexis, which does not yield to mere mimesis, carries its own power. On the other hand, what is happening on the second floor, though inspired by the picture in the book, must be quite original in New England. The old man is not using the instruments of the Congo but the instruments that he has used for time out of mind on the sheep and pigs; and what is done out of doors in the Congo the old man accomplishes in a closed room on a second floor. Living in the New World, the old man has had to construct his own procedures.

"The Music of Erich Zann" is closely analogous to "Cool Air," for here once more the narrator is telling his story because of the remarkable character of the man who lives above him. And this man is as much an original, creating his own modes and procedures under the influence of an exterior inspiration, as the old man and his use of the Pigafetta volume. As Peter Cannon (150) has remarked, each of the men in the upper story, Dr. Muñoz and Erich Zann, is intensely interested in communicating his tale, but each attempt fails, in the one case because of the wind from outside the broken window and in the other because the narrator decides to burn the documents. The odd detail in "The Music of Erich Zann" is that the house in which the two men live has two outsides, the daily life of a French city and a demonic storm that is the source of Erich Zann's music. It is as though the source of the ideal lies at a further remove than simply in the room of Erich Zann. This story, however, like "The Picture in the House," affirms the power of art in the protagonist's admiration for Zann's music, even though on the night of the climax he enters the large garret "shivering with cold and fear" (*DH* 88). In "Cool Air" Dr. Muñoz is not an artist, but the protagonist admires his cultured aspect, the way in which he has created himself, with something of the same passion as the narrator of "The Music of Erich Zann," albeit with some ambivalence because of the man's livid appearance and "coldness of touch" (*DH* 202).

In contrast to these three stories let us consider "The Dreams in the Witch House" and "The Dunwich Horror." The former has something of the same configuration, though the protagonist of that story is not driven to live in the house because he is a wounded soul like the three previous narrators. The house does provide cheap lodgings, true, as do the apartments in the other stories, but Walter Gilman actively desires to live there because of its connection with the witch Keziah Mason and, as a good mathematician, because of his admiration for her art. The upper loft above his garret is utterly cut off from him. He only enters it through his dreams, just as through his dreams he also enters the world of multi-dimensional space, which is so much spacious than the world below, rather like what happens in MacDonald's *Lilith*. Most of these dreams are horrific; we would use the word nightmare to describe them, and Lovecraft does describe remark on "the nightmare shape of Brown Jenkin" (*DH* 268). Gilman returns from this nightmare space with a sunburn in a fever, drenched in cold perspiration; whatever the space he had found himself in, it "burns frore." Meanwhile, life proceeds as it does for a student; he fails some courses and succeeds in others, believing that in some fashion the ancient history of Keziah Mason may have something to do with his studies.[3] Moreover, he is in some confusion between the Keziah Mason he sees in his dreams and an old woman he first sees near the docks and later in the slums who seems to persecute him with her stare.

Now for the sake of the contrast I wish to discuss a story that in several ways is radically different from those we have discussed

---

3. Much of this detail about his studies, his failures and his brilliance and his sickness, may have to do with HPL's own breakdowns and failures that prevented him from entering Brown University.

so far, "The Dunwich Horror." Despite its difference, however, it highlights certain details that we have already noted. No one comes to live with Wizard Whateley, his daughter, and his grandson, no one would wish to although their lives, studious and matricidal, are simply an everyday life; but something has entered into the house in the upper story which they gradually enlarge until it forms a "vacant abyss" (*DH* 166) above their heads. By this time in their "great siege of carpentry" Wizard Whateley and his putative grandson have "knocked out all the partitions, [. . .] leaving only one vast open void between the ground story and the peaked roof" (*DH* 166). Whatever lives there is invisible because it is unspeakable; the vision of it at the end of the story merely says that in its relation with its brother Wilbur it plays out the story of Jacob and Esau, though this story ends tragically. The metaphoric usurpation of all space that we noticed in Mac-Donald's *Lilith* is literal in Lovecraft's narrative. What shall we say? Does the unconscious, which never reveals itself except through its effects, devour the daily life? The unconscious, as MacDonald would have it, pervades the daily life (16), though to the suffering protagonist it seems a usurpation. The creature itself, once we obtain some sense of what it looks like, has "great bulgin' eyes all over it" (*DH* 194), rather like Argos, the very emblem of the superego, at least that which Hera projects when she sets his hundreds of eyes to guard Io. Once the Dunwich Horror breaks out of the house it finds its way, as though by natural instinct, to Cold Spring Glen, from which the whippoorwills had poured on the occasion of Wizard Whateley's death (*DH* 166). It descends into the cold before it ascends to the lightning-wracked Sentinel Hell and the climactic scene of the story. It has no problem in that ascent, for "it could scale a sheer stony cliff of almost complete verticality" (*DH* 181). Though in the latter part of the story it has little resemblance to the kinds of stories we are interested in, it does not release this theme of verticality.

I wish to add another story to these exceptional witnesses, Thomas Pynchon's early story "Entropy," a story that we must note the author has come to dislike intensely because of its too constructed manner. The story is built upon a stark contrast between one story and that above it. On the lower story Meatball

Mulligan is celebrating the second day of chaotic lease-breaking party, while on the upper story an aesthete called Callisto, who had years before been "a young man at Princeton" (72) but who is now "in the sad dying fall of middle age" (73), and his Eurasian mistress Aubade are attempting to hold the temperature of their hothouse apartment, which they never leave at a steady temperature, while outside an early spring in February seems to be holding at a steady 37 degrees Fahrenheit. I shall not enter into the physics or metaphysics upon which the story is based nor the allusions to Adams, Gibbs, Boltzmann, Maxwell, Tait, and Clausius. No doubt the story is overweighted by physical argument. For us the point is that Callisto like Dr. Muñoz is terrified of losing control of the temperature. The world is a heat-death engine against which he is waging a series of hopeless stratagems, "helpless in the past" (84). In the climax Mulligan rises out of the chaos of his lease-breaking party and takes some responsibility for it, asserting a certain order, even calling a repairman to fix the refrigerator that is broken (84), while above him Aubade breaks the glass of the hothouse and opens it up to a life-giving or death-giving chaos. As Pynchon puts the matter more pointedly in his novella *The Crying of Lot 49*, we shall only live through a belief in the possibility that Maxwell's demon shall deliver us from the closed system in which we seem to live a life-in-death existence. Callisto cannot even give life to a bird that is dying in his hands. The only sign of life in the story comes from the party below, the music and the noise that ascends to disrupt the hothouse: "The architectonic purity of [Aubade's] world was constantly threatened by such hints of anarchy: gaps and excrescences and skew lines, and a shifting or tilting of planes to which she had continually to readjust lest the whole structure shiver into a disarray of discrete and meaningless signals" (73). In this appeal to geometry and a splintering shiver, what could be more Lovecraftian? But the people at the party are not in any way aware of the desperate couple above them.

We now need to look at these stories through more direct comparisons. What, for instance, are we to make of these protagonists? Most are in retreat from the world. They take up residence in rooms that shall cost less than they can afford because the outside world threatens them, sometimes actively as in the storm that forces the narrator of "The Picture in the House" to find refuge, sometimes more subtly because they have been psychologically wounded. Even more Dr. Muñoz, Erich Zann, and the old man in "The Picture in the House" are in retreat, though two of them deny their dependence on the outside world. Though he develops a fever, Walter Gilman seems the great exception, and his desire to live in that particular house may be the reason that this story is so different from the others. The temperature is not in question at all; he enters spaces of a very different heat but he had not meant to. In "Entropy," however, the man in retreat is Callisto in his upper room, fearful of the outside world as its temperature hovers at 37 degrees Fahrenheit; Aubade is also in retreat, apparently from the horrors of the French colonialism in South-East Asia.

To push this point further, we must admit that a great difference in these stories lies in the anonymity of the first-person narrators in "Cool Air," "The Picture in the House," and "The Music of Erich Zann." Each of these characters is in some way wounded or in threat. One has a bad financial situation and a bad heart, one is young and rather naïve astride his rational bicycle,[4] and one is poor and neurasthenic. They do not possess the exuberant confidence of the Whateleys or Walter Gilman. They have no name, and no more primitive sign of weakness or lack exists.

A striking point to me is that in most of these stories something is broken. In "Cool Air" the ammonia apparatus is broken so that the temperature begins to rise. In "The Picture in the House" something has broken in the upper story so that the blood has begun to drip through the ceiling; that is never clarified. In any case the entire house is broken by "the titanic thunderbolt of thunderbolts; blasting that accursed house of unutterable secrets" (*DH* 124), which comes swiftly upon the two men's recognition of the

---

4 The knowing narrator of Angela Carter's story "The Lady of the House of Love" argues: "To ride a bicycle is in itself some protection against superstitious fears, since the bicycle is the product of pure reason applied to motion. [. . .] Beneficial to the health, it emits no harmful fumes and permits only the most decorous speeds. How can a bicycle ever be an implement of harm" (97). Nevertheless, in both stories, that of Carter and that of HPL, the bicycle delivers its rider to the door of an irrational, deadly creature.

drop of blood. In "The Music of Erich Zann" the window is broken by the power of the supernatural wind. In "The Dunwich
Horror" the Whateley house is broken apart as the creature within
it attempts to escape into a freer life. In "Entropy" a lease-breaking
is the life of the party (though it is unclear whether the party
celebrates the breaking of the lease or exists in order to break the
lease—if the latter, the invisible landlord seems to be holding out
against the madness). One of the characters has a telling account
of a dispute with his wife: "She ended up throwing a *Handbook of
Chemistry and Physics* at me, only it missed and went through the
window, and when the glass broke I reckon something in her
broke too" (75), a passage that presages the climax of the story
when Callisto's mistress Aubade breaks the windows of the hothouse and holds up "her two exquisite hands which came away
bleeding and glistening with splinters" (85)—witnesses, exquisite
witnesses, to the urge toward chaos and life and death. In every
one of these stories something needs to broken; anything that
maintains life as it is, other than it might be, must be broken.
Otherwise life and death shall not be affirmed.

Another aspect of this breakage lies in the word *shiver* with its
two different but related meanings: "to shake with or as if with
cold [. . .]. To quiver or vibrate, as by the force of the wind." Or
"To cause to break suddenly into fragments or splinters" (*AHD*
"Shiver"). In my account of these stories we have met the word in
its various meanings a number of times. Dr. Muñoz, for instance,
lives in a "shivery place" (*DH* 203), and it is the question why the
narrator does "shiver more than others upon entering a cold room"
(*DH* 199) that leads to the story proper. It seems that the cold and
the terror that causes a character to shiver operate on two levels,
one quite physical, the other symbolic. Through the terror the
character is shivered, suddenly broken into fragments. Walter
Gilman almost shivers at the "seemingly unmotivated stare of the
beldame" near the wharves (*DH* 268). When Luther Brown shivers on the occasion of the Dunwich Horror's first attack the word
seems to stand in the place of an earlier phrase, "convulsed with
fright" (*DH* 177). Anyone who shivers experiences horrification,
the hair standing on end. The wholeness or purity that Dr. Muñoz
and Callisto attempt to attain is unacceptable. We have some un-

certainty, incidentally, what might be the provenance of the word *pure*. The *American Heritage Dictionary* plumps for "to purify, cleanse" ("Peue-"), whereas the *Etymological Dictionary of Latin* plumps for "clean [. . .], unmixed," as does the *OED*, and suggests that it is related to the Greek word πῦρ, fire, to which it is cognate. I cannot decide this puzzle, though we grant that the American dictionary is more recent. Still, the notion of purification through fire is attractive, and we can see how it would lead to the meaning "unmixed"; we shall see, furthermore, that, paradoxically, fire does seem to be a subtext of these stories; but despite Dante's witness, in these stories not even purification by fire is sufficient to redeem the soul.

The access to the upper story varies from work to work. In "The Picture in the House" this access is unproblematic; the protagonist does not attempt to go to the upper story, to which he gives no thought at all and no interest at all until the blood of the slaughter house begins to seep through the ceiling. In "The Music of Erich Zann" the narrator reminds the reader a number of times how steep the street and the house are, and the musician is intensely shy about his art in the upper reaches; it is a laborious ascent. In "Cool Air" the upper story is perfectly accessible, though to the taste of the narrator rather cold, and the narrator does not take the ascent into account until the cooling apparatus fails the first time and until he has an incipient heart attack; at this point he realizes that despite the cold he has a very immediate need for the doctor in the upper story. In "The Dreams in the Witch House" the loft above Gilman's garret is utterly sealed off; he does not apparently enter it and learn of its mysteries unless through his dreams, but he does dream profusely, thanks perhaps to his ability to manipulate Riemannian geometry and thanks also to the aid of Keziah Mason, for he is not at all in command of his dreams as he would wish. Though the upper story apparently offers much to the questing protagonist, he also encounters several difficulties, difficulties that are increasing in this series of fictions, just as the protagonists in MacDonald's stories encounter. It is not easy to avail oneself of the knowledge that lies in the upper regions of the unconscious.

Let us now be more specific about that upper chamber, which seems, hidden away as it is, to have much to do with the uncon-

scious. The upper rooms in the MacDonald stories with their allusions to cosmic order and the Holy Spirit have much in common
with the superego, the rigorous part of our unconscious that is
rich and prolific in moral demands. Callisto is the spokesman for
the superego, demanding that the world be saved from entropy by
the paradoxical and futile construction of the hothouse, a place
constructed on the principles of complete order. Callisto, paren-
thetically, was a nymph in the train of Artemis; Zeus seduced her
and at the threat of the offended goddess set her and her son in
the form of bears set among the constellations. As a sign of elegant
perversions and as a sign of the hermaphrodite Callisto bears the
name of a woman who is elevated to the stars and thus associated
with the cosmic order, the Great Bear that never sets and which
points to the pole star (Graves 1.84). On the other hand, bears are
noted for their hibernation, the state that the narrator of "Cold
Air" yearns for, "a bearable place to hibernate" (*DH* 200), and Callisto through his entire story is lying in bed, but like the transformed nymph Callisto now eternally awake. It is this aspect of
these upper rooms, their connection with cosmic order, that Maurice Lévy cannot accept, believing that the way up is the same as
the way down and that therefore a step upward is simply a step
downward into the abyss with which Lovecraft is so often preoc-
cupied (64), as in "The Rats in the Walls" and *The Case of Charles
Dexter Ward.* I would argue that the step upward is simply that, a
step upward, into the light, and that we need to read these stories,
with of course every qualification necessary, as engagements with
the terrifying superego and the ideal. The system is not communicative, despite the authorities of Heraclitus and Bachelard; 2×3
does not equal 3×2, and the way up is not the same as the way
down, mainly because of the dense specificity of the two paths.
Thus I disagree with my earlier remarks on this thematic structure
(Waugh 225). Nevertheless, I think that Lévy is right in insisting
that many of these upper rooms in these stories contain abysses.
The question is how we shall understand these abysses and the
ways in which they interact with the character of the superego.

II

> If unmelodious was the song,
> It was a hearty note and strong.
> Who lists may in their mumming see
> Traces of ancient mystery. (Scott, 6 Intro. 72–75)

> For O, for O, the hobby-horse is forgot. (*Hamlet* 3.2.122)

With this problem—how we are to reconcile the abyss with the superego—we return to the peculiar nature of "Cool Air" and to the possibility that it may contain, in the manner of James Hillman's work, a trace of mythic material. The "almost bearded" landlady Mrs. Herrero is a likely place to begin (*DH* 200), a figure of the potent hermaphrodite of the fertility rites in the Morris-dances of England, that many scholars believe originated in Spain; this is the Maid Marian or Malkin who was played by a man ("Morris-Dance" 18.873). "Malkin," however, has come to mean more than Maid Marian, whose reputation in the ballads is not as pure as it has come to mean in our later tradition. A "malkin" is "a slut, slattern, drab [. . .], the proper name of a female spectre or demon [. . .], an effeminate man" (*OED* "Malkin"). "Herrero" means a male blacksmith (Castillo and Bond, "herrero"), but the good landlady is a "slatternly" woman (*DH* 200). We should add that this figure is often called the Betty (Needham and Peck 84) and that this word has a verbal meaning, "To fuss about, like a man who busies himself with a woman's duties" (*OED* "Betty"). The Morris-dance was usually performed in May, another indication that it may have been originally a part of a fertility ritual; but in time its characters were liable, in an act of cross-pollination, to appear with the masked characters in the Mummers' performance, which takes place in the winter solstice and often presents a comic version of the story of St. George ("Mummers" 18.966), in which the good saint dies many times only to rise again and in various clumsy ways defeats his vile, supernatural opponents. As we survey the other figures of the Morris-dance not many offer themselves to our inspection, unless it be the silly jokester the Hobby Horse. This

horse, distorted and elevated in the comic mode as it is, leads us to
Pegasus, and we did want a story that had something to do with
the vertical axis of human experience. Bellerophon rode Pegasus to
conquer the Chimaera, a composite monster part lion, part goat,
and part dragon, in Hesiod's account so horrific that it sports the
three heads of the three beasts (*Theogony* 321–22), so horrific that
Horace at the beginning of the *Ars Poetica* seems to take it as the
example of what a poet should not attempt. Later Bellerophon attempted to ride the horse to Olympus in order, Pindar intimates,
to join the company of the gods in immortality (*Isth.* 7.39-47); but
Zeus prevented the attempt and the horse with better sense than
its master cast him off so that he wandered the world thereafter
wretched and half-mad (Graves1.254). This story warns against the
attempt to ascend into that world which is peculiarly the gods', to
escape our human mortal state.

There is sufficient madness in Lovecraft's story. Despite his attempt to maintain his own sobriety, the doctor rages; he cannot
help but rage. And his own mental disturbance causes a variety of
shocks in others. A young man who had come through the Great
War safely suffers epilepsy when he looks at the doctor (*DH* 205);
the man the narrator had hired to maintain the doctor's supply of
ice fled "mad-eyed" (*DH* 206); and the narrator himself began to
"rage almost as violently" as the doctor himself (*DH* 206). We
have seen in other Lovecraftian stories how carefully we must
treat the narrations of the narrators. This narrator claims, in a
break from the early realistic trend of the work, that "Fiendish
things were in the air" (*DH* 206) with no attempt to clarify their
nature. Despite the sober nature of the story's opening, it de-
bouches into hints of madness.

Let us consider Horace's version of the story, that he joins to
the story of Phaethon, as so often in the form of a concise moral
platitude:

> Terret ambustus Phaethon avaras
> spes, ut exemplum grave praebet ales
> Pegasus terrernum equitem gravatus
> Bellerophontem. (*Odes* 4.11)

[Scorched Phaethon deters eager / hopes, and winged Pegasus offers a heavy / warning weighted by the earthly rider / Bellerophon.]

The vertical axis which has so concerned us is evident in both stories, but in this case I am interested in the word *ambustus*, which signifies not only "scorched" or "burned" but also "frost-bitten" (Smith and Lockwood, "amburo" 41); in the height, in the domain of the gods, hot or cold, cold or hot, may seem interchangeable. But whether Olympus is hot or cold or simply a state for which we have no word, it is dangerous to a mortal. MacDonald writes stories about the glories of that domain, and within it the Princess is healed of her injuries, but even MacDonald warns against its dangers; and Bellerophon is never healed. As the crisis approaches in "Cold Air" the cold that the doctor demands in order to maintain him alive in his death is utterly inimical and unbearable to mortals.

Bellerophon's mad attempt brings us to the story we should perhaps have had in mind from the beginning, the story of Prometheus. In addition, we should note that in Aeschylus' play the remarkable figure of Io appears, the woman raped by Zeus whom Hera has now transformed into a cow, dancing through her pain and performed of course by a male actor; and thus this character does seem to play the part of the Betty that we have already taken note of. As for Prometheus, not only is he the Titan who brought fire down from Olympus to aid mankind, he is in Aeschylus' account the true founder of civilization. In *Prometheus Bound* he provides a list of the benefits he has given humanity, but these benefits extend beyond mere aids. In one version of the myth he is the actual creator of humanity. In the words of Goethe's poem "Prometheus" he announces to Zeus:

> Hier sitz' ich, forme Menschen
> Nach meinem Bilde,
> Ein Geschlecht, das mir gleich sei,
> Zu leiden, weinen,
> Genießen und zu freuen sich,
> Und dein nicht zu achten,
> Wie ich. (46)

[Here I sit, forming men / In my image, / A race that is like me, /

To suffer, weep, / Enjoy and rejoice, / And to pay no attention to
you at all, / Like me.]

This Prometheus acts directly against the order established by the
Olympian gods. He is not interested in order but in change and
ecstatic rebellion, that rebellion desired by the general movement
of *Sturm und Drang* that Goethe initiated and participated in as a
young man. His punishment for ascending to Olympus and the
theft of fire is to be chained by the smith Hephaistos to the Cau-
casus Mountains, exposed to the sun, frost, and snow (*Pro.* ll. 22–
25, 992–94); he must, as Milton says of hell, "burn frore." When
that punishment is not sufficient, the eagle of Zeus descends to
tear at his liver daily. In stark contrast to the doctor and the musician, however, Prometheus is at last released from his torture and
in Athens is celebrated by torch races (Burkert 171).

Dr. Muñoz, on the contrary, is a Prometheus who is not un-
bound but increasingly more bound into fetters, frozen fetters, of
his own devising, the ammonia pipes and pump that he modifies
so that his room can be refrigerated to 28 degrees; the second half
of his technological response to his state is his bath accompanied
by spices, incense, and "the pungent chemicals" (*DH* 204). In the
last two pages of the story, however, he deserts his fetters in the
bathroom where he had so striven for his purity to find his way to
his desk and write his final confession; this desertion of his fetters
and his Pegasus, for his technology is the Hobby-horse of the Morris-dance, is in remarkable contrast to the other figures we are
concerned with. Callisto seems bound not only to his hothouse
hermetic room but to his bed, in the final throes of his own para-
noia that edges into the distressed madness of Bellerophon; we
cannot say whether he is released by Aubade's shattering of the
glass. Erich Zann is bound to his music and to his mad pen; perhaps even more he is bound to his inarticulate voice—in his case
so unlike Prometheus who in Aeschylus' rendering of the story is
remarkably articulate, and if he is released by the shattering of his
window he is only released into madness and death. Though we
never see the old man of "The Picture in the House" in his upper
room, we can well imagine that there he is bound to the picture
that is such a tickle to him that it compels him to his butcheries.

Walter Gilman discovers that he is bound to a series of revelatory nightmares through the power of Keziah Mason. Wilbur Whateley, though in many ways he seems the emblem of freedom, must bind himself into his tight clothes if he is to enjoy that freedom; when the watchdog rips the clothes from him he dies; but his brother dies when the fetters of his invisibility are made manifest through the silly apparatus of "a powder in this long distance sprayer" (*DH* 191).

We should notice that Horace's account of Phaethon and Aeschylus' account of Prometheus have something in common, the juxtaposition of hot and cold; but we should distinguish one peculiarity about this relation. Though when we touch something cold it may seem hot, something that is hot never seems cold. The relation, like that of the journey up and the journey down, is not communicative, and it thus reinforces that theme: the way up is not the same as the way down and thus bears within itself its own fatality.

If we survey the stories from the angle of the Promethean gift we see great differences among them. Clearly Callisto has no gift for Meatball Mulligan, though he is dictating to Aubade an apologia of his life that is more intended to clarify his life to himself than to enlighten any of the *vulgus profanum*. The Whateleys have no gift for the people of Dunwich, far from it, although from their own peculiar point of view they may regard the spawn of Yog-Sothoth as a gift; and though Walter Gilman is a perfectly decent young man, he very much pursues knowledge for its own sake. The old man in "The Picture in the House" doubtless means to kill the narrator, but before that fatal moment he seems compelled to justify his own long life and happily to share the picture. Erich Zann and Dr. Muñoz are very different from these characters, Erich Zann writing at a great pace what we assume shall be an explanation of his work for the narrator, though his notes will be flung away by the chaos outside the window that inspires them, and Dr. Muñoz writing "long documents of some sort" (*DH* 205) through the last weeks of his apparent life which he requests the narrator to communicate to certain occult sages, one of them a famous French doctor "now generally thought dead" (*DH* 205), a request that the narrator refuses, for he destroys the documents after the doctor's death. In comparison to those documents Dr.

Muñoz's treatment of the narrator's heart trouble is rather minor. So among these characters only the composer and the doctor are Promethean. Like Moses because wisdom comes down from on high, although this comparison is admittedly a stretch, they hope to bring down the law, the shape of the world as it is, from the mountain, saying with as much irony as James Joyce contrives, "with the light of inspiration shining in his countenance and bearing in his arms the tables of the law, graven in the language of the outlaw" (7.867–69). The composer and the doctor are marginal figures in their societies, and Lovecraft has little hope that their aspirations shall aid mankind and little belief that they should.

When we consider the stories of Bellerophon and Prometheus it becomes clear that the characters in "Cool Air" fulfill these roles in a fractured manner. The single figure of the Greek myths becomes double in Lovecraft's story; that is to say, from the standpoint of the myth the narrator and the doctor are both Bellerophon with his touch of madness and Prometheus in his stubborn rebellion. Or to say it in another way, the narrator is already the wounded figure, suffering from a heart disease, that the myth assures us the hero shall undergo. Dr. Muñoz in his suffering becomes bound to his own machine; he dare not escape from the instrument of his own torture, which is his noble steed, until at last he deserts it without yielding the point that the horse has thrown him, as though he had so far agreed to his own fetters, and yielded to his own death, dead as he is of course and unable to escape his slow proper death. So to the question whether Dr. Muñoz is such a Promethean figure we answer resoundingly yes, except that, as we have seen, Prometheus is at last released from the fire, the snow, and the eagle nibbling his liver. A part of the reason I want to deal with that figure is his involvement in the question of heat.

But also, though he does not create humanity, he is not only a doctor devoted to the physical well-being of humanity; he is a doctor who means to recreate humanity "nach meinem Bilde" so that he shall be at last able to endure eternal life. It is, however, at the price of the eagle that shall have his liver.

One puzzle remains: What we are to make of the "strange, dark place" where Dr. Torres took Dr. Muñoz when he nursed him back from death into the death he has lived for the last eighteen years (*DH* 207)? It is a secret that necessarily remains a secret, though we can guess at it when we realize that this is, I believe, the only story Lovecraft wrote in which the bathroom plays so prominent a role, providing the bathtub in which the doctor incessantly washes himself. Next to the bathtub of course stands the toilet. Early in the story we learn that Mrs. Herrero's son Esteban buys food for him (*DH* 200), a job that the narrator later accepts (*DH* 204). Now if the doctor eats, despite the problems he has with his inner organs, we must assume that he also defecates and that, as I once remarked of the landscape in the dream world, "the somatic process delivers a sarkotic object" (225). Let us recall again the appearance of the shoggoth in *At the Mountains of Madness*, a transformed and transfigured black dung. The "strange, dark place" is the place where we shut ourselves in to defecate and thus produce the emblem of our mortality. It is the symbol of the great theme that Lovecraft shares with St. Paul, "Who shall deliver me from the body of this death?" (Rom. 7:24). But he does not share St. Paul's answer, and neither does the raging, broken Dr. Muñoz who has ascended to the upper story and its "strange, dark place" in order to achieve immortality.

Let us review this material. First, as we began, everything that happens in the story occurs in the framework of a verticality, a lower story and an upper story. The often anonymous narrator who represents the world as it is in the lower story is in some fashion in retreat from that world, but he knows nothing of the upper story until the person who lives there and who hopes to triumph there invites the narrator to ascend; there is always some difficulty involved in the ascent as well as in the descent in which, since the way down is not the same as the way up, one is liable to be lost or maddened. Therefore some technology is almost always involved which both narrator and protagonist are too dependent on, represented by the figures of the hermaphrodite and the Hobby-horse; Io, however, is as much in need as the ammonia pump that goes bust. The consequence of this difficulty is breakage, a shivering and a splintering in the face of a cold that burns, an *ébranlement* that is ecstatic but also joyless. The two phrases "blind hand" and "burns frore," mixed metaphor and oxymoron, indicate the extent to which rationality cannot comprehend this space. We understand thereby how the space within which this experience occurs is highly disturbing, physically and mentally; madness and harm resides there that may be experienced as a punishing superego; Zeus first has Prometheus nailed to the rock through the agency of the divine blacksmith Hephaistos, the god of our human technologies, and then sends the eagle daily, so that in time the Titan learns that his immortality partakes of the mortal world in a much more intimate way than anything implied by his words, "Nach meinem Bilde." He takes on the image of the mortals he meant to aid. But the range of this superego may be indicated by the upper room devoted to numbers that imply the heat death of the universe and the upper room that is a slaughter house. No one escapes this death.

Works Cited

Aeschylus. *Tragoediae*. Ed. Gilbert Murray. 2nd ed. Oxford: Clarendon Press, 1957.

American Heritage Dictionary. 3rd ed. Boston: Houghton Mifflin, 1992.

Burkert, Walter. *Greek Religion: Archaic and Classical*. Trans. John Raffan. Cambridge, MA: Harvard University Press, 1985.

Cannon, Peter. "Letters, Diaries, and Manuscripts: The Handwritten Word in Lovecraft." In Schultz and Joshi, *An Epicure in the Terrible*. 148–58.

Carter, Angela. *The Bloody Chamber*. London: Penguin, 1981.

Castillo, Carlos, and Otto F. Bond, with Barbara M. Garcia. *Spanish-English English-Spanish Dictionary*. New York: Washington Square, 1961.

Encyclopaedia Britannica. 9th ed. Edinburgh: A & C. Black, 1875–98.

Graves, Robert. *The Greek Myths*. Baltimore: Penguin, 1955. 2 vols.

Goethe, Johann Wolfgang von. *Werke*. Vol. 1. Ed. Erich Trunz. Hamburg: Christian Wegner, 1948.

Hesiod. *Theogonia Opera et Dies Scutum*. Ed. Friedrich Solmsen, R. Merkelbach, and M. L. West. Oxford: Oxford University Press, 1970.

Horace. *Opera*. Ed. Edward C. Wickham and H. W. Garrod. Oxford: Clarendon Press, 1901.

Joshi, S. T, ed. "Introduction and Notes." In *The Call of Cthulhu and Other Weird Stories* by H. P. Lovecraft. New York: Penguin, 1999.

Joyce, James. *Ulysses.* Ed. Walter Gabler. New York: Random House, 1986.

Lévy, Maurice. *Lovecraft: A Study in the Fantastic.* Trans. S. T. Joshi. Detroit: Wayne State University Press, 1988.

"Luis Muñoz Rivera." Web. Accessed 29 September 2010.

MacDonald, George. *Lilith.* Grand Rapids, MI: Eerdmans, 1981.

———. *The Princess and the Goblin.* New York: Macmillan, 1951.

Milton, John. *Complete Poems and Major Prose.* Ed. Merrit Y. Hughes. New York: Odyssey, 1957.

"Morris-Dance." *Encyclopaedia Britannica.*

"Mummers." *Encyclopaedia Britannica.*

"MUNOZ—Name Meaning & Origin." Web. Accessed 20 November 2010.

Needham, Joseph, and Arthur L. Peck. "Molly Dancing in East Anglia." *Journal of English Folk Dance and Song Society* 1, no. 2 (December 1933). 79–85.

Pindar. *Carmina cum Fragmentis.* Ed. Brvno Snell. 3rd ed. Leipzig: Teubner, 1959.

Pokorny, Julius. *Indogermanisches Etymologisches Wörterbuch.* Bern: Francke Verlag, 1959. 2 vols.

Pynchon, Thomas. "Entropy." In *Slow Learner.* New York: Bantam, 1984.

Schultz, David E., and S. T. Joshi, ed. *An Epicure in the Terrible: A Centennial Anthology of Essays in Honor of H. P. Lovecraft.* Rutherford, NJ: Fairleigh Dickinson University Press, 1991.

Smith, William, and John Lockwood. *Chambers Murray Latin-English Dictionary.* Cambridge: Cambridge University Press, 1987.

Scott, Sir Walter. *Marmion.* In *The Complete Poetical Works.* Ed. Horace E. Scudder. Boston: Houghton Mifflin, 1900.

Tucker, T. G. *The Etymological Dictionary of Latin.* 1931. Chicago: Ares, 1985.

Waugh, Robert H. "Landscapes, Selves, and Others in Lovecraft." In Schultz and Joshi, *An Epicure in the Terrible.* 220–43.

Lovecraft's "The City"

R. Boerem

Lovecraft's poetry rewards its readers who pay attention to his classical references as they might to its reflections of his fiction. "The City" is a fair example.

The poem had its genesis in a dream Lovecraft had May 1918:

> Several nights ago I had a strange dream of a strange city—a city of many palaces and gilded domes, lying in a hollow betwixt ranges of grey, horrible hills. There was not a soul in this vast region of stone-paved streets and marble walls and columns, and the numerous statues in the public places were of strange bearded men in robes the like whereof I have never seen before or since. . . . I felt that I had once known it well, and that if I could remember, I should be carried back to a very remote period—many thousand years, when something vaguely horrible had happened. Once I was almost on the verge of realisation, and was frantic with fear at the prospect, though I did not know what it was that I should recall. But here I awaked . . . (*SL* 1.62)

This dream inspired the story "Polaris," published that same year, and "The City," published the next year in the *Vagrant* under the pseudonym Ward Phillips. The tie to the story certainly deepens the poem, but an easy explication of that relationship leads a reader, perhaps, to ignore the resonances within the poem itself.

Its first stanza introduces the City of light—golden, splendid, wondrous, and glorious (*AT* 46, ll.1–5). A city of light could be a heavenly city like Jerusalem or Shiva's Banaras in Hindu mythology, or it could be the epitome of civilization, as Paris and other great cities also described as "cities of light." As a vision, it certainly represents an ideal city and, as a symbol, the ideal of civilization. But this vision is "suspended / In deeps of the night" (ll. 3–4), contrasting the brilliance of the city with a darkness that surrounds and contains it.

The second stanza makes two points: first, that the vision occurs in the depths of winter and, second, that winter is a time of "unreasoning" (l. 8) and madness. Winter itself is the cause of madness and suffering, but it is not clear whether this vision is part of winter's madness.

In the third stanza, the vision in the sky is conflicted by light from the constellation Orion, which causes a sleep filled with dim memories of the obscure past (ll. 11–15).

The next four stanzas detail the description of the city's beautifully carved architecture, alluring avenues and plazas, and bright, fragrant gardens. In some sense, the city may be an ideal, but it is also very much a place of physical beauty and comfort.

The poem makes clear that this vision is drawn from the memory of the visionary (ll. 15, 34), who is captivated by the array of stone figures in the plazas, figures of grave, commanding men. One of them "stood dismantled and broken, its bearded face batter'd away" (l. 30). If only one of the many statues had been broken and battered, this suggests it had been a deliberate desecration meant to be a public condemnation of the man represented by the image. In ancient civilizations, public images were literally carved representations displayed in public. Since many of these were, quite deliberately, too ponderous to simply remove, they were disfigured by later powers who wished to condemn to oblivion the memory of those represented by the statues and engravings. An obvious example is the determined erasure of Ikhnaton, the apostate pharaoh, from Egyptian statuary.

The visionary, in stanza eight, "strove to remember / The aeons behind" (ll. 38–39), but receives a "horrible warning" (l. 41) and, in the last line of the poem, flew in panic from the knowledge of terrors forgotten and dead.

The poem opens with a conflict of opposites, a bright vision of splendor in the depths of darkness. Successive images continue this conflict: fragrant, warm ("Halcyon clime," l. 25) gardens are experienced during a cruel winter. The statues are awesome, but one is disfigured. Finally, the striving to remember provokes a panicked flight from knowledge. Before deciding on the nature of the conflict, however, it is worth examining the imagery in greater detail.

Lovecraft was versed in both astronomy and classical literature,
and this knowledge is used to advantage in the poem. One example is his use of "Halcyon clime." By the dictionary definition, this
would mean that the city existed in a calm, peaceful, even prosperous climate, but the Greek myths from which the term derives
give more meaning to the reference. One myth has Alcyone,
whose husband drowned in a shipwreck, throwing herself into the
sea, whereupon the gods mercifully changed her into a seabird, a
kingfisher. In another version, Alcyone was among sisters who,
comparing their happiness to that of Zeus and Hera, were punished by these gods by being transformed into kingfishers. In any
case, the gods, seeing that the kingfishers' shoreline nests were destroyed by the stormy winter waves, had enough pity to command that the waves be calm during the kingfishers' nesting
season, the seven days before and after the winter solstice.

The poem has two references to December. Orion (l. 13) is a
winter constellation that first appears in December, and the Halcyon days are the two weeks before and after the winter solstice
on or about December 21. Given these, it is possible to identify
the "mad time of unreason" (l. 8) as the Saturnalia, the Roman
celebration of the age of Saturn, under whose beneficent rule
there was "universal plenty" and "no division into bond and free"
(Macrobius 58–59). This "mad time" overturned, temporarily, the
bonds and ranking of society so that slaves and masters could exchange roles and the strictures of morality were loosened. The
Saturnalia was celebrated about the winter solstice, the 17th
through the 23rd of December (Speake, "Saturnalia").

Nevertheless, the "mad time of unreason," like the other contrasting images in the poem, points not only to the golden age of
Saturn, but directly to the "brain-numbing days" of tortuous winter.
Indeed, each positive image is engulfed by a negative one. The
"Halcyon clime" of the City, then, is not simply a pleasant climate,
but a climate contrasting the climates that preceded and followed
it. just as the City appears as a light in the darkness, its climate is an
oasis of calm between eras of storm. This suggests that, of the other
contrasts, the brighter of them is the rarer of them. The vision of

light is surrounded in the dark quotidian, a period of joy is in the midst of a season of madness, and civilization itself, symbolized by the City, is but a punctuation between eras of barbarism. The visionary is attracted to the memory of the City with its stately mansions, fragrant gardens, and awesome figures, but there is also the omen of the dismantled statue—an ancient disgrace—and finally the warning against remembering too much of the distant past.

That the warning is "like the ominous morning / That rises in red" (ll. 43–44) refers to the old saying: "red skies at night, sailor's delight, red skies at morning, sailors take warning." It is appropriate that this is an ancient adage dating at least as far back as the Bible (Matt. 16:2–3). Instead of remembering "the aeons behind" (l. 38), the red warning sends the visionary fleeing in panic from "the knowledge of terrors forgotten and dead" (l. 45). What had seemed to be a tempting revival of a glorious past existence was, at the same time, a threatening exposure to terrible knowledge better left forgotten.

It is interesting to note that the constellation Orion, interpreted in Egyptian mythology as a version of Horus, is depicted as a warrior "running away and looking backward" (Müller 57–58), just as the visionary in "The City," revealed in "Polaris" to be a warrior *manqué*, is fleeing the past. Lovecraft may have known of this reference, for the source cited here was originally published in 1918 in Boston as part of a popular reference to world mythology.

At a time of cold and misery, the visionary is shown the glory of an era long past, a vision into which one might wish to enter more fully but, like everything else, the ancient City of light was surrounded by its own terrors, so the vision should not be inhabited too deeply lest those terrors be evoked. Since every positive image in the poem is not merely contrasted with but surrounded by a negative one, the poem strongly implies that any positive experience, even the poem itself, must not be examined too closely, as there is always the danger of destroying the pleasure by recognizing the terrible truth beyond.

This much can be gained just by a reading of the poem itself, but the terrible knowledge might be the "Aletheia Phrikodes" (Greek for "frightful truth") detailed in "The Poe-et's Nightmare," written two years before "The City" (*SL* 1.59) Here, the truth is specifically announced as "omnia risus et omnia pulvis et omnia nihil"—all is jest, dust, and nothing (*AT* 20). Here, too, the soul of a seeker "fled without aim or knowledge" (24, l. 263) rather than know "the final truth" (l. 261).

There are also reflections of "The City" in *Fungi from Yuggoth* (*AT* 64–79). In stanza III, the narrator contemplates accessing memories of lost aeons, and in V he is promised a return home to a marble city of terraces and domes. In XXXIV he awakens a man out of time, no longer feeling himself a part of what had been his familiar life. The last stanza of the poem leaves the narrator sensitive to the essences of things past, "Of locked dimensions harbouring years gone by, / And out of reach except by hidden keys."

The story "Polaris," inspired by the same dream as "The City," gives the City a name, Olathoë, and a location in the land of Lomar on the plateau of Sarkis, south of Zobna, between the peaks of Noton and Kadiphonek (*D* 21–22). The specificity of this description pertains to the reality of the narrator's dream experience. As the visionary of "The City," the protagonist of "Polaris" has visionary experiences on those few nights he could sleep, when the pole star shines "through long hellish hours of blackness" (*D* 20) like an eye that once has a message to convey. He also mentions the movement of Aldebaran, one of the brightest stars on the horizon and one in the constellation Taurus, close to Orion. (Halcyone is also a bright star in Taurus.) The City has marble towers, columns, domes, pavements, and pillars with images of grave, bearded men (*D* 21).

Unlike in "The City," in "Polaris" the narrator remembers his previous life in detail, including at least one "frightful truth" that he might have wanted to forget. He was a scholar of Olathoë, honored with the crucial mission of watching from a tower to give immediate warning about when and from which direction the enemy Inutos came to attack the city, without which knowledge it would certainly fall. Tragically, he is hypnotized by the Pole Star, which commands him:

> Slumber, watcher, till the spheres,
> Six and twenty thousand years
> Have revolv'd, and I return
> To the spot where now I burn. (*D* 23)

Now, he has seemingly awakened enough to his memories of aeons past to want desperately to awaken as well from the "dream" of the present in which there is no northern kingdom in a region inhabited only by the "Esquimaux" who resemble the conquering Inutos.

As in "The City," red is a threatening color. The passage of time is marked by the movement of red Aldebaran, and the "red and sinister" (D 22) moon is a distant accompaniment to the Pole Star's disastrous influence. The warning is a torture to the narrator who cannot awaken from his "dream" of the present to complete his task and redeem his honor by warning the City, so he is trapped in a present that provides certain evidence of his treasonous failure. This is, perhaps, the reason for the disgraced statue in "The City" and the source of at least some of the "terrors forgotten and dead" from which the narrator of "The City" flees.

"Polaris" proposes that Eskimos are the descendants of the Inutos (Inuit) who, squat and dishonorable, vanquished the "tall, grey-eyed men of Lomar" (D 22). This fits a fanciful German pseudo-history about Aryan forebears, perhaps survivors of Atlantis, coming from the Arctic to found western civilization (Jordan 181). Where Lovecraft picked this up is not clear, as most of the German writings were not published until after the composition of "Polaris" and were not translated into English.

August Derleth wrote that "the best of H. P. Lovecraft's poetry is only a minor portion of his work, but it is filled with echoes of his fiction and is clearly related to it" (5). "The City" demonstrates that even a shorter poem rewards an attentive reader who doesn't need to consult the fiction to explore a satisfying depth into the poetry. It also shows that the best of Lovecraft's poetry is not merely an echo of the fiction, but a complement to it.

Works Cited

Macrobius. *The Saturnalia*. Trans. Percival Vaughan Davies. New York: Columbia University Press, 1969.

Derleth, August. "Preface." In *Collected Poems* by H. P. Lovecraft. Sauk City, WI: Arkham House, 1963.

Jordan, Paul. *The Atlantis Syndrome*. Phoenix Mill, UK: Sutton Publishing, 2001.

Müller, W. Max. *Egyptian Mythology*. Mineola, NY: Dover, 2004.

Speake, Graham, ed. *A Dictionary of Ancient History*. Oxford: Blackwell, 1944.